Giu~~~~

Also by Deborah Hart Strober and Gerald S. Strober

Billy Graham: A Narrative and
Oral Biography

His Holiness the Dalai Lama:
The Oral Biography

The Monarchy: An Oral Biography
of Queen Elizabeth II

Reagan: The Man and His Presidency

Nixon: An Oral History of His Presidency

"Let Us Begin Anew": An Oral History
of the Kennedy Presidency

Giuliani
Flawed or Flawless?

THE ORAL BIOGRAPHY

Deborah Hart Strober
Gerald S. Strober

BICENTENNIAL
1807
WILEY
2007
BICENTENNIAL

John Wiley & Sons, Inc.

Copyright © 2007 by Deborah Hart Strober and Gerald S. Strober. All rights reserved

Published by John Wiley & Sons, Inc., Hoboken, New Jersey
Published simultaneously in Canada

Photo credits: page 122, photo by Diane Bondareff, Associated Press; pages 112 (bottom) and 113, courtesy of Brother Peter Bonventre; page 116, photo by Clarence L. Haynes, New York City Transit Police Department, courtesy of Albert O'Leary; page 115, photo by Mark Lennihan, Associated Press; page 121, courtesy of Sally Regenhard; pages 117–119, courtesy of Sanford Rubenstein; page 120, courtesy of Lori Strober Sterling; pages 111 and 112 (top), courtesy of Deborah Hart Strober; page 114, courtesy of Richard Thornburgh, Papers of Dick Thornburgh, 1932–, AIS 98:30, Archives Services Center, University of Pittsburgh

Design and composition by Navta Associates, Inc.

For general information about our other products and services, please contact our Customer Care Department within the United States at (800) 762-2974, outside the United States at (317) 572-3993 or fax (317) 572-4002.

Wiley also publishes its books in a variety of electronic formats. Some content that appears in print may not be available in electronic books. For more information about Wiley products, visit our web site at www.wiley.com.

Library of Congress Cataloging-in-Publication Data:
Strober, Deborah H. (Deborah Hart), date.
    Giuliani : flawed or flawless? the oral biography / Deborah Hart Strober, Gerald S. Strober.
        p. cm.
    Includes index.
    ISBN 978-0-471-73835-0 (cloth)
 1. Giuliani, Rudolph W. 2. Mayors—New York (State)—New York—Biography. 3. New York (N.Y.)—Politics and government—1951– I. Strober, Gerald S. II. Title.
    F128.57.G58S77 2007
    974.7'1043092—dc22
    [B]
                                                                            200620141
Printed in the United States of America

10 9 8 7 6 5 4 3 2 1

*To our grandchildren, with deep love and
appreciation of your uniqueness*

Eyal Jonathan Benjamin
Ran Michael Benjamin
Kai Wesley Philip Sterling
Marley Grace Sterling

CONTENTS

PART IX
LIFE AFTER CITY HALL

Illustrations follow page 110

ACKNOWLEDGMENTS

Giuliani: Flawed or Flawless? The Oral Biography could not have come to fruition without the participation of our interviewees, all of whom provided valuable insights into the life and career of our subject.

We would also like to thank Calvin Alexander, Maryann McHugh Feeney, Marc Rosenbaum, and Nancy Watson.

At John Wiley & Sons, we wish to express our appreciation to our editor, Hana Lane, who encouraged us to go forward with our oral biography of the former mayor, and whose editing skills we greatly admire. We also appreciate the efforts of Hana's very able assistant, Naomi Rothwell, and our production editor, Kimberly Monroe-Hill.

We are truly fortunate in having a circle of friends who have supported us in all of our literary undertakings and who offered special encouragement as we went about exploring the complexities and political activities of Rudolph Giuliani. They include Bonnie Cutler and her husband, Mark Heutlinger; Evelyn and Raphael Rothstein; Marcia and Rabbi A. James Rudin; Florence and Harry Taubenfeld; Sarah and Ze'ev Shiff; Elaine and Martin Zuckerbrod; and Sheila and Herbert Zweibon.

And how could we have made it through these many months without the devotion of our family? We want to express our deep appreciation to Judith and Dr. Mortimer Civan; Mindy and Myron Strober; Joseph Hochstein; and Ruth Hockstein.

Through our children, we are privileged to know and to count among our close friends Dorrit and Meir Nocham, parents of Jeremy's wife, Gabi; Daphne and Hummarde Sterling, parents of Lori's husband, Bryan; Gene Meyers, father of Robin's friend Michelle; and Gene's wife, Jan Book.

Lastly, we want to pay tribute to our beloved, always supportive children and their partners: Jeremy Benjamin and Gabi, parents of Eyal Jonathan and Ran Michael; Lori and Bryan Sterling, parents of Kai Wesley Philip and Marley Grace; Jonathan Strober; and Robin Strober and Michelle Meyers.

THE INTERVIEWEES

Floyd Abrams, an attorney specializing in First Amendment issues, is a member of the firm Cahill Gordon & Reindell. He represented the Brooklyn Museum in Mayor Rudolph Giuliani's suit against that institution. Mr. Abrams has served since 1994 as the William J. Brennan Jr. Visiting Professor of First Amendment Issues, Columbia University Graduate School of Journalism. He was interviewed on September 18, 2005, in New York City.

Eric Adams, a now retired captain in the New York City Police Department (NYPD), first interacted with Mayor Rudolph Giuliani in the 1980s, when Captain Adams served as chairman of the Grand Council of Guardians, a coalition of African American police officers. He later commanded a precinct in Manhattan's Greenwich Village. He was interviewed on October 6, 2005, in New York City.

Steven R. Andrews, an attorney, represented James Dahl, an associate of Michael Milken's at Drexel Burnham Lambert. He is a partner in the firm Andrews Moye, located in Tallahassee, Florida. He was interviewed on October 18, 2005, by telephone.

Herman Badillo, an attorney, is a founding partner of the New York City firm Fischbein Badillo Wagner Harding. He served as borough president of the Bronx from 1966 to 1970; as a member of the U.S. House of Representatives (D-NY) from 1971 to 1978; and as deputy mayor of the City of New York from 1978 to 1979. Mr. Badillo was a candidate for comptroller on the Giuliani fusion ticket in 1993 and served as fiscal monitor of New York City's public school system during the Giuliani administration. He was chairman of the City University of New York's board of trustees from 1999 to 2001. He was interviewed on May 16, 2005, at his law offices in New York City.

Lilliam Barrios-Paoli came to the Giuliani administration following her service in the administration of Mayor Edward I. Koch. Under Mayor Giuliani, Ms. Barrios-Paoli served as commissioner/city personnel director of the New York City Department of Personnel from 1994 to 1996; as commissioner in the New York City Department of Housing Preservation and Development from 1996 to 1997; as commissioner/administrator of the Human Resources Administration from 1997 to 1998; and as executive director of Lincoln Medical and Mental Health Center, a division of the New York City Health and Hospital Corporation, in 1998. After leaving city government, Ms. Barrios-Paoli served as senior vice president and chief executive for Agency Services of the United Way of New York City. In October 2004, she became the president and CEO of Safe Space, a not-for-profit organization serving needy families in New York City. She was interviewed on June 23, 2005, at the offices of Safe Space in New York City.

Carol Bellamy, a classmate of Rudolph Giuliani's at New York University Law School from 1965 to 1968, went on to serve as a member of the New York State Senate from 1973 to 1977 and as president of the New York City Council from 1978 to 1985. She was then named director of the Peace Corps, in which capacity she served from 1993 to 1995. Appointed executive director of UNICEF in 1995, she held that post for ten years. Ms. Bellamy is currently president and CEO of World Learning, an organization devoted to globalizing young Americans, with education and development programs in one hundred countries. She was interviewed on November 17, 2005, by telephone.

Brother Peter Bonventre, a Sallian (De La Salle) Christian Brother, was the assistant principal at Bishop Loughlin Memorial High School, in Brooklyn, New York, during Rudolph Giuliani's years as a student there. Now in his third tour of duty at the school, he serves as a guidance counselor. He was interviewed on June 1, 2005, in his office at the school.

Benjamin Brafman, an attorney, is a partner in the New York City law firm Brafman Associates, P.C., where he practices criminal law. In 1986, Mr. Brafman represented Simon Berger, a lock manufacturer who was prosecuted by then U.S. attorney for the Southern District of New York Rudolph Giuliani on bribery charges and acquitted. He was interviewed on May 20, 2005, at his law offices in New York City.

Steven Brill, a contributing editor and columnist during the 1970s with *New York* magazine and *Esquire*, in 1978 founded *The American Lawyer*, for which he served as editor until 1982, when he became chairman and CEO of American Lawyer Media, L.P. In 1991, Mr. Brill founded and served as president, CEO, and editor in chief of Court TV. He then served for five years as chairman and CEO of Brill Media Holdings, L.P., where he founded *Brill's Content* magazine, and for two years as chairman and CEO of Media Central. Post-9/11, Mr. Brill became a columnist/consultant for *Newsweek* and the author of *How America Confronted the September 12th Era*. In 2003, he founded Verified Identity Pass, creator of a voluntary, private biometrically secure national identification card. He was interviewed on October 14, 2005, in New York City.

Charles M. Carberry served from 1979 to 1985 as assistant U.S. attorney for the Southern District of New York and from 1985 to 1986 as deputy chief of its Criminal Division. Mr. Carberry then became chief of the Securities and Commodities Fraud Unit for one year. He is currently a partner in the international law firm Jones Day. He was interviewed on September 23, 2005, in New York City.

Glenn Corbett, a professor of fire sciences at the John Jay College of Criminal Justice, in New York City, is the editor of *Fire Engineering* magazine. He also serves as a volunteer fireman in New Jersey. Professor Corbett testified at the 9/11 Commission hearings. He was interviewed on October 20, 2005, in New York City.

Saikou Diallo, a Guinean-born businessman, is the father of Amadou Diallo, the twenty-three-year-old immigrant killed on the evening of February 4, 1999, in the vestibule of his Bronx apartment building during an action by the NYPD's Street Crime Unit. Mr. Diallo now lives and works in New York City's borough of Queens, where he serves as president of the Amadou Diallo Educational, Humanitarian & Charity Foundation. He was interviewed on June 28, 2005, at the foundation's offices in Maspeth, New York.

David Norman Dinkins served as a member of the New York State Assembly and as the city clerk of Manhattan prior to his election as borough president in 1985. Four years later, in 1989, he was elected mayor of New York City, defeating Rudolph Giuliani. Following one term as mayor, he was defeated in 1993 by Mr. Giuliani. Mayor Dinkins is currently a professor of public affairs at Columbia University's School of International and Public Affairs. He was interviewed on November 28, 2005, in New York City.

Marie Dorismond is the older sister of Patrick Dorismond, the twenty-six-year-old security guard with the 34th Street Partnership who was shot and killed on the evening of March 16, 2000, on a Manhattan street near his workplace by an undercover narcotics detective during an attempted drug bust. Following her brother's death, Ms. Dorismond, who then worked with the mentally disabled at St. Clare's Hospital in New York City, moved to Florida. She was interviewed on September 28, 2005, by telephone.

Raoul Lionel Felder, an attorney, is a partner in Raoul Lionel Felder, P.C., a New York City firm practicing matrimonial and family law. He represented Nancy Capasso in her divorce from Carlantonio "Andy" Capasso and Rudolph Giuliani in his divorce from Donna Hanover. He is a confidant of both Mr. Giuliani and the humorist Jackie Mason. He was interviewed on May 16, 2005, at his law offices in New York City.

Stanley Friedman, the former Democratic Party leader of the borough of the Bronx, was prosecuted in 1986 by then U.S. attorney Rudolph Giuliani on a variety of charges relating to corruption during the administration of Mayor Ed Koch. Convicted of racketeering, conspiracy, and mail fraud, Mr. Friedman was sentenced to twelve years imprisonment but was released in 1992. He is the manager of the Staten Island Hotel on Staten Island, New York. He was interviewed at the hotel on July 13, 2005.

Sukhreet Gabel, née Julie Bess, was in 1988 the chief witness against her mother, Judge Hortense Gabel, in then U.S. attorney for the Southern District of New York Rudolph Giuliani's prosecution on a variety of charges, including conspiracy and bribery, of the judge, the former Miss America Bess Myerson, and Myerson's companion, Carlantonio "Andy" Capasso. She was interviewed on May 17, 2005, in New York City.

Jay Goldberg, an attorney, is the founder of Jay Goldberg, P.C., a New York City firm, where he practices general civil and criminal law. He represented Carlantonio "Andy" Capasso and Bess Myerson, both of whom were prosecuted in 1988 by then U.S. attorney for the Southern District of New York Rudolph Giuliani on conspiracy and bribery charges. He was interviewed on June 15, 2005, in New York City.

Mark Green, a Democrat, served as New York City's commissioner of Consumer Affairs during the Dinkins administration, from 1990 to 1993. He was then elected to the office of public advocate, which he held from 1994 to 2001. Mr. Green was his party's mayoral candidate in the race against Michael Bloomberg in 2001 but would have succeeded to the mayoralty had Giuliani run for, and been elected to, the Senate in 2000. He was interviewed on September 13, 2005, in New York City.

Malcolm Hoenlein served as executive director of the New York–based Jewish Community Relations Council until 1986, when he was named executive vice chairman of the Conference of Presidents of Major American Jewish Organizations. He was interviewed on July 21, 2005, in New York City.

Edward Irving Koch, following his eight years (from 1969 to 1977) as a member of the U.S. House of Representatives (D-NY), served as mayor of the City of New York from 1978 to 1989. Also an attorney, he is a member of the New York City firm Bryan Cave LLP. A frequent contributor of articles and columns to publications, Mr. Koch is also a prolific author. Among his books is *Giuliani: Nasty Man*, written in 1999, during Mr. Giuliani's second term as mayor of the City of New York. He was interviewed on May 13, 2005, at his law offices in New York City.

Gerald Lefcourt, an attorney specializing in criminal defense, practices in Manhattan. He served as president of the National Association of Criminal Defense Lawyers from 1997 to 1998. He was interviewed on July 18, 2005, in New York City.

Frank Luntz was associated with the New York *Daily News* when in 1993 he was selected by Rudolph Giuliani as pollster for his second mayoral campaign. He went on to conduct polling during both terms of the Giuliani administration. Mr. Luntz continues in his role as pollster to major political candidates. He was interviewed on July 11, 2005, by telephone.

Ruth Wyler Messinger, a Democrat, served as a member of the New York City Council from 1977 to 1989 and as borough president of Manhattan from 1990 to 1997. In 1997, she was her party's losing candidate against the incumbent mayor, Rudolph Giuliani. She currently serves as president of the New York–based American Jewish World Service. She was interviewed on May 17, 2005, at her home in New York City.

Albert O'Leary served as press officer for the Department of Sanitation from 1973 to 1980; as press officer at Police Headquarters from 1983 to 1987; as director of media services for the Transit Police Department from 1987 to 1995; as director of employee communications for the New York City Transit Authority from 1996 to 1998; and as vice president for public affairs for the Transit Authority from 1998 to 2002. He has served since 2002 as director of communications for the police union, the Police Benevolent Association. He was interviewed on June 15, 2005, in New York City.

John O'Leary, as Brother Aloysius Kevin, was from 1951 to 1968 a member of the religious order the De La Salle Christian Brothers. From 1958 to 1961, he was a teacher and mentor to Rudolph Giuliani at Bishop Loughlin Memorial High School. While serving in that capacity, Brother Kevin, as he was then known, became a confidant and guest of the Giuliani family. After leaving the religious order, he resumed the name John O'Leary. He is married and lives in California. He was interviewed on July 5, 2005, by telephone.

Sally Regenhard is the mother of the late Christian Michael Otto

Regenhard, one of the 343 members of the New York City Fire Department who died on September 11, 2001. The twenty-eight-year-old Christian, still on new-hire probation with Engine Company 279, was last seen alive on that morning in a lobby of the World Trade Center. Impelled to activism, Ms. Regenhard, formerly the public relations director of the Hebrew Hospital Home, and later a private consultant, became an activist on behalf of the victims of 9/11 as the founder and chairperson of the Skyscraper Safety Campaign. She was interviewed on September 27, 2005, in the Bronx, New York.

Fran Reiter was chairperson of the New York State Liberal Party when Rudolph Giuliani was considering his first run for the mayoralty of New York City. She served as Giuliani's deputy campaign manager for operations in his second mayoral campaign, in 1993; as deputy mayor during his first term, from 1994 to 1997; and as campaign manager for his reelection campaign, in 1997. Ms. Reiter went on to serve as president and CEO of New York City's Convention and Visitors Bureau from 1998 to mid-1999, and as executive director of the Public Theater. She is currently a partner, with Martin Begun, in Reiter-Begun Associates, L.L.C., a Manhattan-based consulting firm. She was interviewed on June 21, 2005, in New York City.

Edward D. Reuss, who in his twenty-nine-year career with the NYPD reached the rank of captain, joined the police force in 1963. He served as a sergeant from 1973 to 1981, as a lieutenant from 1981 to 1989, and as a captain from 1989 to 1992, when he retired. He is the founder of NY COP, an online magazine to which he contributes articles. He was interviewed on June 20, 2005, in New York City.

Sanford Rubenstein, an attorney, is a partner at Rubenstein & Rynecki, a Brooklyn, New York, firm. A longtime activist on behalf of the Haitian community, in 1997, during the Giuliani mayoralty, he represented Abner Louima, as well as Mr. Louima's family. He also serves as the personal attorney to the Reverend Al Sharpton. He was interviewed on June 2, 2005, at his law offices in Brooklyn, New York.

Gene Russianoff serves as senior attorney with the New York Public Interest Research Group (NYPIRG). In that capacity, he led many campaigns on behalf of citizens' organizations during the Giuliani administration. He continues to advocate on behalf of the citizens of New York City. He was interviewed on June 3, 2005, at the NYPIRG offices in New York City.

George Schneider was a classmate of Rudolph Giuliani's at Bishop Loughlin Memorial High School in Brooklyn, New York, from 1957 to

1961, as well as at Manhattan College, in Riverdale, New York, from 1961 to 1965. He was interviewed on July 12 and August 24, 2005, by telephone.

Derek S. Sells, an attorney, served as a staff attorney with the Public Defender Service, in Washington, D.C., from 1990 to 1995. Since that time, he has been a partner at the Cochran Firm, founded by the late Johnnie Cochran. Mr. Sells represented the family of Patrick Dorismond, a young Haitian American security guard shot by a New York City police officer on March 16, 2000. He was interviewed on August 22, 2005, at the Cochran Firm, in New York City.

The Reverend Al Sharpton has been an activist in the African American community for several decades. President of the National Action Network, he mounted demonstrations during the Giuliani era following the brutalization of Abner Louima and the murders of Amadou Diallo and Patrick Dorismond. Mr. Sharpton ran in the Democratic Party's presidential primary in 2004. He was interviewed on June 14, 2005, in New York City.

Fred Siegel is the former senior editor of *City Journal*, published by the Conservative Manhattan Institute; he served as an unpaid adviser to the mayoral campaign of Rudolph Giuliani in 1993. A prolific writer, he is the author of *The Prince of the City*, published in 2005. He is a professor at Cooper Union, in New York. He was interviewed on July 7, 2005, in New York City.

Henry Stern, a member of the Liberal Party, was a member-at-large of the City Council from 1971 to 1981. He served as commissioner of the New York City Department of Parks and Recreation both during the administration of Mayor Edward I. Koch, from 1983 to 1990, and that of Mayor Rudolph Giuliani, from 1994 to 2001. He was a cofounder, in 2002, of New York Civic, a New York City public interest organization. He was interviewed on August 11 and September 1, 2005, in New York City.

John Sturc, an attorney, served as associate director of the U.S. Securities and Exchange Commission's Division of Enforcement from 1984 to 1990. He is a partner in the firm Gibson, Dunn & Crutcher, LLP, in Washington, D.C. He was interviewed on October 24, 2005, by telephone.

Richard Thornburgh was a colleague of Rudolph Giuliani's from 1975 to 1977 in his capacity as assistant attorney general in charge of the Criminal Division of the U.S. Department of Justice. Elected governor of Pennsylvania in 1978, he served two terms. He was then appointed attorney general of the United States, serving in that position from 1988 to 1991. From 1992 to 1993, Governor Thornburgh was undersecretary of the United Nations. He was interviewed on August 24, 2005, by telephone.

Alan Vinegrad, an attorney, served as deputy chief of the Criminal Division of the Eastern District of New York from 1995 to 1997, later becoming chief from 1998 to 1999; as deputy chief assistant U.S. attorney for the Eastern District of New York from 1999 to 2001; and as U.S. attorney for the Eastern District of New York from 2001 to 2002. He is at present a partner in the New York City office of Covington & Burling. He was interviewed there on June 28, 2005.

Robert Volpe is the father of Justin Volpe, the NYPD officer who pled guilty in the August 9, 1997, attack on Abner Louima. Robert Volpe served in the NYPD, where he rose to the rank of captain. As a noted undercover art theft detective he was the subject of the book *Art Cop Robert Volpe, Art Crime Detective*. Now retired, he visits his son monthly at the Minnesota prison where he is serving his thirty-year sentence. He was interviewed on July 7, 2005, in New York City.

Rudy Washington, an African American construction industry entrepreneur who had been the target of mob violence, met Rudolph Giuliani after having decided to endorse him in his second mayoral campaign against David Dinkins. A member of Mayor-elect Giuliani's transition team in 1993, Mr. Washington served in the Giuliani administration as commissioner of the Department of Business Services from 1994 to 1996, and as deputy mayor for Community Development and Business Services from 1996 to 2001. He was interviewed on July 20, 2005, in New York City.

Stephen C. Worth, an attorney, served as assistant district attorney for Kings County from 1976 to 1980. He later founded various firms on Long Island, where he practiced from 1981 to 1998. That year, he became a founding partner in Worth Longworth & London L.L.P., which is under contract to the Police Benevolent Association to represent its members in criminal and disciplinary cases. In that capacity Mr. Worth represented Police Officer Charles Schwarz, a defendant in the Abner Louima case, and Police Officer Edward McMellon, a defendant in the Amadou Diallo case. He was interviewed on July 14, 2005, in New York City.

PART I

The Softer, Gentler Rudy Giuliani

Chapter 1

THE MAYOR'S POIGNANT LAST STATE OF THE CITY ADDRESS

I'm never going to have a better job.

—Rudy Giuliani, at the conclusion of his final
State of the City address, January 8, 2001

Rudolph William Louis Giuliani—"Rudy" to friend and foe alike—had a lot on his mind as he entered the City Council Chamber at City Hall on that January day to deliver his final State of the City address. The last year had not been a good one. On Thursday, April 27, 2000, the penultimate year of his final term as mayor of New York City as dictated by term limits, Rudy had stunned New Yorkers by disclosing that he was engaged in the fight of his life, having been diagnosed only the day before with prostate cancer, the disease that had killed his father nineteen years earlier.

Then, on May 10, following several years of rumors about friction in his marriage of sixteen years to his second wife, television personality and actress Donna Hanover, and one week after a photograph of him strolling with his new love, Judith Nathan, appeared in the *New York Post*, Rudy announced, without informing Donna, that they were separating. That revelation would lead to the public airing of many of the messy details of their troubled union.

And there was more to come: on May 19, Rudy, who had announced his intention to run for the Senate seat being vacated by the veteran Democrat, Daniel Patrick Moynihan, pitting him against First Lady Hillary Rodham Clinton, the Democratic Party's declared candidate, further stunned New Yorkers by announcing that he was dropping out of the race. It was a terrible decision for Rudy to have to make. While he had seemed almost

3

ambivalent about the race prior to the disclosure of his illness—infuriating some of his closest advisers, who thought he could have deflected attention from his marital mess by trouncing Hillary—Rudy told a standing-room-only press briefing at City Hall simply, "This is not the right time for me to run for office. If it were six months ago or it were a year from now, maybe it would be different. But it isn't different and that's the way life is."

By year's end, the lame-duck mayor's legacy, despite the many achievements of his first term, was in question. His heroism on September 11 lay months ahead. Now he was being castigated for igniting the very racial strife he had pledged to eradicate, and his approval rating had slid precipitously, reflecting the electorate's dissatisfaction.

———————

Stanley Friedman, former Democratic Party leader, Bronx, New York; prosecuted in 1986 by then U.S. attorney Rudolph Giuliani   He was a *dead*-duck mayor before 9/11. It was cumulative; his reputation had finally caught up to him and he was just not the right person for the job anymore.

Raoul Felder, attorney practicing matrimonial and family law at Raoul Lionel Felder P.C., in New York City; represented Rudolph Giuliani in his divorce from Donna Hanover   People get tired of your face after a while. Look at Churchill—after winning a war, the Man of the Century was voted out of office. I don't think he [Giuliani] was at a disastrous level, but he had fallen a lot, and there was complacency. But he was still an important enough figure because he had the book contracts [for *Leadership*, with Ken Kurson, 2002; and a memoir, which was scheduled for publication in September 2005] *before* 9/11—they were healthy contracts—so he was not such a has-been, not a bit of a has-been, even.

Fran Reiter, New York State chair, Liberal Party; deputy campaign manager for operations, Rudolph Giuliani's second mayoral campaign; deputy mayor, administration of Mayor Rudolph Giuliani (first term); campaign manager, Giuliani's third campaign   The Rudy Giuliani who took office that second term was a very different person than the one I saw towards the end of the campaign, where term limits, and the prospect of term limits, weighed very heavily on him and I didn't see a lot of joy in Rudy when he got reelected. I mean, he got reelected by this *huge* margin: he's not just a Republican winning election again; he wins by sixteen points! He should have been *ecstatic*. He wasn't, and I have to believe it was from two things: one, it was the beginning of the end, and the truth is, it's not necessarily that he *would have run* for a third term if he could have, but just the *prospect* of being able to run and not being viewed as a lame duck. Psychologically, it makes for a very different approach to governing. This weighed very, very heavily on him and influenced how he governed in that second term. He seemed to lose his passion for the big projects. He got nitpicky.

Benjamin Brafman, attorney; represented Simon Berger, prosecuted in 1986 by Rudolph Giuliani   Rudy was not at a good place in his personal or public life: he was being criticized throughout the city, by various groups, as being either wrong on certain issues, or too tough, or not sympathetic. And his personal life was in the tabloids on a daily basis and he had been personally embarrassed.

Herman Badillo, candidate for comptroller on the Giuliani fusion ticket, 1993; fiscal monitor, New York City public schools, during the Giuliani administration; chairman, City University of New York board of trustees   He was in a decline because of relations with Donna. People didn't think that he had behaved properly then: as a matter of courtesy, you go and talk to your wife and say, "I want a divorce." You don't have a press conference to announce it. And you don't parade your girlfriend around town. That, certainly, people felt, was inexcusable behavior. That, I think, was the thing that brought him down [in the public's estimation].

Ruth Messinger, borough president of Manhattan, 1990–1997; defeated Democratic Party candidate against incumbent mayor Rudolph Giuliani, 1997   The most revolting thing about this man is the way in which he divorced his wife. I'm sure the health thing was serious, but this is not a man who lets things stand in his way to get what he wants. I think that he was given information that he would have a hard time [running for the Senate against Hillary Clinton].

Not one to be deterred, though, the mayor launched into his final State of the City address with his customary oratorical flair, displaying anger at one moment, humor the next. Speaking extemporaneously as he moved back and forth to more fully connect with his audience, Rudy Giuliani was, as he would state the following year in his memoir, *Leadership*, "in full organizational mode," outlining his plan to re-create the Office of Emergency

Management and the Administration for Children's Services as "permanent freestanding agencies" and to "merge the Human Resources Administration and the Department of Education, to further the goal of turning HRA into an employment agency."

John O'Leary, formerly Brother Aloysius Kevin, one of Rudolph Giuliani's teachers at Bishop Loughlin Memorial High School, 1958–1961   Emotionally, his thoughts are very positive. I think it has as much to do with the personality he has genetically as any of his religious training. All that training was important but was absorbed into that kind of straightforward, positive personal psychology he has. He tends to look on the bright side of things and doesn't get down and think about all the things that won't work; he's not that kind of person. He's upbeat, and this is the Rudy *I* knew. It's not just his religious convictions and his strength of character, but his *personality*; he has a very positive personality.

Herman Badillo   At these State of the City things, he spoke extemporaneously; he didn't have any notes or any power points [PowerPoint presentations] or anything like that, which made him very effective because he'd just get up and talk about whatever the issues were—and then point out how he felt about being mayor.

Raoul Felder   I was at all the State of the City speeches. He went on without notes. At the first one after he was reelected, he introduced the commissioners and someone thought he had a thing in his ear—that someone was prompting him, so they asked him later, "How did you *do* that for an hour and a half or two hours?" He said, "I treated it as if I was making a summation to a jury and I had all the points in my head. And once you have that, it's simple."

Mark Green, public advocate, City of New York, 1994–2001; Democratic Party mayoral candidate, 2001   I attended every one of his State of the City addresses and they were tours de force. To watch him speak an eighty-minute State of the City address was exhausting but impressive. But I learned something from him: while most politicians in that situation would read a speech for twenty or thirty minutes, *he* would speak into a mike, without a podium, a prompter, or notes, for *eighty* minutes. And so when I announced for mayor, or when I now give a speech of consequence, I try to write it and learn it in my head and not read it, literally.

As he spoke, the mayor gathered steam, exclaiming at one point, "We should be ashamed that we don't have the political courage to take on the unions, the special interests, and everything else." Then, as if to affirm his place in history despite his low approval rating, he displayed two contrasting blowups of *Time* magazine covers, published a decade apart. The first one, from 1990, bore the legend "The Rotting of the Big Apple," while the second, dated January 1, 2000, featured a photograph of the massive millennium Times Square celebration that had taken place only days earlier in a safer, cleaner, more economically viable New York City.

His proud, defiant expression giving way to wistful reflection, the always politically ambitious and often contentious Rudy Giuliani confided to the several hundred administration workers who had crowded into the Council Chamber to hear his final State of the City address, "I'm never going to have a better job."

Richard Thornburgh, assistant attorney general in charge of the Criminal Division, U.S. Department of Justice, 1988–1991, and colleague of Rudolph Giuliani's, 1975–1977   His passion for the city was pretty evident [going back to the 1970s, when Thornburgh served with Giuliani in the Department of Justice]. In addition to his competence as a chief magistrate, he had kind of a cheerleader quality to him that came through when he talked about New York.

Frank Luntz, selected by Rudolph Giuliani as pollster for his second and third mayoral campaigns, in 1993 and 1997   I met him for the first time when I was pitching him, when I wanted to do business for him. I was surprised at how he really, truly loved New York City. He believed that New York was worth fighting for.

Fred Siegel, adviser to the mayoral campaign of Rudolph Giuliani, 1993; author, *The Prince of the City*, 2005   He loved the job; he likes doing things and accomplishing things as opposed to simply filling out his résumé. He submerged his own enormous ego into the well-being of the city.

Mark Green   He was sincere that day. And of course he would be emotional in his last State of the City, when, by law, he couldn't serve any longer and he had just withdrawn from a national election because of illness. I think he's a sincere bully and I agree that many other times he thought that bullying was the way to get things done. To say this in 1994 would have been regarded as way too personal an analysis; to say it in 2005 is simply to say what now everyone believes, even his closest friends. I guess in the law a judge would *stipulate* that he's a bully and you'd have to figure out whether you like it or not.

Stanley Friedman   It's the best job that anybody can have because he knows in his heart of hearts that he can make positive changes for eight million people in the City of New York. They want it because of the challenge, because of the ego, because of the arrogance, because of the drive.

Fran Reiter   It's generally viewed that had 9/11 not happened, he would have limped out of office still being remembered for this unbelievable first term, which was a metamorphosis, creating a metamorphosis in the way New York was governed. But, in fact, the second term was pretty lackluster, and you see him overreacting or under-reacting to very public issues. What do I think happened? His personal life was in *total* upheaval—the kids were at the most vulnerable age; his marriage was a disaster—this was his *second* marriage, not his first; this is a very religious guy, this is a Catholic. These were important issues to him from a religious standpoint. He got through the '97 campaign and, frankly, I think he was depressed. I have no proof of that, but my sense is that he was psychologically somewhere else.

Herman Badillo   He was pretty much close to tears, but he was very emotional *generally*. I'm sure he would have loved to stay as mayor, if he could have, for another three or four terms.

Lilliam Barrios-Paoli, commissioner, New York City Department of Personnel; commissioner, New York City Department of Housing Preservation and Development, 1996–1997; commissioner/ administrator, Human Resources Administration, 1997–1998   Then you add to that the fact that now that he may be ready for a private life, he doesn't have a private life anymore; he's met somebody—clearly he's somebody who likes ladies—and then he finds out he has cancer in the most vulnerable place that a man can have a cancer. Something had knocked the wind out of him. I think the fact that he knew that he couldn't be reelected certainly mattered and counted. I don't think he was entirely sure what else he wanted to do. It is very difficult after you're mayor of the City of New York to go to Albany and be governor. And going back into private practice didn't seem like the most thrilling thing on earth. It was sort of like: what do I do *now*?

Benjamin Brafman   Rudy was known as a tough guy. There is a softer, kinder, gentler Rudy Giuliani today. It's a natural evolvement for someone who has gone through an upheaval in their personal life, is in a new relationship in which he appears to be happy, and is going through cancer. That is a defining moment—my wife and I went through breast cancer together and it was a defining moment for us—and it gives you a different perspective on life.

Raoul Felder   You don't have to get past the cancer; he was in the throes of that treatment and he isn't the kind of guy who wants to give half an effort to anything. He was not in good shape physically. Not a lot of people know about it, but he got two kinds of treatment, the seeds and the radioactive. I knew two other people who went through the same thing and they were literally out of action—they'd come in a couple of mornings a week. He could not run the city and do both; it was just physically impossible. I don't think he ever had a question about beating it.

Ed Koch, mayor, City of New York, 1978–1989   His health was very important to him; I don't think there was anything false about his comments at the time. He would have been very difficult as an opponent. Never, *ever* underestimate him.

Herman Badillo   Having prostate cancer upset him more than I thought it should have because these days, it's not *that* serious a problem. I think it had to do with the fact that, apparently, he was diagnosed accidentally—he had always been terrified of getting the PSA [prostate specific antigen] test, and then he found out that he had cancer and he was really scared to death because he didn't know enough about it. And then he went around talking to all kinds of doctors; he circled around, talking to more doctors than I thought was necessary. I was diagnosed with prostate cancer, and I went to New York Hospital, I talked to my doctor, and I got seeds, which he eventually agreed to do, but I didn't need hormones or all the other stuff. He went to my doctor; he went to Mount Sinai; he went to [the University Hospital of the] Albert Einstein [College of Medicine]; he went all over the place—and I couldn't understand why he had made such a big to-do about it, but I guess it was because he had never taken the precaution of taking the PSA test every year and he was worried and very upset about it.

Lilliam Barrios-Paoli   And his father died of it, so the sense of his vulnerability; his humanity; his frailty; the end of a job he loves; the end of a marriage that, whatever it was, *meant* something. I think a lot of it was that in the city he loves so much, not everybody loves him back. Ed Koch used to say that if everybody who was angry at him [Koch] would get together, he would lose, and it happened. And if you've been there long enough to pique a lot of people, they come at you. And then the rhetoric in New York City was abysmal, especially around race. Was he compassionate? No. But did he have anything remotely resembling to do with any of the incidents? No. Did he incite the police? No, the police don't need to be incited; they do their own thing. Could he have been a more compassionate mayor? Yes, but from there to accuse him of practically doing it, that's a little extreme. All of that, I'm sure, had a lot to do with it.

Mark Green   He had worn out his welcome because of his difficult personality. Giuliani's public temperament was so angry and off-putting in this multiracial city that people had just had enough of him. And then his personal difficulties with his marriage and with his Nixon-like "enemies list" led to a public exhaustion with him.

Steven Brill, founder and former editor, *The American Lawyer*; founder and former president, CEO, and editor in chief, Court TV   It could be that they wanted Rudy without the *Rudy*. The marital stuff revealed the hard side of him that people didn't like, as did his reaction to the Dorismond case. Maybe people felt: he's a good manager, but maybe there's someone else who can do it without those rough edges.

———

While the usually tough political personality who strode from the dais on that January day in 2001 was decidedly subdued, the mayor had clearly demonstrated that there was a lot more fight in him. Then, by his rare public display of vulnerability, he acknowledged what his close political associates and friends have always believed—that there exists a softer, kinder Rudy Giuliani capable of feeling personal pain. Who *is* that man?

Chapter 2

WHO *IS* RUDY GIULIANI?

I actually think I am a very polite person.
—Rudy Giuliani, quoted in *George* magazine, April 1999

Gerald Lefcourt, attorney practicing criminal defense; president, National Association of Criminal Defense Lawyers, 1997–1998 Not long ago, a woman invited me to the opening night of a play she was producing. We were seated on the aisle, in the second or third row, and she noticed that Rudy was seated across from us. She asked if I knew him. When I said yes, she wanted to meet him, so I took her across the aisle and tried to introduce her, and Rudy said to me, "What are *you* doing here?"

First Encounters/First Impressions

Steven Brill I met him in the early years when I had started *The American Lawyer* magazine. I remember it vividly. He was kind of shy and certainly didn't quite fill a room. I was interviewing Harold Tyler—"Ace" Tyler as he was known—who was Rudy's mentor. He was a partner in a law firm and we were talking in his office at Rockefeller Center, and he said, "I want you to meet one of my guys" and he told his secretary, "Send Rudy in." He [Rudy] was an eager guy who was about my age, a couple of years older. He came in, shook hands with me, and said hello, and the last I heard from him until he was associate attorney general was when one of our reporters did a piece about the Reagan administration's immigration policies, which Rudy was running; there was a particular controversy over people coming in from Haiti, and he was the guy in charge of the Crone Detention Center, which was out in the Florida Everglades. The reporter wanted to interview him about that and he was kind of elusive, so I called him and set up that interview. And then he became U.S. attorney [Giuliani first joined the U.S. Attorney's Office in 1970, remained there for three years, joined the U.S. Department of Justice in 1973, and became the U.S. attorney in 1983]. At about that time, I was writing my book about the Teamsters Union [*The Teamsters*, published in 1978] and I talked to him a lot because he was prosecuting a lot of organized crime cases in New York. Then, for our fifteenth anniversary, we did a cover naming about ten lawyers who had made a big difference in the world, and Rudy was on the cover, along with a guy named Joel [E.] Hyatt—he had started a chain of legal clinics—and Joe Flom, who had founded Skadden, Arps [Meagher, Slate and Flom]. He [Rudy] was then U.S. attorney and he happily went up to Joe Flom's office to have the picture taken there. He's been a friend of mine since. I've talked to him about the business I'm now doing and I've talked to him on and off a lot since then.

Gerald Lefcourt   In the mid '70s, when Rudy was chief of narcotics in the Southern District, I had a drug case before Judge [Robert] Carter, who made a ruling that was perceived to be against the prosecution. Rudy came down to the judge's courtroom to try to have it undone. The whole thing had been litigated in front of the judge, and I thought it was pretty arrogant to try to get him to change his mind because Rudy was chief of narcotics. The judge didn't change his mind. Rudy was not disappointed; he was *offended*.

Jay Goldberg, founder, Jay Goldberg, P.C.; represented Carlantonio "Andy" Capasso and Bess Myerson, prosecuted in 1988 by then U.S. attorney for the Southern District of New York Rudolph Giuliani   It was the *comb-over*! I said to myself, Why couldn't his wife tell him how stupid that is? So he's bald. I'm happy that he's "listened" to me [Mr. Giuliani has abandoned his comb-over for a more conventional style]. Now his only impediment is a speech defect, his lisp.

Mark Green   I lived at 444 East 86th Street [a high-rise cooperative apartment building in the Yorkville section of Manhattan's Upper East Side] from 1980 to 1982, on the thirty-fourth floor; Rudy Giuliani lived at 444 East 86th Street on the thirty-fifth floor, in what, obviously, was a pure coincidence, so I saw him periodically in the building we both lived in before we became citywide officials. And I knew him as a prominent Justice Department attorney, and I was a consumer advocate. I thought, he looks like a can-do Republican.

Malcolm Hoenlein, executive vice chairman, Conference of Presidents of Major American Jewish Organizations People had told me about Rudy, but I had not known him before I took him and his wife, Donna Hanover, to Israel in the early '80s in a program I had initiated in the late '70s identifying people who were or would be influential in the future. I had Chris Matthews, Tim Russert, David Dinkins, and Ed [Edolphus] Towns [member, U.S. House of Representatives, D-NY]. Rudy was certainly a high-profile person at the time and he was very interested; he asked good questions and was clearly deeply moved by the trip. He talked about it many, many times afterwards. He blended in, and Donna was *incredible*: she was intelligent, on top of everything. We had a reunion of all the people who had gone on our trips. We did a very funny slide show: I had taken pictures of them all sleeping at different stages of meetings and on the bus—we had a lot of congressmen—and Donna was the emcee. She did it with such humor. She was really incredible.

David Dinkins, mayor, City of New York, 1989–1993, having defeated Rudolph Giuliani I have a vague recollection of having met him when he was U.S. attorney and I was Manhattan borough president. The fellow who was first deputy U.S. attorney said that Rudy had an interest in politics and he thought it would be interesting if we met. We had a mutual friend who had been an assistant U.S. attorney under Bob Morgenthau and so I said okay and we met. I had no particular impression of him other than that he was ambitious.

Fred Siegel I met him in late '92. My first impression was of intelligence; he's very bright. He takes in a vast amount of information very quickly and makes coherent sense of it.

Malcolm Hoenlein To me the barometer [on politicians' visits to Israel] was always how they reacted at Yad Vashem [located in Jerusalem, the Holocaust museum and memorial to the six million Jews who perished in the Nazi death camps]. I had some who went through Yad Vashem who walked in and walked out and that was it, and I had some who were literally inconsolable for twenty-four hours. Giuliani was clearly deeply moved and was more knowledgeable than many of the others about some of the things that were on display.

Lilliam Barrios-Paoli   The first time I ever met him was for a job interview [in December 1993]. Randy Mastro, who was the chief of staff, had asked me to come and interview with him, and I assumed that it was going to be very brief—it was a Saturday morning—but I sat with him for about an hour and a half. I was astounded. He struck me as a very, very, very intelligent person—somebody who came to the mayoralty with a real agenda of what he wanted to accomplish. I was very surprised; I was not expecting that.

Floyd Abrams, attorney specializing in First Amendment issues; represented the Brooklyn Museum in its suit against Mayor Rudolph Giuliani   I was invited to have lunch with him by one of his partners to welcome him back to the private bar [in 1989, when Mr. Giuliani joined White & Case]. He represented the [*New York*] *Daily News*, and we discussed some First Amendment issues. I don't think that I, or our First Amendment discussion, interested him very much; he was indifferent to claims of civil liberties and the First Amendment. I also thought that he thought civil liberties was for sissies. It's not that he was against free speech or that it was his priority to destroy free speech in America, but that this was not the stuff of strong men. Walking away, I didn't think any better of him than when the lunch had started.

The Fun-Loving Rudy

Despite his Dickensian visage, Rudy Giuliani has a fun-loving side, which was evident during his eight years in office. He loved dressing in drag for Inner Circle dinners, sponsored by New York City's press corps, which take place annually and feature skits lampooning newsmakers.

Ed Koch   He can be absolutely charming over lunch and he does have a good sense of humor.

Richard Thornburgh   He wasn't a stiff by any stretch of the imagination. His sense of humor is sardonic, but he enjoyed a good laugh. He wasn't a jokester or anything like that. But he had an appreciation for some of the absurdities of life. And we were working hard during that period because we had a very important charge: the Department of Justice had in many quarters been discredited by its role in the Watergate investigation, and we had an attorney general of unquestioned integrity, who took quite seriously his obligation to restore integrity in the department itself. So all of us were under the baleful eye of [Attorney General] Edward Levi as we went around our tasks. But Rudy had worked for the late Judge Tyler, who was possessed of a twinkle in his eye and a great sense of humor himself, so while we worked hard and there was a lot of grinding that went on, it was not steely-eyed and without any respite. All of us enjoyed and appreciated the chance to be there. It was an exciting time.

Steven Brill   He laughs a lot. Last year, I was at a Yankee play-off game and I was standing on line to get a soda with one of my kids and this guy comes up from behind and puts his hands on my back and says, "What are *you* doing here?" I turn around and it's *Rudy* with his bodyguard. He's a good guy.

Raoul Felder   He does stuff in accents a lot. I can't even do it, but the *Godfather* business. He has a sense of humor, but I don't know if that comes across when you see him. He does things that nobody would dare to do—the Inner Circle stuff, dressing up like a woman; and Jackie's performance, where he put on a wig and rode this motorcycle a couple of feet in. He had enormous energy and he had a friend who owned a cigar bar, Elliot Cuker, and he used to unwind there at night—go on and on; he was the last one who wanted to go home.

Frank Luntz   The single most pleasant moments of my entire political career were sitting with him on the porch at Gracie Mansion, listening to him tell stories of when he was a prosecutor, when he worked for the Justice Department and as a prosecutor up in New York. He would go until two or three in the morning. His whole staff would leave because they'd either heard these stories before or they'd lived them and they didn't want to hear them. *I'm* a sucker for it; I *loved* it.

   We were at a steak restaurant on the far west side of town and I asked him about one of these stories and all around me I heard, "Oh, no!" And at this point—this was later in my relationship—I said, "What's your problem?" And they all looked at me and said, "We've heard this a dozen times already. We're going out for a smoke; you can sit and ask him questions." They knew that he was going to start telling stories.

Rudy, the Yankee Fan

Raoul Felder   He loved ball games and all that stuff; he was a great Yankee fan. The Yankees were playing in the World Series, and my son-in-law wanted to go. I'm not a great baseball fan, so I asked Rudy if he could get tickets and he said, "Be my guests; I'll treat you." They were not free tickets; he paid and he didn't make that much money. We go to Grand Central [a railway station located on Manhattan's East Side]—there's a Yankees Express train painted with the Yankee stripes—and we meet Pataki there. It's a night game, the longest game in the history of the World Series, and I was just jumping out of my skin. Finally we get back to Gracie Mansion, and Rudy is peppy—it must have been two or three in the morning—and he's just, "Why don't we do this again *tomorrow* night!" My son-in-law was about to say something, so I kicked him.

Frank Luntz   He talked about what it was to be a Yankee fan in Brooklyn. But what he was really saying to me was that he genuinely loved baseball, deep in his heart. This is a guy who doesn't like things because they are popular. He likes things because they mean something to him; they have a value to him that you can't quantify. It also said that he was tough, that he could withstand criticism. If you can survive as a Yankee fan in Brooklyn, you can survive *anything*, *anywhere*, by *anyone*.

Rudy, the Music Lover

Raoul Felder   He enjoys himself. I was with him once when he was conducting the symphony. He *loves* all that stuff. He's an authority on opera. When he was getting the radiation treatments, he used to play opera.

Brother Peter Bonventre, assistant principal at Bishop Loughlin Memorial High School, Brooklyn, New York, during Rudolph Giuliani's attendance   He *loved* opera, and when he appeared for an intermission feature on the Metropolitan [Opera intermission broadcast quiz] a few years ago and answered questions as part of the panel, I sent him a little congratulatory note.

Does He Have Close Friends?

Herman Badillo   He has a group of people that he meets with regularly, like Howard Koeppel. That's another thing—living in an apartment with two homosexuals [after the breakup of his marriage to Donna Hanover]; there's nobody in the Republican Party like that. All of those things are okay in New York City which would not be acceptable in Middle America.

Frank Luntz   Rudy tends to keep people around for years; people who were with him twenty years ago are still with him today, to a great degree. Peter Powers [the mayor's counsel, former deputy U.S. attorney, and colleague at the law firm White & Case], Denny Young [Jr.], and [Department of Justice colleague] Ken Caruso knew him way back *when*.

Malcolm Hoenlein   We became friends. I had opportunities to sit with him once in a while at Gracie Mansion, mostly when I would come with somebody, and I never felt ill at ease with him; I never felt pressure. And I don't remember him saying: It's too much; why are you guys coming here? And all the Israeli officials wanted to see Giuliani; he has a tremendous reputation there—even before 9/11—and he made himself available when they came; his door was always open to them. He established especially close ties with [former mayor of Jerusalem and member of the Knesset, the Israeli parliament, Ehud] Olmert and the prime minister. There's truly an emotional tie between him and Israel. I saw him there a couple of times and I was with him after a bus bombing in Jerusalem. He insisted on going on the bus when everybody said to him, "Don't do it." He said, "No, if we're going to show the people of Israel that we're really with them then you've got to go and *show* them."

Does the Intense Rudy Ever Relax?

Steven Brill   Rudy came to an anniversary of Court TV, a big party at the Metropolitan Museum, and I remember kidding him. I said, "Floyd's here" [Floyd Abrams, the noted First Amendment lawyer who was then representing the Brooklyn Museum in Giuliani's suit against that institution], and he said, "Oh really, where?" I said, "He's over there. He's going to win those cases." And he just laughed. It struck me that he didn't care.

Raoul Felder   I used to go to City Hall sometimes. He'd say hello and he was the most relaxed person in the world; you'd think he didn't have a care in the world. The guy has marital problems—that can destroy anybody; he's recovering from cancer; and the World Trade Center happens, and he went with it.

PART II

Beginnings: Brooklyn and Long Island

Chapter 3

A YANKEE FAN IN "GOD'S KINGDOM": BISHOP LOUGHLIN MEMORIAL HIGH SCHOOL

> *I played hooky to play baseball, and*
> *somehow I survived it to become mayor.*
>
> —Rudy Giuliani, quoted in the *New York Daily News*,
> October 24, 1998

Rudy Giuliani never wanted for his next meal as a small boy growing up in Brooklyn. But life was far from pleasant. His father, Harold, a saloon keeper, would send the puny, sallow-skinned boy out to play wearing a Yankees cap, making him a sure target for the jeers of the neighborhood's rabid Dodgers fans. To ward off attacks by the angry fans, Harold, who kept, and occasionally used, a baseball bat to deal with unruly customers in his saloon, gave Rudy boxing gloves when he was only two years old.

While Rudy, ever loyal to his father, would become a Yankees fan in his own right and remain one, he would pay a heavy price: as a toddler he developed a nervous tic in one eye, would later suffer from insomnia, sometimes staying awake for 48 hours at a stretch, and would be described many years later, in a profile prepared for the *New York Observer*, as possessing a "predominantly aggressive nature," as well as being a "hostile enforcer," that term defined as applying to individuals who "tend to act as though they believe they have a monopoly on divining right and wrong, good and bad . . . believe that they have a right and the obligation to control . . . are unrestrained in discharging their hostile impulses against the weak, the powerless, and the contemptible—ostensibly in the public interest."

Brother Peter Bonventre   I'm sure he was teased. It wouldn't destroy him *at all*.

21

Fred Siegel   I empathize because I'm a Yankee fan from Brooklyn. There is a certain against-the-grain perversity to it that prepares someone to take on tough opponents—a willingness to cut against the bias.

Frank Luntz   When he was five years old, they were actually going to string him up—the kids were going to hang him from a tree, not understanding that you can *kill* somebody that way. He cracks jokes about it; he tells that story with a smile on his face. But if you get him to tell the details, they're actually very violent. These were tough kids. This is New York! New York produces tough kids; tough kids become tough adults. It was his uncle who actually got him down, who saved him.

Rudy had other problems while growing up. One of his uncles—his mother's brother—was a loan shark with mob connections. To his parents' credit, they moved from Brooklyn to Long Island in order to get Rudy away from such bad influences and closer to better role models, namely other uncles, who were either firefighters or policemen.

Harold Giuliani was also a role model, admonishing Rudy, "Never lie; never steal." In 1981, at the age of seventy-three, suffering from prostate cancer, and on his deathbed, Harold told his by then well-known son, "Courage is being afraid but then doing what you have to do *anyway*." It seems the dying Harold could not summon the courage to tell Rudy of his not-so-savory past: in the 1930s, he had served a five-year sentence at Sing Sing. His crime? The armed robbery of a milkman.

Or *had* he told Rudy of his criminal past? Rudy insists that he would only learn of his father's conviction and incarceration in 2000, following its revelation by a Giuliani biographer. Can we really believe that the doggedly zealous and exceedingly ambitious Rudy, by that time a young prosecutor on the political make, knew nothing of Harold's criminal record? Or did Rudy know about it but, fearing that public knowledge might thwart his career, decide self-servingly to keep his own counsel?

John O'Leary, formerly Brother Aloysius Kevin   There were occasions where Harold and Rudy and I would go for a walk on a visit to his home. I sensed a close relationship between Rudy and both of his parents. I don't think that he was closer to Helen than he was to Harold. He was close to both of them. In about 1960, when there was the presidential race between Nixon and Kennedy, Rudy was a big Kennedy fan, whereas his mother was a Nixon fan and Harold was for Kennedy. But there was no bitterness or any kind of argument. They just admitted that they were for different people and we talked about that for a while at his home.

Bishop Loughlin Memorial High School

Established as an all-male, diocesan institution—it would become coeducational in 1974, incorporating girls from Bishop McDonald Memorial High School, in the Crown Heights section of Brooklyn—Bishop Loughlin Memorial High School originally occupied a gracious Victorian mansion built circa 1878 for, but only occupied for a short time by, the first Bishop of Brooklyn, John Loughlin. The house is now used as a residence for its faculty members, La Salle Christian Brothers. In 1933, a more utilitarian building was constructed next door—one whose architecture is typical of high schools all over the United States—and that is where, from 1957 until his graduation in 1961, Rudy Giuliani spent an intellectually and vocationally stimulating four years.

Bishop Loughlin is in a sense the educational offspring of St. James High School, established in 1851 in downtown Brooklyn. When the new Bishop Loughlin building opened in 1933, St. James closed and its students were brought there. As a diocesan school, it drew—and still does—students from Catholic parishes throughout the Diocese of Brooklyn, which is comprised of Brooklyn and Queens, as well as youngsters from Long Island, Manhattan, the Bronx, and even Staten Island, some of them not even Catholic, but enrolled there by parents seeking a better educational and social environment for their children.

In Rudy's day, any student who wished to attend a diocesan Catholic high school had to take the "Co-op Test"—it is now called the TACH (Test for Acceptance to Catholic High Schools). Standards were—and still are—rigorous: there were openings for only two young men from each parish, and scholarships were available to deserving students, 95 percent of whom went on to college. Rudy Giuliani, who lived in the Rockville Centre, Long Island, Diocese, was one of the lucky two from his parish who made the cut on both counts.

Back then, as Rudy commuted via the Long Island Railroad to Brooklyn, he would come up from the station early each school day morning and stroll through a vibrant working-class neighborhood, where the residual population from the days of the fabled Brooklyn Navy Yard still lived and worked.

Brother Peter Bonventre   It wasn't as gentrified as now. You can't live here anymore; it takes a million and a half dollars to buy a brownstone; you can't get into these new condos that they're building on Greene Avenue— what's left begins at $600,000, what's *left*, one-bedroom apartments. Would you *believe* it? It wasn't like that at all then. There were brownstones—who even thought that brownstones were important in those days? He would come from the train station and he'd walk up the way the students did. There was a little church, a Polish Roman Catholic church, and many of them would drop in there—it was converted to the Paul Robeson Theater, although it doesn't have much activity at all. Many of them liked just to mount those stairs, go into the church for a minute and then move on to the school. I'm sure he did that, too; not necessarily every day. What was the school like? It wasn't an affluent area at all, as it's becoming. There are articles in the *New York Times* about Fort Greene—about the restaurants— it wasn't that way then.

In those days, we had a lot of brothers of every age. When I first came here, in '54, I had about five years of teaching, so I was pretty young—in my midtwenties. We had a dress code in those days. The brothers—there were no priests on staff—wore a traditional habit going back to the 1700s; we were a French order [founded in 1683 by St. John Baptist De La Salle, 1651–1719.] The students had to wear a jacket and a tie at that period, unless you had a varsity sweater with a varsity letter. Otherwise you had to wear a shirt and tie. Our dress code is considerably different now: we have a uniform, but you don't have to wear a necktie and you don't have to wear a suit coat, but there is a school emblem, with a lion. I will wear clerical garb only on a very solemn occasion. At the present time I generally wear black pants and shoes and a shirt and tie [on the occasion of the authors' interview, a patterned, brightly colored tie].

There was a very, very close involvement with the students. We ran most of the activities. The editor of the yearbook would have a brother in charge. The Diocese of Brooklyn never allowed—nor did we want— American football. It was too expensive, too risky—injuries and all—and we didn't have volleyball; we have it now, for the girls. We didn't have soc- cer—soccer was not popular at that point in the U.S. But we did have all those traditional sports—tennis, swimming, baseball, handball, track—we had a professional coach; basketball.

We always considered religion an academic subject, and everybody was required to take the traditional courses—English, a language, mathemat- ics, social studies, science, phys ed, and religion, so about half of the year was taken up with religion. There was so much for them to do in their academic program that it would be very hard to squeeze in more than half a year. We followed the Regents curriculum and they took the Regents [examinations].

Rudy at Bishop Loughlin

Brother Peter Bonventre   He would come in here [to the assistant principal's office] on occasion. He was a very vivacious personality, full of spirit, a lively individual who got into the life of the school. And whatever talents he had, he used *those talents*. He was not a track star or a baseball star, but he was in intramurals for four years. And he started an opera club near the end of his stay here. He was not in the orchestra and he was not in the band. He could have been in one of those musical things, or even a chorus, but he was not. So as far as that goes, he probably is someone, like myself, who simply enjoys good music but has no ability, except to turn on the radio. I'm sure, like most of us, he sang someplace—maybe in the shower. But he didn't have any ability that I am aware of to sing. *Perform*, yes; he performs in all sorts of ways, but not musically, that I am aware of. But whatever he got into, he put his heart and soul into it.

Rudy's Intellect

John O'Leary, formerly Brother Aloysius Kevin   In 1958, when I first met Rudy, I had 250 or more students every day. I was a member of the De La Salle Christian Brothers. But I left that order in 1968—I had been a member almost seventeen years by that time—and now I'm just an ordinary member of the Church. Bishop Loughlin was a scholarship school, so all of the students were very bright and they were there because they wanted to learn. If I were to classify Rudy as a student, I would say he was above average, very bright and willing to learn. But at that point in his academic career, he lacked a little discipline. Some boys in high school are notorious for being a little disruptive and not altogether motivated. Rudy certainly had lots of energy; that became very evident to me as the year went on.

George Schneider, classmate of Rudolph Giuliani at Bishop Loughlin Memorial High School, 1957–1961   We first met as freshmen, when we were in the same class. We weren't in classes [together] after that. My impression was that he was very, very glib—very quick in responding in class and in anything that he did—and that he was outgoing and laughed easily. He certainly was not shy.

John O'Leary, formerly Brother Aloysius Kevin   My image of Rudy in those days is of a young man with a big smile on his face. He had serious moments, of course, but I think of him, generally, as a very sociable, happy, smiling person.

George Schneider   He seemed intelligent. Physically at the time, he was a bit overweight—he even was in college. We went to Manhattan College. When he was the D.A. in New York and he showed up on television on one of the magazine shows, I hadn't seen him for many years and I was just amazed at the way he looked. He looked very different; he was so *slim*.

Brother Peter Bonventre   At that point, nobody paid tuition although they did pay an activity fee. All of them were quality kids, very bright, handpicked by their parishes. Rudy was from the onset a very bright boy: he was on an elite honor roll. I'm sure that he did well in all of his subjects. If he did shine in any particular subject, it was probably social studies.

Among Rudy's classmates at Bishop Loughlin was Peter Powers, whom Rudy would later describe as his "lifelong friend." Peter would one day serve as Rudy's campaign manager and deputy mayor.

John O'Leary, formerly Brother Aloysius Kevin   I had Peter in class, but I don't remember him nearly as well as I remember Rudy. Peter was quieter than Rudy and Rudy attracted people to him; it was more Rudy's charisma that attracted Peter more than anything else.

George Schneider   When you had a conversation with Rudy, he was ready with a quip and also ready to laugh if someone else said something. He was pretty relaxed talking to people, pretty outgoing.

John O'Leary, formerly Brother Aloysius Kevin   He had a good sense of humor. It was a kind of an intellectual sense. Whenever the occasion offered, he could make a joke and laugh. He didn't make fun of people, and it certainly wasn't sardonic or sarcastic. He was a very cheerful person, someone who smiled a lot and was friendly.

Brother Peter Bonventre Every year we would have a Christmas Assembly—we still do, just before we leave for the holiday—and in his senior year, Rudy played Santa Claus. There was a lot of entertainment by the students and then, near the end of the program, he marched down the aisle with a couple of elves and sat on a large chair on the stage and regaled the audience. They brought out the gifts that they were going to give out to faculty members. Rudy was so *out there* as Santa Claus: he had this infectious smile and enjoyed being in the limelight. It's obvious from his public life that he enjoys the limelight. He's gregarious, he likes people, and all of that was certainly part of what he was here.

George Schneider He was *perfect* as Santa Claus; a little chubby, and he laughed easily. He was outgoing, you know, and he did that very well.

Did His Parents Interact with Faculty Members?

Brother Peter Bonventre They would come to parents' meetings. One of the brothers [Brother Aloysius Kevin, now John O'Leary] knew the [Giuliani] family and went to their home for dinner. That's not something we generally did.

John O'Leary, formerly Brother Aloysius Kevin Rudy had given me some trouble in class—talking; nothing worse than three-quarters of the rest of the class—and I had a reason at a particular point in the spring of his sophomore year [1958] to discipline him. At the beginning of his junior year, we had an open house and the English Department had its display up on the stage of the auditorium. Toward the end of the afternoon, I noticed a couple standing in the aisle. They came up, introduced themselves as the Giulianis, and said, "Do you remember, you had our son, Rudy, last year?" And I said, "Yes, I do." And they said, "Do you remember the time you had to discipline him? I said, "Yes, I do." And they said, "Well, we want to thank you because it made a big difference in his life; he has come along, and as far as his grades are concerned, they went up, and he's just a better student all around, and we're very grateful for what you did." Well, that took me by surprise. Then they asked me out to visit them in their home. I agreed to go. Rudy was very hospitable, very friendly, very nice, as were his parents. Rudy and I had nice conversations—there was a lot of laughing—and we had a good time. We struck up a conversation about subjects that we had never talked about in school, and I discovered that Rudy liked the opera. I was an opera buff—I *loved* the opera, and a friend of mine at the school used to treat me to the opera—so we talked a lot about that on the first occasion. And that led, a few weeks later, to the founding of an opera club at Loughlin.

Rudy's Budding Interest in Politics and Government Service

Brother Peter Bonventre   He was on what we called the "Student Court." In the Senior Poll, seniors voted for one another as the "best dressed" and all that other silly stuff, like "most handsome." He was voted "class politician." Now, why was he voted "class politician"? Maybe he was a politician even *then*. The class may have been prescient enough to foresee that.

John O'Leary, formerly Brother Aloysius Kevin   When he was a sophomore, when I had him in class, I don't remember his being particularly political. I wasn't teaching Rudy for the rest of his high school career, but I remained a friend even though I didn't have him in class, and he used to talk to me about what he was doing in terms of school politics. And, of course, he was the campaign manager for George Schneider, who didn't win.

Brother Peter Bonventre   He was a great devotee of John [Fitzgerald] Kennedy. He really admired him and I think that entered into his bloodstream. When he came to this auditorium—he announced his candidacy for mayor the first time in three different schools and he came here first—he spoke to our students and encouraged them to go into public office to serve, that you go into public office to help people. He's a believer and his own moral code came to the fore and one of the principles of that moral code is how you treat other people. He is genuinely interested in people and in service to the people. And that's what he told our students in his first candidacy. I think that John Kennedy's "Ask not what your country can do . . ." was *ingrained* in him and that he carried it out in his various positions in the United States.

John O'Leary, formerly Brother Aloysius Kevin   He was very strong for Kennedy in 1960. In fact, he took off from school once just to see Kennedy give a talk in Queens. He had, technically, played hooky. But, of course, it was a very understandable day off, to go and see a presidential candidate.

It was a big crowd and he was so very, very excited. And then he came back to school after the talk was over to see me, to tell me that he had seen Kennedy. He said, "I *saw* him, Brother Kevin, I *saw* him! I saw *Kennedy!*"

George Schneider   I didn't become aware of that until he was actually becoming my campaign manager [for Student Council president] in our junior year. He did a lot of the stuff. But he also worked with some of the students and got a little bit of funding for us.

Brother Peter Bonventre   We had three parties, the Gold Party and the Purple Party—purple and gold are our school colors—and we also had a White Party. This was a big thing: it was a whole week where they did nothing but parade around. They would be in the neighborhood either before school or after school to hawk their own candidates, to try and sell what they were going to do for the school, and they had signs all over the school—Vote for So-and-So. It was just a lot of fun and all of their creative energies went into it.

John O'Leary, formerly Brother Aloysius Kevin   Rudy was very flamboyant as far as his political work for George was concerned. They had big signs and Rudy was something of a glad-hander, making sure everybody knew that George was running. And anything that the campaign manager in this school that was fairly straitlaced and rather carefully disciplined could do, *he* did.

Why Didn't Rudy Run?

George Schneider   There was a nomination process in which the students had something to say about who could. The brothers had some role in picking the final candidates. After the nominations were in, they sorted through them and selected six people, so that you had three presidential candidates and three vice-presidential candidates. So he [Rudy] would not have had full control over it.

John O'Leary, formerly Brother Aloysius Kevin   A group of people all got together as friends and decided: you're going to run and I'll be the campaign manager. It all came out of socialization among this group of kids. It wasn't that big a deal to be president of the student council; there wasn't that much to do.

Election Day

George Schneider   That morning we came in early. We had a U-Haul trailer being pulled by a car, and there was a bunch of us in the back with signs as to what party we were. They were playing music in the back and we were waving and saying hello and tossing things into the crowd as we were driving along. The colors of Bishop Loughlin are purple and gold. We were the third party and they needed another color so they called us the "White Party," and we were going around in this interracial neighborhood with signs saying "White Party." It had nothing to do with being black or white; it just had to do with the name of our party, but we didn't think about that until afterwards. But it didn't result in any incidents. There were three of us in the race—myself, Tony Shanley, and Joe Centrella— and Joe wound up winning by two votes over me and I was three votes over Shanley, so five votes separated the three presidential candidates; that's how close it was. The race was unbelievable!

Could You Have Imagined Then That He Would Have a Successful Political Career?

Brother Peter Bonventre   No; they were kids who could get into anything. I didn't look ahead and say someone was going to be *this* or *that*, and I wouldn't be able to say that about Rudy. He went on to Manhattan College, he studied law, and we wanted him to do his best. It's that way with each of our students; they surprise us. We try to get them to the next step in their development; we try to challenge them to be the best they can be. And then they move on and they go on to college and they begin to see the variety of things they can do.

———————

Although Rudy was clearly interested in secular issues such as politics during his years at Bishop Loughlin, it was evident to his mentors there that he had a strong religious vocation. And in fact, he seriously considered becoming a priest.

John O'Leary, formerly Brother Aloysius Kevin   He was religious and he was very sincere and it wasn't a big surprise to me that he wanted to enter the priesthood. We talked it over and it seemed the right choice at that time, as I saw it for him. Remember, in the 1950s there was a big surge in religious practice and interest throughout this country, particularly among Christians who are Catholic. Thomas Merton [1915–1968, an American Christian religious personality] wrote books and was a Trappist monk, and he's an example of the kind of mentality that had taken over in postwar Catholic America. There were fairly large numbers of young men entering the priesthood and the brothers during the '50s and early '60s. It pretty much ended by the mid '60s, but when Rudy had made his decision he certainly wasn't the only one.

Brother Peter Bonventre   I wasn't surprised at all that somebody did, or *didn't* [want to enter the priesthood]. He came from a religious elementary school. Then he came to a high school where he was surrounded by priests and religious purposes. And we had vocation lessons in the religion class—questions like: What do you think you can try to discern in vocation? Should you be a married man? Should you be a priest? Should you be a brother? So they were almost forced to think about it, even in some subconscious way. It wouldn't surprise me that he asked those questions of himself.

Most parents of that period were more open to their children becoming priests or holy sisters. And we did have at that period, and a little after, a number of young men who went into the priesthood and the brotherhood. And many, especially the brothers, left. They had, maybe, tried it for a few years and said, "It's not for me" and eventually left because they needed something else for their lives. Now a lot of those people are in what we call the *Signum Te Dei*, the Sign of Faith—the translation of a Latin term. It's really one of our emblems, a brothers' symbol, so a large group who were brothers have maintained a relationship with the brothers and with each other. It's like a social club for them—they meet periodically and have picnics and things like that.

How Sincere Was Rudy's Interest in Becoming a Priest?

John O'Leary, formerly Brother Aloysius Kevin   He had the intention of going into the Montfort Fathers [a religious order whose members served in the world's most destitute nations], which no longer exists. It was named for St. Louis de Montfort, a French saint in the eighteenth or nineteenth century. He founded the order. They did ordinary parish work most of all. But I'm sure they did mission work as well. New York was the center of this group—they had training on Long Island [in Bay Shore]—and he had stated very definitely that he had contacted them [during his senior year at Bishop Loughlin]. Things were in the works for him to enter that group. Then Harold got sick—it was during second semester of the senior year. Harold's illness was a concern because if he [Rudy] had entered the priesthood, he would have had to leave home and Rudy didn't feel that that was a good thing for him to do. Given the state of his father's health, he didn't want to leave his mother there alone. He didn't exactly abandon it [the brotherhood]; it was that he was putting it off until a later date, when he felt his family would be in a situation that they could support his decision to be gone.

———————

Interestingly, despite Brother Kevin's having ascribed the most noble of motives to Rudy's change in plans, Rudy himself confides in his memoir, *Leadership*, "I signed up to enter the Montfort Brothers. . . . But then, as June turned to July, I realized I had a problem: my budding interest in the opposite sex was something that wouldn't be suppressed." Rudy goes on to say that he decided instead to attend Manhattan College, "hoping that perhaps I'd be better prepared for celibacy after a couple of years."

John O'Leary, formerly Brother Aloysius Kevin　It's important to understand that in the mid '60s, so much had changed within the Church and so many people had left the priesthood and were leaving religious orders. It was only a number of months after I saw Rudy at that evening at Manhattan [in the 1960s] that I myself left the brothers. Vatican II occurred in the mid '60s and that changed a lot of what was going on in the Church and the views of a lot of people. So it wouldn't have been a surprise that Rudy had decided not to become a priest.

Higher Education

John O'Leary, formerly Brother Aloysius Kevin　He graduated from Loughlin in 1961 and went to Manhattan College. I left this country in 1963—I went to East Africa and taught there for four years—so during most of Rudy's college years, I wasn't in contact with him. I do know that he became more interested in politics when he was in college and that he made some contributions to the Manhattan College student newspaper in politics. I would imagine that [he was affected by] the people he met; your companions make a big difference in how you think about your government and what you do.

George Schneider   Both Bishop Loughlin and Manhattan were Christian Brothers schools, so when the teachers would be talking to you about schools [colleges], frequently that name would come up. There was a sense of continuity with our high school education, so a large number of Bishop Loughlin students went on to Manhattan. Rudy was a commuter [the Giulianis lived in Hicksville, Long Island, at that time]. He wasn't in my fraternity and he was in a completely different program, so we didn't interact that much. I would see him around campus and say "Hi!" or we'd chat. The emphasis on extracurricular activities was not as intense. In high school almost everybody joined the track team; you felt compelled to do it. At Manhattan, you didn't feel as much a part of that as you did in high school.

Manhattan College was a big influence on everybody and it was a good school. You wound up taking more credits than you did in most places. A part of that was influenced by the fact that for the first two years, you were taking theology in addition to your other classes. So it was a very busy, full day, and there was homework as well —the follow-up work associated with the lectures—and in my case [engineering] labs. You typically had to move around quite a bit, going up and down the hill, from one classroom to the other. So it was usually pretty intense. There was always some opportunity to have lunch and hang out for awhile in the middle of the day. But there wasn't a lot of free time.

I don't know if I would have picked law school specifically [for him], but Rudy's decision to enroll at New York University didn't surprise me. From a capability point of view, he always seemed very bright and interested in doing *more*.

Carol Bellamy, classmate of Rudolph Giuliani's at New York University Law School, 1965–1968   It was a class of about three hundred, not a small class. It's an urban setting so you're kind of off on your own and you tended to get to know the people in the projects you were working on. It's not as though we were off in some kind of a green-fielded campus where you got to know more people. We went to school and we went to work and we did whatever we did. If you look at our class, there are some who are still practicing law and are very good lawyers, but a number of us did that for a while and then went on to do other things. I think it had less to do with NYU Law, although I'm a big fan of NYU Law and I would point out that the Nobel Peace Prize winner this year [2005] is an NYU Law graduate. It had much more to do with the '60s—a period of some degree of turmoil, a very interesting period.

PART III

Crime Buster

Chapter 4

FROM STREET-SMART RUDY IN THE IVY LEAGUE SOUTHERN DISTRICT OF NEW YORK (SDNY) TO NUMBER THREE IN THE U.S. DEPARTMENT OF JUSTICE AND U.S. ATTORNEY FOR THE SDNY: A SMALLER POND IN THE SWIM TO CITY HALL?

I was twenty-six when I became an assistant U.S. attorney. I had a mustache—it was 1970.

—Rudy Giuliani, in his memoir, *Leadership*

After graduating magna cum laude from New York University Law School in 1968, Rudy set his sights on becoming a federal prosecutor, first cutting his teeth locally by clerking for a judge in New York's Southern District— no easy accomplishment being that those coveted entry-level positions usually go to Ivy Leaguers (think John F. Kennedy Jr.). But Rudy was impressive, and although then a Kennedy Democrat, he caught the eye of Lloyd MacMahon, a prominent Republican lawmaker and the chief judge of the Southern District, who, unimpressed by pedigree, saw Rudy's good points—his street smarts, driving ambition, and tireless dedication. Becoming Rudy's mentor, the judge even helped Rudy to avoid military service in Vietnam—a deferment that would one day come to haunt candidate Rudy.

In 1970, Rudy joined the U.S. Attorney's Office, moving up rapidly— within three years—to become chief of the Narcotics Unit of the Department of Justice. From there, at Judge MacMahon's behest, the young narcotics warrior was taken on by Deputy Attorney General Harold Tyler, who made him an associate deputy attorney general of the United States—a position viewed by Rudy as the first stepping-stone in pursuit of his ultimate goal.

Richard Thornburgh   In 1975 I had just been appointed to head the Criminal Division in the Department of Justice, here in Washington, and Rudy was an associate deputy in Judge Tyler's office. Right in the immediate post-Watergate period, we were the cleanup team in the Ford administration, and we intersected a fair amount on issues relating to national security and the like, growing out of the Church Committee hearings [the late Senator Frank Church, D-Idaho, who in 1975 with Representative Otis Pike, D-NY, cochaired hearings in both the U.S. House of Representatives and the Senate resulting in the sharp curtailment of the CIA's ability to carry out covert operations in Central America]. The Rockefeller Commission [President's Commission on CIA Activities Within the United States, headed by Vice President Nelson A. Rockefeller during the administration of President Gerald R. Ford] report had been rendered, looking at irregularities in the intelligence and law enforcement communities in the late '60s and early '70s, and it was our job in the Criminal Division to look into any potential criminal violations and it was generally under the supervision of Judge Tyler's office. So at a working level we interacted with Rudy through my then deputy, the late Jay Waldman. Obviously, he impressed me as a very astute and insightful lawyer. He'd been a litigator with the U.S. Attorney's Office in New York. I was the U.S. attorney in Pittsburgh before I came to Washington in '75, and at that time, Rudy was an assistant to Mike Seymour, who was the U.S. attorney in Manhattan, who was a cousin of mine. I didn't know Rudy then, but I knew the work that was done in Mike's office, and the impression that I retain from our first encounter during that two-year period was of a very sharp and highly motivated, able lawyer of whom we all expected great things.

Was Rudy Contemplating a Political Career during That Time?

Richard Thornburgh   I don't know if we focused on it so much at the time. We were so involved in the business of the Department of Justice that nobody was really speculating on politics. But we spent a lot of time shooting the breeze, as younger lawyers do. Of course, Rudy went on to his political career after his service as U.S. attorney in New York. He was obviously a very bright guy. We expected that Rudy would have a meaningful career, whether it was in politics or within the Justice Department or as a judge.

In 1977, the young prosecutor joined the law firm Patterson, Belknap, Webb & Tyler. Then, four years later, on February 20, 1981, he was nominated by President Ronald Reagan as associate attorney general in the U.S. Department of Justice.

Charles Carberry, assistant U.S. attorney, Southern District of New York, 1979–1985; deputy chief, Criminal Division, 1985–1986; chief, Securities and Commodities Fraud Unit, 1986–1987 When he was in Washington there had been tension between Washington and New York: Washington wanted to step on New York's independence, so there may have been some concern that we would be less independent because he was part of the Washington bureaucracy.

Rudy returned to the U.S. Attorney's Office little more than two years later. On March 16, 1983, Senator Alphonse D'Amato, a future adversary, recommended that he be named U.S. attorney for the Southern District of New York. President Ronald Reagan agreed, nominating Rudy for that post less than a month later, on April 12.

George Schneider I was watching television—a magazine show, *60 Minutes*—and there's Rudy! He was in the process of talking about some of the indictments that were being brought against organized crime, and I said, "Wow! Look where Rudy is!" You see someone you know who's in such an important position. And he looked so slim. I could recognize him immediately, but his physique was so different than it was in high school. That was before the mayoral election and it did surprise me to know someone who had risen to such a high level—not necessarily that he *could* do it. I was impressed with that. And I'm not shocked that Rudy could do it. But surprised? Yes.

Richard Thornburgh I don't think he had a restoration job to do in the Southern District; it had been in good hands. But I do think he had a task in participating in restoring people's confidence in the capability of the law enforcement community to deal with things like white-collar crime and organized crime, which were plagues in New York at the time.

Rudy Washington, member, transition team, first administration of Mayor Rudolph Giuliani, 1993; commissioner, Department of Business Services, 1994–1996; deputy mayor for Community Development and Business Services, 1996–2001   I respected him from a distance. I had an impression of him—being real or in my imagination—because prior to meeting him I came out of heavy construction and I was crossing swords with people like Sammy "the Bull" [Gravano, a Mafioso who eventually cooperated with Giuliani in bringing down John Gotti] and the Gambino family [leading Mafia racketeers who controlled, among other operations, garbage pickup from city business enterprises, prosecuted by Giuliani during the 1980s]. I had always been involved in politics. I had run for office in my midtwenties and won, only to have the Queens County organization go after me because I beat them: within one year, I was audited *twice*. I couldn't even pay my mortgage or write a check because they would put a lien on my account. I'd go through the audit and when it was finished, the auditor would say, "Well, Mr. Washington, I don't know how you got into the system; we're sorry to put you through this. I'm sorry." Nothing's wrong and you clear the audit, only to have them say, "But you see this little emblem here, in the computer? We're going to do this again." And I would say, "You just finished auditing me. Why are you going to do this *again*?" And they would say, "Because it's *there*, and if I take it out and it turns out you're a criminal, I'll lose my job." And that was Queens County, Donald Manes's organization, I was fighting against. [Manes, the late Queens borough president, committed suicide in March 1986 amid a major corruption scandal and prosecution by U.S. Attorney for the Southern District Giuliani.] So I found myself in a situation where the enemy of my enemy was my friend: Rudy, the U.S. attorney, was breaking up the Queens County organization; he was trying to put those folks that were making my life miserable in jail. So as far as I was concerned, Rudy was a champion and could do no wrong. And I had never even *met* him.

Gene Russianoff, senior attorney, New York Public Interest Research Group [NYPIRG]   I've had three or four encounters with the former mayor and they've all been different. We held a conference on corruption in government in 1986. It was timely because the city municipal scandals had broken and [Queens Borough President] Donald Manes had killed himself and it was really major news. [The late] Jack Newfield, of the *Village Voice* at the time, got us to have Giuliani as the keynote speaker. He's definitely different than you and I—the famous are different than you and

I—and he came at the last minute and was a big hit; people *loved* him. I can't really make an assessment for myself because I'm so cynical about the political game.

Ed Koch   I was mayor and he was the U.S. attorney and I met him in that context. He asked me to speak to his colleagues at the U.S. Attorney's Office, which I did, to my recollection, and he also offered to get involved in indicting drug offenders, setting aside what he would refer to as a "Federal Day" when they would be making arrests and indicting people here in New York City, so we had a good relationship.

In Forsaking His Position in the Department of Justice for a Smaller Pond, Did Rudy View It as the Better Pond in Which to Swim toward His First Political Goal, City Hall?

Charles Carberry   Rudy had been an assistant U.S. attorney; he had been in the system and many people knew him. We were not surprised that he left the Department of Justice to come to the Southern District. This was regarded as a step up. Traditionally, at least in the eyes of New York, the premier federal prosecutor position in the country was the Southern District. It was viewed by its alumni as the second most important position in the Justice Department. At the time, I had no idea that he was looking at a political career. The mind-set among his colleagues was that this was the job he really wanted.

Steven Brill   The U.S. Attorney's Office in New York is the key, hands-on prosecutorial office in the world. As associate attorney general you've got a lot of the trappings of power; you're sitting in the Justice Department. But you're number three and you're a long way from number one. I think that the right person, with the right talent, will feel more fulfilled as the U.S. attorney than as the associate attorney general.

Richard Thornburgh   That's where the action is! I've held a variety of positions in public life, and I'm often asked which ones I liked the best and I invariably respond that from a professional point of view, being the U.S. attorney was the best. It's a lawyer's job, but it's also a very high-profile, high-impact job and very satisfying. So it didn't surprise me at all when he left the Reagan administration to go back and assume the position of U.S.

attorney in the Southern District because that's probably the preeminent U.S. attorney's job in the country. And, from Rudy's standpoint, that was an opportunity not to be passed up. He had served in the U.S. Attorney's Office under Mike Seymour and Paul Curran previously, so he knew exactly what went on there and he had been for a couple of years with the Reagan administration, at the upper levels, as associate [attorney general] and this was a natural career move from his standpoint.

Steven Brill   I never saw him in the U.S. Attorney's Office or at Justice as someone who was aching to run for political office. I don't think he was until after he left. When he left the U.S. Attorney's Office, he took a job at White & Case, and I wrote a story in *The American Lawyer* in which I said it was an awful pairing of talent and law firm—that they were just ill-suited to each other, which, it turns out, I was right about. They're a stiff, arrogant, miserable group of people and that's just not *Rudy*—Rudy's an iconoclast in a lot of ways. It's not that he doesn't like the money or isn't comfortable with people with that kind of power, it's just personality-wise. It was obvious to me that Rudy was never going to work out in that place. Rudy didn't mind the article at all; *White & Case* minded the article. I had lunch with him some months after that, when he was thinking about running for mayor, and it was the first time I had thought of him as a political guy.

Charles Carberry   I think the sense that Rudy Giuliani might be looking at a political career changed over time. That was not my impression when he started at the Southern District. I thought being U.S. attorney was about as good a job as you could get. By the time I left, there was speculation that Rudy was interested in a political career, but this did not start on day one.

Benjamin Brafman   I wasn't surprised because he got a lot of mileage out of being in the U.S. Attorney's Office. We were at a time when the city was falling apart in many ways and a lot of people saw that having a "tough cop" in charge might be good for the city. The city was suffering from highly visible quality of life crimes that were making our streets not only appear unsafe but *unsavory*, and Rudy ran on [the platform of]: I'm going to clean this place up just like I did when I was a prosecutor. That was Rudy, *quintessential* Rudy: I'm a tough guy and I can do it better than anyone.

Taking Time Out to Attend to Personal Matters

In 1968, while still clerking for Judge Tyler, Rudy had embarked for the first time on the sea of matrimony, marrying his second cousin, Regina Peruggi. While the two would remain husband and wife for fourteen years, Rudy was known to have a roving eye, and theirs would soon become a marriage in name only. Then, in 1982, shortly after becoming associate attorney general in the Reagan Department of Justice, Rudy had their marriage annulled, claiming he hadn't known that he and Regina were so closely related.

Lilliam Barrios-Paoli   I knew Regina well when I was commissioner of Employment and she was in charge of Adult Continuing Ed. at CUNY [the City University of New York]. And because CUNY had a lot of contracts with the Department of Employment, we had a lot of interactions and we liked each other a lot. I was on her board at Marymount [Marymount Manhattan College, a small Catholic institution located on Manhattan's Upper East Side, of which Peruggi became president in 1990] and we're still good friends. I found out about the whole Giuliani thing in 1989. I was driving up to Albany with her in the car, and we were testifying on unemployment—I was driving and there were two people from the Department of Education, somebody from my staff, and Regina. We were sitting there, babbling, and I said something like: "Oh God! I hope Koch wins [the primary]; I don't know that I really want to work in a Dinkins administration. And forget about a *Giuliani* administration!" And Regina said, "Stop! Disclosure time, disclosure time! You know, I was married to him for fourteen years." I remember looking at her and saying, "I'm not even going to ask you how you went on a first date with him. But I would like to know how you went on a *second* date."

The end of Regina's marriage to Rudy was mutual, not acrimonious. I think they had separated emotionally by the time they decided to do it legally, so I don't think that the drama that we saw in his second relationship was there. Regina's not a particularly religious person, and in her mind if he was going to be a politician, if that was important, he did what he thought he had to do. And if she was going to be upset at anyone, she'd be upset at the church, not at *him*. It was not a pleasant thing, but I don't think she felt: Woe is me! The only comment she ever made to me about it was that she was surprised that he thought it was that important.

We talk about it at certain times. She is the essence of discretion and because of many family relationships they share, it's very complicated. I think that at many levels she's fond of him, regardless of what happened between them. After she left Rudy, she had a very good relationship with someone else [Jim Hall, a prominent African American educator and the dean of the Department of Adult and Continuing Education at York College, where he shared an office with Peruggi, and with whom she lived for twelve years, from 1980 until his death in 1992]. Unfortunately, he died, but she was very happy and she has no bitterness about the whole thing. You know, first marriages are only remembered with terrible memories if you've never managed to get into a different life. But if you're happy afterwards, it's like your high school days.

They have a very cordial relationship now. In fact, I had dinner with Regina not long ago and she said they were at a funeral of somebody they knew very well from many, many years ago and Judy, his present wife, was extremely nice to Regina—that they couldn't do enough for her and gave her a ride. And Regina also has a very cordial relationship with Donna.

On June 3, 1983, the newly single Rudy was sworn in as the U.S. attorney for the Southern District of New York. But his bachelor status would soon end: shortly after having obtained his annulment from Regina, Rudy cast his gaze on a comely blond Florida-based television news reporter, the recently divorced Donna Ann Kofnovec Hanover. She accepted Rudy's proposal of marriage and they tied the knot on April 15, 1984, at St. Monica's Catholic Church, in Manhattan.

Chapter 5

PROSECUTORIAL HITS AND MISSES

*I spent a lot of years being a lawyer, assistant
U.S. Attorney, U.S. Attorney. I've dealt with
a lot of disturbed people; sometimes you
can just hear it in their voice.*

—Rudy Giuliani, addressing a call-in listener to his program,
as quoted in the *Village Voice*, May 23, 2000

Richard Thornburgh   When I became attorney general in 1988, Rudy was the U.S. attorney in New York. At that time he was in the midst of a number of investigations that he was working on with the Department of Justice, which I was personally aware of—the Milken case, the Teamsters' case, and other organized crime cases—and when Rudy left the U.S. Attorney's Office in 1989, he gave me a memo with some recommendations that I was able to implement with regard to creating the kind of fraud task forces that he had used in white-collar cases in New York. We replicated those across the country, most notably in dealing with the savings and loan cases.

The U.S. attorney is a presidential appointee—he's not like the regional manager of HUD [Housing and Urban Development] or HHS [U.S. Department of Health and Human Services]—and, therefore, is due a great deal of deference by the attorney general, who is also a presidential appointee. They seldom get at loggerheads. But, theoretically, if they do, the only person who can settle that difference between two of his appointees is really the president. Needless to say, that doesn't happen: a wise U.S. attorney keeps the Justice Department fully informed of directions in which he's going and seeks guidance and ultimately, in a number of cases, sometimes by statute, approval of the attorney general and the Department of Justice for any action he's going to undertake.

Gerald Lefcourt   Under Giuliani, the public relations staff went from a part-time person to five people. It became a PR machine. That is my ultimate biggest problem with Rudy because to me that position is so important and so powerful that to use it for political purposes is the worst of all possible crimes. Unfortunately, that is what he did, to a large extent. That is not to say that *all* prosecutions were tainted, but the office became tainted—he polarized that office. Assistants would leave that office with announcements that said, "Prosecuted Congressman Garcia." Prosecutors aren't supposed to be concerned with that. They are supposed to be concerned with justice, not self-aggrandizement. That you should be regarded because of the names on your belt is wrong and dangerous.

Rudy Giuliani, ever-mindful of his Catholic upbringing, would apply strict religious and moral principles in his unmerciful punishment of lawbreakers.

Richard Thornburgh   Rudy is not a stiff-backed guy and not a doctrinaire guy. But I knew from the very beginning that he was tough and a true believer in his mission in law enforcement. Whether that qualifies him for the priesthood, I don't know.

Benjamin Brafman   He was a very strong-willed prosecutor. I think the fact that he was of Italian heritage himself made him a tough prosecutor; he wanted to bend over backwards to root out and successfully prosecute organized crime because he felt that Italian Americans suffered unfairly by gangsters being Italian and he resented it. But it's also that he was in the U.S. Attorney's Office at the right time: white-collar crime was breaking out all over; the sentencing guidelines were coming into play where the position was being taken that white-collar defendants should no longer be coddled and that they should be prosecuted severely.

He was scrupulously honest; you could never corrupt Rudy Giuliani by offering him anything of value to do something that he didn't think was appropriate. But at some point, it goes to your head—you become *the* most important prosecutor in the country, so the more cases you bring, the more notoriety you bring upon yourself. That office was criticized a lot for summarily arresting white-collar defendants, represented by counsel, who would have surrendered when called. It was unnecessarily exploiting arrests, grabbing headlines. But that was part of the climate—it was happening all over the country.

Charles Carberry   He was an exceptional lawyer. In terms of legal analysis and factual understanding, he was very quick. He didn't make up his mind before he knew the facts. He could be very persuasive. Like many successful men, he is driven. He works very, very hard and is very single-minded. He never asked me to do what I thought was unprofessional. He was easy to deal with as a boss.

Benjamin Brafman   I am not Rudy's greatest fan or his greatest critic: I think he has very real strengths in many ways. I know him and we've always gotten along on a personal level. When you look at any long-term U.S. attorney administration, you will see some cases that are stunning successes and some cases that end in dismal failures, and in my now thirty years of being involved in the criminal justice system, I have seen more than a handful of cases brought by prosecutors all over the country that, in my judgment, should never have been brought. I was a prosecutor for five years; you had enormous responsibility, enormous power, and enormous discretion, and how you use that discretion as a prosecutor is one of they key factors that people look to when they determine your legacy as a prosecutor.

Prosecuting Organized Crime Figures

Gerald Lefcourt   I probably had more dealings with him on substantive issues than most defense lawyers. Early on, I was involved in a so-called organized crime case involving a person named Matthew Ianniello. The government took a position which I thought then—and I still do—was the height of outrageousness. It was Rudy's first big case and it had to do with the garbage industry. Con Ed [Consolidated Edison, a New York utility company] was allegedly the victim of a fraud that went something like this: Con Ed had a list of garbage companies they would do business with and a list of companies they wouldn't deal with. They decided they didn't want to deal with Mr. Ianniello's company. Lo and behold, they gave a contract to a company that was on the verge of bankruptcy and thus couldn't fulfill the contract. This company assigned the contract to Mr. Ianniello's company. Now the government thought that Con Ed had been defrauded out of its policy not to hire Mr. Ianniello's company because of his alleged involvement in organized crime. As we ended up arguing to the jury, it's like you have a deal with Joe to cut your lawn, but Joe doesn't cut it, *Steve* does. But your lawn is still cut exactly as you agreed to pay for it. And, in

Con Ed's case, the garbage was picked up exactly as they agreed to pay for it, so they didn't claim they were defrauded out of money, but were defrauded out of their policy not to deal with Mr. Ianniello. When the government announced the indictment, Giuliani restrained all of the assets of all of the defendants by going to a judge ex parte, on his own, without hearing from defense counsel. He got an order which, in effect, pauperized the defendants. They couldn't afford to hire lawyers. This was the first time that that was done and it led to a national policy in many prosecutorial offices to try to seize assets of defendants and forfeit them—even to forfeit legal fees. So the first order of business in the Con Ed case was to litigate whether these defendants could use their own money to defend themselves. It was a big fight and it was Rudy's big entrée into this whole world. To him it was okay that the defendants were pauperized and had to get public assistance to defend themselves.

I was chairman of the criminal advocacy committee of the Association of the Bar of the City of New York. We looked into that very controversial policy. We held public hearings where many former U.S. attorneys and chiefs of the Criminal Division talked about how dangerous this idea was to prevent people from defending themselves and really making them indigent. Rudy was the only person who appeared at the hearing in defense of this policy. He did so by going back to the origins of organized crime and how dangerous organized crime was, as if his policy would only be used in organized crime contexts. But, of course, it became a powerful prosecutorial tool.

Steven Brill   I'm quite familiar with his RICO [Racketeer Influenced and Corrupt Organizations Act] cases, his basic approach to organized crime. He made it on to the cover of our magazine at that time as someone who really made a big difference over a decade. Before Rudy was U.S. attorney, organized crime in places like [the Fulton Fish Market near the] South Street Seaport was just taken as a *given* and you could sort of nip at the edges of it, but someone who said: "I'm going to overturn these [crime] families; I'm just going to do this," would be seen as crazy. And he got most of that done and you have to give him credit for that. Whether he's good on the points of evidence in a courtroom, I don't know that; he probably is. But I appreciate someone who looks at something and just doesn't accept the explanation that it's always been that way and there's just nothing we can do about it.

Drug-Busting with D'Amato

On a summer day in 1986, the ever-zealous Rudy Giuliani, decked out in Hell's Angels garb, joined Senator Alphonse D'Amato in a staged-for-the media undercover drug buy-and-bust operation in Manhattan's Washington Heights, a notorious selling area. The object of the exercise was to boost the senator's chances for reelection. The two "thugs" in fact made only two real buys, purchasing mostly ordinary powder.

Albert O'Leary, director of media services, Transit Police Department, 1987–1995; director of employee communications, New York City Transit Authority, 1996–1998; vice president for public affairs, New York City Transit Authority, 1998–2002 He looked foolish. I can't use the words that the cops would use to describe him and Al D'Amato going out to buy crack. It was just *stupid*; they looked like a couple of jerks. It was all media. At that time, if you put on one of those outfits and went into East New York to try and buy crack, you were lucky if you came out alive. I don't know where that [the idea] came from. But it was ill-advised and the cops just laughed at it.

A Hit: The Prosecution of Bronx Democratic Party Leader Stanley Friedman

On April 9, 1986, in what has been described by his critics as a blatantly political move to destroy the reputation of Mayor Ed Koch, his potential political rival, Giuliani indicted the very influential and colorful Bronx Democratic Party leader Stanley Friedman on a variety of corruption charges. They included having bribed Queens Borough President Donald Manes—who had committed suicide two months earlier—and Manes's close friend, deputy director of the New York City Parking Violations Bureau Geoffrey Lindenauer, to obtain lucrative collection contracts. While Giuliani often delegated prosecutions to subordinates, he chose to handle the Friedman case himself.

Gerald Lefcourt The Stanley Friedman case was about the biggest Democratic target around at the time and if you had any thought as to your afterlife, this was the case to take. If you have an interest in becoming involved in politics and you want to emerge as did [Thomas E.] Dewey, to whom he [Giuliani] was compared in the *New York Law Journal*, you take the case and you win it at all costs. You do it in order to throw your hat into the political world in a very big way.

There were a number of stories before the trial about other bad acts Stanley Friedman was allegedly involved in. Giuliani was leaking information on an extraordinary basis. He would go on television and say, "Of course I can't talk about the indictment of Stanley Friedman," but you can see the problem where you have only one party [the Democratic Party in the Bronx]; you have corruption and, therefore, Friedman [the Bronx County leader] is guilty.

Stanley Friedman   The evidence is clear that he had a game plan. He was a very ambitious, very intelligent, very motivated, and driven individual and he was going to run for mayor. Why else would he bring his wife to court in New Haven? Why else did he bring his newborn baby [Andrew, born on January 30, 1986] in a carriage and parade him before the jury? Because that's what candidates do.

Gerald Lefcourt   What Giuliani was running up there was nearly a politician's media event. Imagine bringing his baby into the courtroom! I mean, this isn't about you, Mr. Prosecutor, it's about the system of justice and whether there is enough evidence to prove beyond a reasonable doubt that a particular defendant is guilty of a crime. It's not about you glad-handing the press and bringing your wife and child to the courtroom.

Stanley Friedman   One day during the trial, my eighteen-year-old son and I were in the elevator with Giuliani and he said, "If your father does the right thing, then he doesn't have to go to jail"—they wanted to put Koch away—and my son said, "My father *is* doing the right thing." They didn't succeed with Koch because they were on the wrong track, not because Koch got away with anything.

———

The case, which would be tried before Judge Whitman Knapp, relied to a great degree on the testimony of Lindenauer. The prosecution's case was helped considerably by a change of venue to New Haven, Connecticut, where the jury was actually composed of residents of Hartford, located in the center of the state and, according to Stanley Friedman, a conservatively oriented city.

Gerald Lefcourt Assistant U.S. Attorneys [William] Bill Shultz and David Zornow did most of the heavy lifting. Everyone was shocked at Giuliani's opening statement. It was not the way lawyers perform before a jury. The second shock came when in his cross-examination of Stanley Friedman, he brought up points that were clearly inadmissible. When Judge Knapp ruled Giuliani's submissions out, Rudy began to sweat. He didn't know what to do, so he asked for an adjournment to get himself together, even though it was in the middle of the afternoon.

Stanley Friedman Everybody tells me that Lindenauer was the whole case. I'm not here to say that I was wrongly accused. I was *properly* accused—maybe not for every single nail that he drove into the coffin, but I was guilty of attempting to bribe Manes and Lindenauer. But they tried to pile it on; they smeared me in the press with Cablevision, with the taxi industry, with Donald Trump and the Commodore [Hotel] on Forty-second Street, which is now the Grand Hyatt—what some political people say are "legal bribes." Call it what you want, but those things were all done to prejudice me and the other defendants—you try to throw as much paint on the wall as you can and some of it sticks.

Gerald Lefcourt Two months into the trial, Rudy announced that the government would rest its case the next day. I went back to the hotel where the defendants and their lawyers were staying and had a beer with my client, Marvin Kaplan, in a bar in the lobby. I told him the mail fraud counts would have to be dismissed because the government never proved anything was mailed. As I told this to my client, I thought no one was around. The next morning, we go to court and Giuliani asks for more time so that he can call another witness. I asked the judge if we could approach the bench and I told him what I had told my client the previous afternoon in the hotel bar and that I wondered whether this witness had anything to do with Rudy's request. Just then, Rudy tells the judge: "Wayne Barrett [a reporter for the *Village Voice* who was staying at the defendant's hotel] told me last night of this conversation." Barrett was spying on us for Giuliani!

While the prosecution sought twenty years behind bars, Judge Knapp sentenced Friedman to twelve years. He would serve a third of that sentence.

A Miss: The Lock Manufacturer

That fall, U.S. Attorney Giuliani prosecuted Simon Berger, a manufacturer of security locks who stood accused of having bribed a New York City housing official in order to secure a contract for placing his product in a federally financed housing project. That case is of particular relevance concerning the issue of whether there was an atmosphere in the U.S. Attorney's Office that could have engendered what Mr. Berger encountered when he was brought there following his arrest. Apprehended at seven o'clock on a Sunday morning, Berger, a Holocaust survivor who had arrived in the United States penniless after the war, was taken from his Long Island home in handcuffs to Giuliani's office, where he was seated opposite a blackboard on which was written the slogan *"Arbeit Macht Frei,"* the odious words emblazoned on the entry to the Auschwitz death camp, where Mr. Berger had been imprisoned during the Holocaust.

Alan Vinegrad, deputy chief, Criminal Division, Eastern District of New York in the 1990s; chief, Criminal Division; deputy U.S. attorney, Eastern District of New York; U.S. attorney, Eastern District of New York   I can't think of any justification for writing on a blackboard near a prisoner, Jewish or otherwise, "Work Shall Set You Free." There are degrees of being normative, being aggressive, and then crossing the line. And some of that is going to depend on the judgment of the individual prosecutor, or prosecutors, who are involved. Without commenting on that case, specifically, certainly there are cases where a prosecutor feels justified in using lawful, but aggressive, methods to get evidence from a suspect; to try to get a confession from a suspect; or to try to send a message to the public that certain conduct won't be tolerated. There are guidelines and customs, if you will, about what's appropriate and what's *not* appropriate. Sometimes it's going to be appropriate to arrest somebody at six thirty in the morning and put handcuffs on them. Doing it on a *Sunday* morning is a step beyond that because one would know if one was an agent that if you do and there's no judge available to bring the defendant before promptly, that person's going to be spending the night in jail.

Benjamin Brafman   It would be fair to say that Rudy Giuliani didn't even know that Simon Berger was going to be arrested that Sunday morning, so [one shouldn't] blame him for what happened in the office on a day when he was probably not even aware that certain official action was taken. He's a hands-on person in some ways, but it's a big office—at any given time, they have hundreds of investigations—and there are layers of accountability; there are line assistants, supervisors, deputy chiefs, and chiefs. I don't believe for a second that Giuliani *ordered* it to be there; I don't believe for a second that Giuliani knew it was there; and I don't believe for a second that David Zornow, the assistant United States attorney, either *knew* that it was there or had it put there *intentionally*. I know that was what Simon suggested, but I never found any evidence of that and, knowing both Rudy and David, I don't believe either of them would stoop to that level. I always believed that it was a misguided agent who, knowing a bit about Simon's background, thought this was a, perhaps, cool way of making Simon face up to the reality that he was in a position where he could help himself by giving information about others.

Giuliani was quoted by the *New York Post* to the effect that the incident was "reprehensible," attributing it to IRS agents who had allegedly scribbled the deeply offensive words on the blackboard weeks before Berger's arrest. He ordered a thorough investigation, which was conducted by his mentor, the trial judge, Lloyd MacMahon. In rendering his finding, MacMahon stated, "There is not a scintilla of evidence to suggest that the government intentionally directed the phrase toward Berger."

Benjamin Brafman   I don't know that Rudy ever apologized to Simon. But if he didn't, I think that the most he would say is: If it happened under my watch, it was wrong, and I would have fired the person if I knew about it. I've been to a number of different functions where we've chitchatted, but we're not *social* friends. If Giuliani *were* someone I was close to, I would have gone to see him directly about this when it happened. When I confronted the assistant United States attorney, David Zornow, he was terribly, terribly concerned that this not be used in an irresponsible manner to destroy his career or, through him, give the Southern District a black eye. Simon always saw it as part of a sinister plot and to this day, I'm sure he's convinced that it was.

My criticism of that whole affair was the fact that a man like Simon Berger was summarily arrested and not given the opportunity to voluntarily surrender with counsel. It has long been a prosecution tool—I am constantly fighting against it—where they believe that if you scoop someone up early in the morning, when they least expect it, that terrifying moment will cause them to either confess or incriminate themselves before consulting with counsel and opt for cooperating with law enforcement as a way to lessen their own involvement. What they didn't anticipate was that Simon Berger was truly innocent and, having survived Nazi concentration camps, wasn't about to be intimidated by some middle-aged federal agent or a young prosecutor who he met with on a Sunday morning.

To be confronted with the words *"Arbeit macht Frei,"* I can imagine the horrific impact that has on someone who's been through the Holocaust. My maternal grandparents were murdered at Auschwitz and a lot of my family perished during the Holocaust, so I was very sympathetic to Simon. I was the right person, if you will, to both understand Simon's rage and to channel it, because I was convinced that he wasn't going to win the case simply because of that.

A source who would not speak for attribution suggested that Berger was unhappy with his initial attorney, Barry Slotnik, because having complied with the subpoena he believed that he would not be arrested and was shocked when he was. According to the authors' source, the government claimed that either they had forgotten that Mr. Berger had retained counsel or that counsel had only submitted documents on behalf of his company, thus they felt comfortable in communicating directly with the arrested man.

Benjamin Brafman   He had gotten a subpoena and complied with it and retained Barry Slotnik on the date of his surrender. There was no other contact, I believe, with the U.S. Attorney's Office and Slotnik's office. I was called into the case after Simon had already been arrested and had gone through what he claimed happened to him on the date of his surrender. He came to me through Harry Taubenfeld [a practicing attorney with the firm Zuckerbrod & Taubenfeld, of Cedarhurst, Long Island, and a personal friend of Simon Berger and his wife, Rita].

I have developed a trial practice in the last twenty-five or thirty years and I pride myself on being a trial lawyer. But you also need the right client, who is not afraid of the consequences if you go to trial and lose—someone with the intestinal fortitude to withstand it; the resources to pay for it. And you need also the right facts. The Southern District is a very smart group of people and they have a high percentage rate of convictions and many people *do* plead guilty. Simon Berger could very well have, with another lawyer, under different circumstances, taken the position: I don't want to risk going to trial; I *did* pay him and if that's wrong, I'll plead guilty to it.

It was my strong belief that given the fact that we had a very try-able, defensible case, if we tried to defend the case using that issue [of prosecutorial strong-arm tactics] out front, it would blow up in our faces. But we filed a motion, at Simon's insistence, to dismiss the case based on prosecutorial misconduct, an "alleged incident" in our moving papers, which we filed under seal. But we never accused the U.S. Attorney's Office, itself, as being intentionally involved in the misconduct because this was beyond the pale; this was never, in my judgment, anything that anyone in a reasonable degree of authority in that office would authorize. This was offensive not only to Simon and to me but, I believe, personally offensive to Rudy and a source of great embarrassment to him. I *know* him and I don't think he would ever consider doing something like that to a Holocaust survivor. And I know David Zornow; he is himself very involved in work on behalf of Jewish organizations. David Zornow would never be involved.

The case was tried before Lloyd MacMahon but was not prosecuted by the team that had arrested Mr. Berger as they had all left the U.S. Attorney's Office by that time. While Mr. Berger had, in fact, paid a quasi-public official, he had been *the victim* of extortion by that official, rather than the instigator of a bribe. Mr. Berger did not testify, and the case hinged on the defense's cross-examination of the government's witness, Harold Pinckney, who would forfeit his cooperation agreement by lying about crimes *he* had committed.

Mr. Berger was found not guilty following jury deliberations of only a few hours. And in the wake of his acquittal, the government wrote to the court, stating in effect that while Mr. Pinckney had cooperated in the investigation, he had in their view committed perjury, thus they were requesting that he receive a harsh sentence. Judge MacMahon complied, ordering that the government's perfidious witness be incarcerated for seven years.

Benjamin Brafman   When the jury stood up and said "Not guilty," Simon collapsed on to the table, sobbing. He hugged me, and everyone in the courtroom except the jurors was crying and they didn't even know anything about Simon's background—that he was a Holocaust survivor; it had nothing to do with the case. We had no press during the trial and I don't believe his acquittal ever got into the papers.

Another Miss: Going After Miss America and Judge Gabel

U.S. Attorney Giuliani could go to bizarre lengths in pursuit of a conviction, a case in point being his prosecution in the late 1980s of Bess Myerson, a former Miss America, television personality, and city official, on bribery and mail fraud charges. In that instance, crime-buster Rudy took advantage of a troubled, clinically depressed young woman, Sukhreet Gabel, choosing her as one of his chief witnesses against her own mother, the seventy-four-year-old, nearly blind Judge Hortense Gabel, who had figured in Myerson's attempt to have her then lover's alimony payments to his ex-wife reduced. Rudy had clearly overreached in pitting a daughter against her own mother, and both Myerson and Judge Gabel were acquitted.

Jay Goldberg   There was criticism of Giuliani for bringing the case, on the theory that it was too weak and it had been supposedly rejected by [Manhattan District Attorney Robert] Morgenthau. I disagreed with both propositions. There was enough circumstantial evidence that a different jury might have taken a different approach. But any claim that a judge was influenced so that justice wasn't rendered to one of the parties, especially in a matrimonial case, is a very, very serious charge that goes to the heart of our judicial system, and if Giuliani believed that there was enough to do an investigation, he was within his discretion to do so. I *wasn't* in favor of him polluting the atmosphere for the month or two or three before the trial—"Through unnamed sources" or "It has been learned." It hardly paid to go to court, except that the judge did a good job in questioning the jurors and we may even say that they were there to just pass on the evidence.

Bess was in love with Andy—they seemed like a compatible couple—and like every person in love, she wanted to do something to help him because he must have had a tremendous emotional overlay from what had resulted from the judge's order. The allegation is that she wanted to help him and she was willing to take on this person [Sukhreet] who Judge Gabel had tried for years to get placed [in gainful employment]. It had to be pretty sad because Judge Gabel was thought of as a great person and you would think, with her contacts, she certainly could get a position in government for her daughter. But the claim in the indictment was that she couldn't. So then Bess moved in.

Sukhreet Gabel, in 1988 the chief witness against her own mother, Judge Hortense Gabel   What the hell, Mom! What is going *on* here? You mean the best, but you're not young, you're slipping—your mind is not as strong as it once was; you're not as careful as you once were. Perhaps you're not seeing something that's patently obvious because you're just too impaired, and what you would have smelled out and put a stop to *immediately* years ago you're just not seeing. I've got to figure this out. I've got to help you. I'm going to get to the bottom of this. Bess and my mom were Hunter girls [Hunter, a Manhattan college, is part of the CUNY system], my mother ten or fifteen years before Bess, and both women were powerful in politics: Bess was a former commissioner; my mother was a former commissioner [Myerson of Consumer Affairs 1969–1973, during the administration of John V. Lindsay, and of Cultural Affairs 1983–1987, during the administration of Mayor Edward I. Koch; and Gabel a Rent Commissioner]. They were never kissin' cousins, but they certainly were friendly. My dad and my mom often gave dinner parties—they had *salons*: you didn't go there for the food, you went there for the great conversation. I met Ed Koch as a congressman and all of the "goo-goos"—the good government types—would regularly meet and debate, and they were lively and fun. One day, I got a call from my mother, who said, "Oh, by the way, Bess Myerson is coming tonight." "Oh," said I, "aren't *we* getting big in the world!" And Mom said, "It was kind of strange; I've known her for *years*, but she invited herself." That was the first I ever heard of Bess Myerson beyond the public context, and at that dinner party she made an effort to talk to me and I was flattered. But I was not embarrassed; if somebody speaks to me, I'm not going to say "poor little me" because I've had an interesting life *too*, and I'm not a kid, so that didn't cow me particularly.

Suffice it to say that Bess kept inviting herself and invited me to a few things that were either semiofficial or official: It was always fun to travel with Bess and, of course, Bess is such an imposing figure. She's not pretty, not attractive, but *beautiful*. And, of course, she's very, very tall. And she likes to control people; she does it with body language, for example, standing a little too close to a female of average height, say five foot four, and I'm addressing an impassioned answer to her nipples! It's disconcerting, to say the least, and she does that very much on purpose.

Jay Goldberg   It was a wonderful thing for Andy for a time. Bess was liberal and very fine when she spoke; Andy was like rough and tough, but they appeared to get along. Once the case was over, they broke up. But they lived together out in West Hampton and when he was incarcerated on a tax case, during every recess she would bring food to him. I don't think *my wife* would do that, but she was very dutiful. But I can't say he was nice to *her*: the prettier they are, they can't find the right person. And these men resort to physical violence against them.

Mayor Koch had appointed a very well-known, famous judge, retired, Harold Tyler, who did an exhaustive investigation of the allegations before the trial. He came to the conclusion that there was more than an adequate basis. Morgenthau passed on it and Giuliani was more courageous. It could be that he also had an agenda, but that doesn't detract from the fact that the case should have been brought. He was faced with a report that was done at the urging of Koch that came to the conclusion that bribery and obstruction of justice had occurred. And what was he to do if Morgenthau passed on it, but there it was, hanging out there, a thirty-page analysis by a super-respected retired federal judge that there was more than enough to proceed with the case. I knew Bess Myerson for some time, and when the investigation happened, I met with her and with Mr. Capasso and I decided to bring in a lawyer to represent Ms. Myerson, Fred Hafetz [an experienced defense attorney and a former state and federal prosecutor], who I respected, and I represented Mr. Capasso. I never met Sukhreet before the trial. She was not well—she had had shock treatments and her memory was like Swiss cheese.

Sukhreet Gabel　　The night that Marcella [Maxwell, then the commissioner of Human Rights] fired me, my mother said, "Please don't fire her; let her resign. She'll *kill* herself." Why are these women talking about *me*? I don't like this! I would not kill myself for the likes of Marcella Maxwell! Are you *kidding*? I don't think much of that woman and I'm certainly not going to commit suicide over that. Mom! How little you know of *me*! It was obscene! I floundered. I lost a fiancé because I wasn't working. I got very, very, very sickly depressed. And that was when the crazy rumors started: here's this sweet, vulnerable girl, this tragic figure who's had *shock treatments*.

The first investigation was by the city commission investigating Bess. I told the truth. There was a moment of truth in my mind during that questioning: Do I lie by omission or do I spell it all out? Part of me said: I am sick and tired of being the fall guy for the big people. If Bess wants to treat me like a child, and if these giants—Bess, my mother, Marcella, this one, that one—want to play ninepins, with *me* as the *ball*, I don't like it; I have a life and a career and, goddamn it, I'm not going to sacrifice *my* career, commit perjury, and give up any of my hopes and dreams to preserve their icon status. My lawyer, Phil Schaeffer, was aghast. The first thing he said to me when we left the room was, "Well, you just cost Bess Myerson *her* job!"—never mind the fact that she cost me *mine*! Then the state commission said, "Don't listen to this woman; she's a crazy bitch." And the state commission people said, "No, we think she's a quite credible witness; anything she said is checked, impeccably, with what everybody else has said. Overruled."

———————

The case was tried by federal judge John F. Keenan, formerly Mayor Koch's City Hall–based personal criminal justice coordinator, who in the early 1980s had found no reason to investigate charges that Myerson had sought to secure favors for Andy Capasso by hiring Judge Hortense Gabel's daughter. Leading the prosecution's team was David Lawrence, who was assisted by Stuart Abrams.

Jay Goldberg   There's no question that at the time the jury was selected in the Bess Myerson case, she was guilty in the minds of everybody. Of the five hundred people that Judge Keenan questioned, everybody believed her, Capasso, and the judge to be guilty. There was so much in the way of leaks. It could have been in the FBI, but I don't think so; the FBI wasn't involved in that case as much. I believe it had to have come from the U.S. Attorney's Office, and it inundated the city with her misconduct and corruption. The sad part of it is that when they were indicted, it was too late for the defense to do anything about it because the judge imposed a ban on counsel to not speak with the press. So the attorneys started out a hundred yards back of the starting line to try to extricate these people. And Giuliani was a very publicity-minded individual. But I guess that's how you move up the ladder politically.

The U.S. attorney committed her [Sukhreet], in effect, to the custody of a nice-looking investigator. I think he probably was responsible for our excesses; he might have said: Let's hear what these people are talking about, or something of that nature. I don't think it [Sukhreet's taping of telephone calls with her mother] was done without a suggestion from the U.S. Attorney's Office.

Sukhreet Gabel   They gave me this clunky tape recorder that they put in the drawer of my desk and if somebody significant was to call, specifically Phil Schaeffer or Bess, I was to push the button and turn the thing on. I'm a mechanical klutz; do not ask me to operate machinery! Which switch? It wasn't labeled. For all I know, I could have turned it on when I had a phone sex relationship with a guy in England at the time—*Dirty Dancing* on an FBI tape! Bess Myerson didn't call; Phil Schaeffer didn't call. *My mother* got recorded. I *still* don't know how!

Jay Goldberg Everything was focused on Sukhreet, in terms of her credibility, and it was very easy to cross-examine her because there were all these inconsistencies: in the grand jury she would say, "April tenth" and on the witness stand she would say "June fifth." She testified that she was present when her mother and Bess met, and the government may have been in a situation where all they could do was call her. If you have thirty areas, maybe you only ask five; if you ask the *sixth*, you'll get in trouble. And the experienced lawyer knows when not to ask that extra question. And if the prosecutor has a number of witnesses, it's better to cut back. But she was the only witness to these meetings and the only one who was able to say what Bess and her mother said. Now, whether the taping should have come out, I don't know. The government brought that out and *that* was the big mistake. The defense would have not realized that the daughter would have taped the mother. And had the government called Sukhreet and refined its questions to just who said what and when the meetings were, that probably would have been enough; they didn't have to play a tape.

Sukhreet Gabel I had, apparently, made a very, very *good* impression on the grand jury and a very, very *bad* impression on the jury. As impressed as I was with their examination of me in the grand jury, I was just as *unim-*pressed with what I considered a shamefully bad performance on their part at the trial. They asked the wrong questions, they rambled—time and time again, I had to ask David Lawrence, "Could you repeat that?" I was tired; I was stressed, but these questions were long and rambling, and by the time he got to the end of asking the damn question, I'd already forgotten the first part of it.

Jay Goldberg We say that our system of independent judges is America's unique contribution to the science of government and if that's impaired, it doesn't serve the public interest. I think Giuliani did the right thing; I think there was more than enough to bring the charge. The jury saw it in a different way and the summation was of monumental significance—this case rested on the summations. We had to put it together and show how stupid it was.

 This was like a two-hour comedy routine because that's what the case *was*. What I did, according to the judge, was to *laugh* the case out of the courtroom.

This was a very good jury. They went out laughing, so they felt good. During the deliberations I asked someone to make sure that Sukhreet was in the first row of the courtroom so that when the jury came back for read-backs and the like, that they would think that she was there, waiting for them to convict her mother.

Sukhreet was viewed with such disdain, and the jury disliked her in such a way that they just couldn't visit the possibility of jail or dishonor of a judge who was remarkable in terms of pioneering women's rights and who was very, very respected. It's sad because it may show how far parents go to help an impaired child. That was very important in the jury's consideration. As so often happens, you can get an acquittal on the seventh floor with one jury and the same presentation could be made on the third floor and you could lose the case. Everything depends on the composition of the jury.

Sukhreet Gabel Rudy had been told by all and sundry: This is an unwinnable case; it's too circumstantial, a tempest in a teapot. I think they realized that they weren't going to win. Clearly, their strategy at that point was to throw me to the wolves. I never met Rudy; I only dealt [with him] on a need-to-know basis, even though I knew he was heavily involved. It was one of his pet projects because he wanted to run for mayor and what could be better than bringing down a judge, a Mafia contractor, and Miss America, Koch's "girlfriend," in one fell swoop? Even if you lose the case, that is many millions of dollars' worth of free publicity. Of course he wanted to run this case!

Jay Goldberg People say that if you have the money and you get the best lawyers, you get acquitted, but that doesn't always work. I remember sitting next to Bess when they announced that there was a verdict—you can actually feel the blood pressure; it goes right through your head—and I looked at her and said to myself: I can't see her in an orange jumpsuit, in prison. She heaved a big sigh.

Sukhreet Gabel After the verdict I called Giuliani—to everyone's great surprise, he got on the line—and I said, "Why did your guys hang me out to dry?" And he gave me some very slick politician's answer—I don't even remember the words; I just remember *the tone*—and I was just ready to spit. The *nerve* of Rudolph Giuliani to have brought this tempest in a teapot, with myself, Bess Myerson, and my mother in an eight-week trial and have the government spend over $6 million on this investigation!

I mean, you talk about putting the em*phasis* on the wrong syll*able*. There were some really, really deep fault lines running through all of those people and all of their issues, but to focus on this particular part of that Gordian mess was absolutely the wrong thing to do, except for the cheap-ass publicity that this guy got. It was *terribly* cynical. That's Rudy in the headlines! Blame it on the jury; blame it on a million different things.

Hits and Misses: The Wall Street Prosecutions

As the U.S. attorney, Giuliani was initially most interested in prosecuting individuals involved in organized crime, drug trafficking, and political corruption. By the mid to late 1980s, however, spurred by actions of the Enforcement Division of the Securities and Exchange Commission (SEC), he and his associates in the Southern District of New York looked closer to home, in a sense, by paying increasing attention to the financial world centered mere blocks from his own offices. Of particular interest were company takeovers and high-risk ventures.Working in close cooperation with the SEC, Giuliani's aides investigated and brought to justice such high-profile figures as Ivan Boesky and Michael Milken. Some observers of his actions would later criticize him for allowing both Boesky and Milken to retain significant portions of their enormous assets.

Jay Goldberg He certainly was the first to focus in on corporate misconduct. I often thought that so much time was spent on Italians and the Mafia while corporate crime —as it is now at the forefront of prosecution—had to be addressed. Previous U.S. attorneys didn't do that. He moved in on the securities fraud area. However, if I had one complaint it was, as one might expect of a person who had an agenda to seek political office, that there was an inordinate amount of leaks and press coverage where there shouldn't have been. That was, in fact, a violation of the Canon of Ethics.

He's a very, very tough guy. He was propelled by his ambition: he's a U.S. attorney and he wants to make his mark. He was very lucky, too, because in his reign an enormous impact was made against organized crime. But that was because the FBI's investigations all ended and were ready for prosecution by the time he was the U.S. attorney—the FBI had been investigating this for eight years and had finished four different investigations when he was there—so he got the credit; it seems like he busted up the mob.

John Sturc, associate director, Division of Enforcement, U.S. Securities and Exchange Commission Cooperation between the Securities and Exchange Commission and the Justice Department was good, but there was not a high level of interest in prosecuting securities cases in most jurisdictions. While there had historically been some level of interest in New York, Mr. Giuliani's office took a higher level of interest. The perception of potential abuse in the insider trading area, particularly among investment banks, was increasing, and there was more of an effort on the part of the SEC to encourage the Justice Department to become involved in these cases. There was a perception at the time that the civil remedies that existed were not an adequate deterrent.

Steven R. Andrews, attorney; represented James Dahl, an associate of Michael Milken's at Drexel Burnham Lambert We never met with Giuliani; he was conspicuously absent from any meetings, any involvement in the case. I don't think any of the defense lawyers even talked to him. My sense was that he wasn't really the guy calling the shots. Maybe he called the ultimate shots. As far as we could see it was [Assistant U.S. Attorneys Jess] Fardella and [John] Carroll making the decisions. Giuliani was never in the case.

When we were trying to figure out what was going to happen to my client, no one ever told us that we had to take this to Rudy Giuliani. I thought that was unusual because when they made the decision to compel Jim to testify, they would have wanted to at least get a sense of the guy. Jim was sort of the Rosetta stone of the whole investigation, but Giuliani didn't meet with him; the day that the decision was made to compel Jim's testimony, Giuliani was not to be seen. He was never in his office, which was actually on that floor.

Charles Carberry I remember Giuliani's phrase that informants are the lifeblood of prosecution. Unless you are getting information, you can't make cases. In security fraud cases we never really faced the question of how repulsive your informant is. Unlike a [Salvatore] Gravano, who killed eighteen people, these were white-collar criminals; they weren't killing anybody.

Steven Brill It's an obligation, if nothing else, because we're all members of the same society and we live in the same place, to report crime. There's nothing wrong with that. It's not violating the adversarial process; he's not saying that lawyers have more obligation to turn their clients in. He's saying, You have an obligation to call the police if, when you walk out of this building, you see someone doing a purse-snatching down on Sixth Avenue.

Steven R. Andrews   I don't have many clients running in to retain me saying, "I feel morally bound to tell the truth."

John Sturc   His office did great work in these cases. So to say, as some do, that we [the SEC] helped launch him is a bit of an overstatement. To be sure, we worked hard to develop cases and we brought them to the attention of his office. That said, it wouldn't have gone anywhere but for the hard work of people in his office. They had the authority to follow through and to prosecute cases very, very well. It was more of a collaborative thing. Both agencies benefited and the public benefited.

Steven R. Andrews   I thought the attorneys in the Southern District were very professional. I took a minority view among the defense counsel. Now understand that I only saw the nice side of it.

John Sturc   He was very supportive. There were times where he was directly involved. He backed his people up, provided them resources, and was prepared to keep going even though some of these cases were not at the time particularly popular within some quarters in New York. The *Wall Street Journal* lambasted him constantly, and there was a concerted public relations effort mounted by Drexel Burnham and Mike [Michael] Milken. They hired the firm of Robinson Lake and took many steps to influence the media. But Mr. Giuliani was not deterred by that.

Steven R. Andrews   From my standpoint—and from that of every defense lawyer in the case that I talked to—Giuliani's name never surfaced once as a decision maker, ever. The odd thing to me—having had a lot of experience in federal criminal cases—was that at some point in time in a case of this importance, the U.S. attorney would have been involved. But his fingerprints weren't on it at all that *I* saw. My sense was that he didn't want his fingerprints on it—that he thought, I don't know where this is going, and who it's going to end up with, and if I have political aspirations, why ostracize a large group of people that are potentially going to be my supporters?

Edward Reuss, retired captain, New York Police Department   What impresses me the most about him is that he went after Wall Street because, to me, this is the seat of power—this is *big* money. He went down there and made a difference. There is always police corruption—where power exists there's that possibility—but the police are at a low level of power; they have the power to arrest and to actually use deadly physical force, but it's easily dealt with compared to higher levels of corruption. These [Wall Street defendants] are people with a lot of money and *real* power. So when he's going after these people, I'm impressed. I think most cops would be.

Benjamin Brafman Many of the cases in the criminal justice system end in a plea and the government has an enormously high success rate by virtue of the fact that people are sufficiently intimidated by the process. Most people *are* guilty of something that they've been arrested for. There is no constituency for defendants in America—then or now—because most people feel like: if you did something wrong, you should be convicted, and there's a "tough on criminal" philosophy, or mentality, that pervades the world today and it's very hard to get an acquittal in court, even in a case where you *have* stuff to work with. And many of my colleagues in the white-collar criminal defense bar rarely go to trial—and have not gone to trial—in many, many cases.

Did Anti-Semitism Figure in the Wall Street Prosecutions?

Steven R. Andrews There was a real undercurrent of feeling at Drexel that this investigation had anti-Semitic overtones to it—that if you looked at all the targets in the investigation, they were all Jewish, with the exception of Jim [James Dahl], who is the biggest goy on the West Coast. Now whether that came from the top or whether that was just misplaced rationalization by defense counsel and the targets, I have no idea. But there were various sorts of conspiracy theories going back to when Saul Steinberg made overtures to Disney. I never personally saw that, but it was certainly the undercurrent that was being talked about; when defense lawyers and their clients would have a drink at night that was the sort of thing they would say.

John Sturc I don't think there is validity to the assertion of anti-Semitism; I think it was purely coincidence. There were a number of cases that involved people who weren't Jewish. I think the assertion is just propaganda. I happen to be Jewish myself and if somebody would have detected anti-Semitism, *I* would have. It could have been a rationalization or a misplaced sensitivity.

————————

During a press conference at the height of the Wall Street investigations, Giuliani—as quoted by James B. Stewart in *Den of Thieves*—addressing his potential targets, said, "If they had some common sense, and some sense of morality, what they would do is cooperate and try to help the U.S. government clean up this mess."

Charles Carberry   The worst thing for a prosecutor to do is to think he's imposing some kind of moral [code] as opposed to the law. I'm not enforcing the Ten Commandments. We can survive as a society without deciding that insider trading is illegal. It's not murder, it's not rape, it's not classical theft. I was enforcing regulations. Now those [Wall Street] guys were making a lot of money in that market; they had an obligation to obey the regulations and they were crossing the line. It was my job to bring these cases, but I never confused myself with the angel of righteousness. Insider trading is not rape. It's an offense.

Every conversation I had with Rudy dealt with technical matters: here are the elements, here are the proofs. I never had Rudy tell me, "Get that guy," or "Get that target." He never asked me to leak any information, and I never did. Rudy the righteous or Rudy the angel of God was not the Rudy I dealt with. Maybe in the organized crime cases or in the narcotics cases his reaction was different. If he showed any emotion, it was not over the case. It was over something going wrong, something that didn't get done on time.

At that time it was not the normal practice to arrest white-collar criminals, and even now it's not the normal practice. But it's not unusual. And, if you have an investigative reason for doing it, you discuss it and then you make the decision. The decision to arrest was basically at our discretion. The people we arrested were put right into federal jail. Quite frankly, these arrests had a huge deterrent effect—at least short term—down on Wall Street. There were several reasons for the arrest of white-collar criminals. One, we were constantly being told by legal aid lawyers and others that white-collar criminals were being treated differently than people from another class. Two, clearly these arrests could be beneficial. When faced with the seriousness of the consequences of their actions, some people quickly made a decision to cooperate. Another reason for doing the arrests is flight. You are talking about people with offshore bank accounts who are much more comfortable living in other places than some postal worker who has stolen a thousand dollars in Treasury checks. One of the people we arrested had cruise tickets and was headed overseas.

John Sturc   I didn't know about the arrests beforehand. It hadn't happened before, so in that sense it was a surprise. Those decisions are made by the Justice Department; they are not decisions that the SEC makes, nor should they be. The Justice Department administers the enforcement of the criminal law across the board. That [Giuliani's decision to arrest Wall Street executives] was their call, but it was rightly their call. I really don't know whether it turned out to be efficacious or not. There was never, at the end of the day, a successful prosecution of the people arrested.

Charles Carberry   The decision to arrest a particular person went from the assistant attorneys to me. They would provide the evidence and the reasons for an arrest. I would then go to the chief of the Criminal Division and then we would present it to Rudy. We would tell him what we wanted to do, what we thought we should do. We also told him that the arrests would attract publicity so he should know ahead of time before we did it. It was basically up to Rudy for him to agree with our analysis or not. I can remember that since he was trying [Stanley] Friedman at the time [in New Haven, Connecticut], discussions were held on a Saturday; he would come back to New York on the weekends and work in the office. I presented what we thought the evidence was and what I proposed we do. It's not a rubber stamp; in no time or place was Rudy a rubber stamp. If you didn't give him all the information he needed, he would ask you questions. But he's not a time waster, either. He's a decisive man and once he has what he believes are the core facts he can make a decision.

One of the most controversial aspects of Giuliani's Wall Street investigations was his decision to arrest indicted individuals in the full glare of the media spotlight.

Edward Reuss   It *was* necessary because you're sending a message: Hey, you're not above the law! Look, they'll arrest a police officer and they'll drag him out in front of his neighbors, and he's a public officer, a high-ranking officer. Don't forget, the people who are in law enforcement need leadership, somebody they can look up to and respect. And when you go after people like that, the little guys down below, the troops, admire that. That's how I think he motivated the New York City Police Department.

Alan Vinegrad   Prosecutors would say there's a legitimate justification in giving that heads-up to the members of the media so that you can send the public message that people who do x, y, and z are going to be held to account. An individual image of somebody being arrested is powerful and long-lasting sometimes, and that's the best way prosecutors can achieve their job, which is deterring other people from engaging in that kind of behavior. That's the prosecutors' side of the view.

Floyd Abrams   I doubt that Rudy Giuliani devoted much thought to the sort of harm being inflicted on someone who had not been convicted of any crime by treating him in that public, disgraced fashion. When he paraded that investment banker out of his office, I doubt that it ever occurred to him in advance that there might be something morally wrong with a prosecutor using his power in that fashion. He probably was told that people would criticize him, but he's used to criticism.

Richard Thornburgh   One of the roles of a prosecutor is to give the public some confidence that wrongdoing is being attended to in their jurisdiction. And while there are always accusations of self-promotion that go along with that—I had my share of that when I was U.S. attorney—you're really trying to build the public's confidence and actually give them a place to go with allegations that might not otherwise be attended to.

Alan Vinegrad   The other side of the view is that often perp walks occur with people who have been arrested but haven't been *convicted*. And the tarnish that you get from that visual image can never be erased if at the end of the day the prosecutor's case is not proven and the defendant is vindicated. And the prosecutor's job is to make sure, as best one can, that you reserve those public displays for the cases where it's truly warranted and where you have a good level of confidence that what you're doing is right. It's a delicate balance. That's why one of the most important things you've got to have as a prosecutor is judgment, especially since you're so powerful.

Charles Carberry   We *didn't* stage perp walks, making them walk to court so they could be photographed by the media. Everyone was handcuffed because once they make an arrest that's federal regulations: if you are transporting a prisoner, you need handcuffs for both your and the prisoner's protection. Wall Street guys were treated according to federal regulations. I have no reason to believe that arresting officers didn't act in a totally professional manner.

Stephen C. Worth, attorney under contract to the Police Benevolent Association to represent members in criminal and disciplinary cases He was looking for publicity, always with a view to furthering a political career. Marching Wall Street brokers out of their offices at ten o'clock in the morning was clearly a media event. He was opportunistic enough to smell the media and to actively seek it out. He overreached *for sure*.

Charles Carberry   There was some criticism of the press conferences. I remember him expressing very articulately the idea that we can't prosecute all crime, so deterrence is important. If you ever saw a Rudy press conference, it's really not what you see in ninety seconds on the news. He would have everybody involved speak. It was a team press conference. His press conferences got a lot of publicity, a lot of deterrence.

Steven Brill   I followed the cases very closely. Boesky wasn't really cooperative. I did a cover story that said: "Is this a sweetheart deal?" and I had a picture of him leaving a squash court while he was out on bail. I think that in many cases, the plea bargains and/or the sentences were too lenient. In some cases the judges didn't push hard enough.

John Sturc   None of the people who were involved in these cases were all bad. None of them were involved in serial killings and I have no doubt that in the course of their lives [Michael] Milken and the other people did many good things. But the issue that was posed was: you have a system of rules and laws designed to create a level of confidence and trust in the securities markets and that it is essential to keep the system going. So maintaining the integrity of the system is critical.

Stephen C. Worth   Boesky and Milken happened and everybody wrote the books. Then everything quieted down. We had a good eight- or nine-year period before all this was stoked up again and it's because all these things collapsed and when they collapsed precipitously, like the World Trade Center, somebody was telling a lie to get to this point.

PART IV

The Political Agenda

Chapter 6

ACT ONE: RUDY THE LOSER

All of my past draws me to take on this challenge,
to restore the city of my grandparents and
parents, of my relatives and friends, and
to offer New Yorkers hope for the future.

—Rudy Giuliani, announcing his
mayoral candidacy, May 17, 1989

Rudy announced his candidacy first at the Metropolitan Republican Club on Manhattan's Upper East Side, and then in stops at his alma mater, Bishop Loughlin Memorial High School, in Brooklyn, in Queens and the Bronx, and on Staten Island. The sincerity of his pledge to restore the culturally vibrant city's reputation, to redeem it from those who had brought it down—street and white-collar criminals, drug dealers, and crooked politicians—was obvious.

Brother Peter Bonventre   All the students were there [on the day that Rudy Giuliani announced his candidacy at Bishop Loughlin Memorial High School]. It was a population quite similar to what it is now—largely African American and Hispanic—but he fearlessly announced that he was going to go up against Dinkins. We had the band playing and a "Welcome Back, Alumnus of the School" banner. He came, did his thing, and left.

Richard Thornburgh   In some ways, the mayor of New York is equivalent to—even more prominent than—the governor of New York because New York City is a major metropolis and attracts a lot of attention, so I wasn't really surprised. I knew that he wanted to continue his public service. I knew his record, knew his character, and encouraged him to do so, and this seemed like a logical step: he knew the city, had served ably, and had a high profile and a high approval [rating] in his job as U.S. attorney.

First Impressions of Mayoral Candidate Giuliani

Eric Adams, captain, New York Police Department   I was introduced to him at a Police Benevolent Association [PBA] event. He was there with [former Republican mayoral candidate] Diane McGrath, who later became his Taxi and Limousine commissioner—she married Bill McKechnie, who used to be the president of the Transit PBA—and she introduced us and we exchanged pleasantries. At the time, I was chairman of the Grand Council of Guardians, the African American law enforcement organization of all the police agencies, and he was interested in getting an endorsement from me and we spoke briefly.

I met him again at his law firm [White & Case]. He felt he was the best person for the job. I was very public at that time regarding the Association, and he believed that in using my relationships within the African American community—he was running on a pro–law enforcement platform because crime was high coming out of the Koch years and going into the beginning of the Dinkins years—any law enforcement person he could pull in would be helpful to his campaign. Not only that, the city was five-to-one Democratic and he was trying to pull together any type of support he could get and Diane was also reaching out to anyone she could bring on board. He mentioned how tough he was on crime and how he believed that he was the best candidate for dealing with public safety. He had a "Vision of a Safer New York" sort of speech. He didn't let his guard down; he just gave me the typical campaign speech—that he would be a great candidate for the City of New York.

Fran Reiter   I met Rudy for the first time at a dinner that was organized by the Liberal Party of New York State. We were starting our deliberations as to who we would nominate for mayor, and ultimately support in 1989. There were many Democrats who were running, or were considering running, all of whom we knew, and we didn't know Rudy Giuliani, so we asked the political leader of the party to reach out to him, to talk to him, and then report back to us. And based on that, we asked this same person to coordinate a dinner with Rudy so that the leadership of the party from the city could meet with him.

He was not uptight—this was a very relaxed guy who was comfortable around a lot of people, even strangers. He certainly could be intense about his desire to be mayor and about why he thought he would be a good mayor. But at the same time, he could joke and relax and look comfortable. In fact, he has a terrific smile, which I got to see a lot more as I got to know him better. But certainly the picture that one has of Rudy, particularly very early on, was of somebody very austere. And I'm sure that went along with and fed my preconceived notions of the tough prosecutor who I wasn't going to like very much. But I found him to be enormously personable. Our first conversation—chitchat over cocktails—was about the movie *The Godfather*, a favorite of his and of mine. Then we sat down—there were probably about fifteen of us around the table—and the format was that he would tell us about himself and why he was running for mayor and then we would ask him questions. I came away from that first meeting with three thoughts about him: number one, he was much more likable than I thought I would find him because, certainly, having not met him, my impression of Rudy Giuliani was that he was this tough prosecutor—we all have our preconceived notions—and I found him enormously personable, with a great sense of humor, and very easy to talk to. The second thing I came away with was that this man was, clearly, *very, very* smart in the way he thought and communicated. The third thing was that he was uneducated at that point about a whole host of urban issues that would confront him were he to become mayor.

Eric Adams   I was very close to my mother, a very spiritual person, and I consider myself to be a very spiritual person and I learned from her how to *feel* people. And when I first met Giuliani, all I can remember is that I felt a very, very bitter, evil spirit coming from him, a lot of hatred, and although he put his best foot forward to be as cordial as possible, I felt very uneasy around him. At no time did I sense when we were talking that he was saying [to himself], This person is black; this person is white. I wasn't getting that at all; it wasn't about race, it was [what Officer Adams perceives to be Giuliani's negative attitude] about *humankind*.

Raoul Felder   I had had contact with him on and off over some years, but the first time I really took a look at him as a potential mayoral candidate was when a book was written by Wayne Barrett and Jack Newfield about the crookedness of City Hall [*City for Sale: Ed Koch and the Betrayal of New York*, 1988]. It's an interesting book in that it had a picture of the beginning of the Dinkins administration. I went with Jackie Mason to the book party at the Village Gate [a Greenwich Village spot that featured cutting-edge entertainment], which is now closed. [Felder and Mason, after reading *City for Sale*, explored Giuliani's political attributes.] We were very impressed by him [Giuliani]. I thought he had a high intelligence level and was a terrific antidote to what had been going on.

Getting on Board for Rudy Giuliani

Rudy Washington   I had no way of reaching Rudy. They [Giuliani's campaign strategists] were shooting a commercial and I just walked up and said, "My name is Rudy Washington; I want to help this guy." And they *looked* at me. And when I showed up at Rudy's office at campaign headquarters, they couldn't be convinced that I was not a spy: an African American of some standing shows up and says he's going to help *Rudy?* He may not admit it, but there was some distrust there: he didn't know me from a hole-in-the-wall; he didn't know if I was working for Dinkins or not. But I had him come out [to the African American community of Queens] and speak to the Rotary Club and he began to break down some of these barriers with black businessmen, and people started saying, "Well, he has a great track record." And when he saw me go down the line with him and stand publicly with him and endorse him and say, "This is the man for the job," he and Peter Powers realized very quickly: this guy's for real; he's not playing games. This is not some organizational plot by the Democrats to torpedo our effort. So he began to bring me in closer. We would go to a Saturday meeting, and afterwards Peter Powers, the mayor, I, and maybe someone else would sit around and talk about how we could get traction within the African American and Latino communities and how we could improve the campaign. And the rest is history.

The Jewish Community and Giuliani

Malcolm Hoenlein   I don't think they knew that much about Giuliani. Some in the business community resented some of his actions. I wasn't really dealing with the local politics of it so much. There was consistency to his positions on Israel. I sat in on some of his meetings with prime ministers and he asked all the right questions. I think his friendship and concern for Israel is not political; it is sincere. A lot of people treat him with great skepticism, but I can tell you that there were things that were done quietly; there were times when we asked him to do certain things and he didn't say no, whether it was to host somebody or to meet somebody or to intercede or to speak to people in Washington. I had known Dinkins for a long time and had a lot of respect for him as a person. And it was before Crown Heights so you didn't have him put to the test of that. But Giuliani did do a lot of outreach into the Jewish community. I think he got more votes than people expected but not nearly as much as when he got elected [in 1993]. And in his second reelection, in '97, he got about 60 percent of the Jewish vote. But Dinkins by then did have Crown Heights and there were a lot of questions—there was the Sharpton factor in all these issues and it was very polarized.

The Failed Campaign

Rudy Giuliani announced his candidacy for mayor on May 17, 1989, and his campaign was in trouble from almost that very moment. He stunned his advisers and negated his manifesto by refusing to take questions from the city's press corps—the first of his many mistakes in dealing with the local branch of the Fourth Estate. In his own mind, Rudy had reason to shut the press out. Only that morning, the *New York Daily News* had disclosed that White & Case, the white-shoe law firm Rudy had joined in 1989, represented and was a foreign agent for Panama, whose dictator, General Manuel Noriega, had been charged by the U.S. government with drug trafficking. As Rudy strode from the platform that spring day, the pursuing reporters peppered him with questions about whether he had known of his firm's Panamanian connection, setting off an onslaught by prominent local politicians—Democrats and Republicans alike. Less than three weeks later, Rudy was forced to resign from the prestigious firm. But the damage had been done: the bad-tempered and inexperienced Rudy had surfaced and the campaign was barely under way.

On the Campaign Trail

Raoul Felder   He was going around, as they all do, to many stops. Jackie Mason and I wanted him to meet somebody on the editorial staff of the *New York Times*—he wasn't getting a fair shake—and so he said, okay, between stops he'd stop off at Jackie's home, which is in the Metropolitan Tower on West 57th Street, right next to Carnegie Hall. We had a few people there. There was some food spread out and he apparently hadn't eaten that day, but he got engrossed in talking, in the give-and-take, and he stayed a few hours. He had these other stops he was supposed to make, but he is passionate about ideas and he got himself all involved.

[On another occasion] Jackie was performing in a theater-in-the-round out on the Island [Long Island, New York]. We went out to eat later and I asked him about his feelings about abortion. I think he was in a transitional state, but he said to me, "You know, as long as you have a situation where people who have money can get an abortion and people who don't have money can't get the abortion, then it becomes a simpler issue: you can't have something where if you have enough money you're able to do it and if you don't, you can't."

And he was very strong on the Israel situation. I remember saying to him, "When did you get so involved and passionate?" Apparently, it turned out, that when he was in the Justice Department, he was in charge of the Klinghoffer case. [Leon Klinghoffer, an American citizen confined to a wheelchair, was a passenger with his wife on the *Achille Lauro*, and on October 8, 1985, was murdered and thrown overboard by hijackers headed by PLO executive committee member Abu Abbas, a close aide to the late PLO chairman Yasir Arafat.] He [Giuliani] said to me, "You're dealing with thugs."

Jackie Mason Is Forced from the Campaign

Rudy had designated the rabbi turned Borscht Belt humorist as his honorary campaign chairman. Returning the favor, Mason, in an interview with the *Village Voice*, published in early October, expressed wonder at how Jews could support the Democratic Party's candidate, Manhattan Borough President David Dinkins, opining that he "looks like a black model without a job."

Rudy's advisers, Ray Harding and Peter Powers, knew that Mason had to go, and they brought Raoul Felder and Mason's manager, Jyll Rosenfeld, into campaign headquarters on the day the *Village Voice* hit the newsstands to insist that Mason resign by three o'clock that very afternoon. Mason did so. But there was more to come. The following week, *Newsweek* magazine reported that Mason, during a luncheon on August 31 attended by Giuliani, had called Dinkins "a fancy *shvartze* [Yiddish slang for person of color] with a moustache." Straining to contain the damage, the Giuliani campaign took out a full-page ad in a Jewish newspaper depicting Giuliani with George Bush and Dinkins with Jesse Jackson emblazoned with the words "Let the People of New York Choose Their Own Destiny."

Was It Very Difficult for Rudy to Distance Himself from Jackie Mason?

Raoul Felder Yes, it was. But you've got to bear in mind, he was surrounded by these professional political people and it was a decision *they* made. And my own supposition is that he would have ridden it out. But in the middle of the campaign like that, they told him to, and they did it gracefully. In fact, after he was elected he was friendly with Jackie; he appeared on the stage, in a motorcycle outfit, with Jackie on an opening night. I remember, on one opening night we were sitting in some building and reading the reviews and he read them aloud to everybody there. So I don't think that either one of them really considered that a death blow to whatever their feelings were.

A Rare African American Voice in Support of Giuliani

Rudy Washington In 1988, when he started to say that he was going to run, I thought, I'm voting for this guy. And it became a tough choice because it was a race against David Dinkins. I live in a predominantly African American community and at that time I was president of my Rotary Club and very active in business organizations—I sat on two or three boards within the community; I started two day-care centers that were doing quite well and were two of the largest, probably, in Southeast Queens—so I was very entrenched. When Rudy got ready to run, obviously, everybody was lining up for David Dinkins—it was coming off the Jesse Jackson race for president in '88 when Jesse had a big turnout within the black community—and it was that vote that delivered David Dinkins. Once again—I was known as a political player but not part of the organization who would wind up fighting the establishment, as opposed to being part of it—I took a very contrary position in the community.

I knew David Dinkins; he's a very nice man. But New York City was going through some tough times: we were in the middle of a crack epidemic; a police officer was assassinated by drug dealers. I don't use the word loosely; literally, he was sitting in a car, guarding a witness's house, and the drug dealers wanted to send law enforcement a message, so they walked up in the middle of the night and ambushed this young kid in his car. If that's not an assassination, I don't know what *is*. So, just on merit, I felt that Giuliani was the guy for the job. A few people followed me; a few people said, "Hey, I was robbed—I've got drug dealers on my corner." And there were a couple who said, "Rudy, if you go, I'm going."

I would have loved to have had an African American mayor, but that was not the time for symbolism and I took that position—I basically used that term—because I didn't know any other way to say it. And a lot of people got very, very upset with me. One time, a woman that I didn't even know walked up to me and said, "You know, I supported you for everything you've ever done." Then she smacked my face and said, "I wouldn't vote for you for *dogcatcher* for supporting Rudy Giuliani over David Dinkins!"

Was Giuliani Assuming That He Would Be Running against Mayor Koch, Not Dinkins?

Fran Reiter   That's very true and it changed the entire tenor of the '89 campaign, if for no other reason than for the racial issues. Here you had David Dinkins, who had defeated a Democratic Party icon, albeit one whose mayoralty was in trouble, but the trouble was not with Koch; *he* was not under investigation, his *administration* was under major investigation for all kinds of corruption. And Koch, like most third-term mayors, was starting to lose a little steam. That happens to everyone. But there's no question that Rudy thought that Koch was still strong enough to beat David Dinkins.

David Dinkins   The question was whether I could even survive the Democratic primary. My opponents were Ed Koch, a three-term mayor who had been very popular in the beginning, not so popular in his third term; [city comptroller] Jay Goldin, who, I believe, is one of the most artic-ulate, knowledgeable people I've ever met in New York City municipal gov-ernment; and Dick [Richard] Ravitch, who was a highly successful head of the MTA [Metropolitan Transportation Authority] with their capital pro-gram. Their wisdom was that each of them was Jewish and that even if I managed to finish second, if nobody got 40 percent, then I would certainly lose in a runoff. Well, we got over 50 percent and the three of them endorsed me the next day.

Frank Luntz   When I produced my survey for the *New York Post* in that very first poll in '89, the writers went to the owner [and real estate mogul] Peter Kalikow—they will admit it today; they wouldn't admit it at the time—and said, "You can't run this" because the headline was "Koch Clobbered." Dinkins was beating him and Giuliani actually was in the mix; he genuinely had a shot and no one ever thought that Koch was going to lose, even though his numbers were bad in the polls; this was just the guy who *always* won—no matter *what* happened. Even when he was supposed to lose to *Cuomo*, he won. He was the comeback kid.

Mark Green   Koch was a very weakened third-term mayor, obviously, because of all the scandals. His poll numbers were dismal. And Giuliani came on as an anticrime white knight and was leading in polls over both Koch and Dinkins at the start. He assumed that it would be a race against Koch and made all his plans based on that assumption. And when it ended up a race against an African American borough president, I do believe it surprised him and it was harder for him to handle. One of the funniest lines I've ever heard was that Rudy Giuliani has such difficulty dealing with racial issues that the only black people he appointed all had the name *Rudy*—Rudy Washington and Rudy Crew; two out of two is a lot. [Jack Newfield, writing in *The Nation* on June 17, 2002, stated, "People began to make jokes that the only black people Giuliani could relate to had to also be named Rudy—a reference to Crew and Deputy Mayor Rudy Washington."] You have to concentrate on what you do because people will racialize anything you do. So Giuliani had to be careful in the general election in which Dinkins started way out ahead because it was such a phenomenal story that the African American borough president feared the big third-term incumbent. Then Koch endorsed Dinkins and so Dinkins started out in a very prized position and then lost ground over time.

Fran Reiter   Dinkins gets the nomination and now, all of a sudden, you have a very, very different kind of campaign: you're a Democratic city where, with rare exception, the winner of the Democratic primary is generally presumed to be the next mayor because Republicans almost never win the mayoralty. And as the nominee of the Democratic Party, you have the first really viable African American candidate. That's a historic occurrence and it shed a whole new light on all this. And, frankly, it hurt Rudy forever after in terms of his relationships with minority communities, particularly the black community, in the sense that I believe that Rudy thought because he was viewed as being the guy who knocked off Dinkins in '93—that he could never recover from that in the way that the African American community looked at him. I think he was wrong because, in fact, he did recover to some extent with African American communities in the other boroughs. Had he been more open to the idea that he could sell the African American community on his mayoralty and the plusses to their community from his mayoralty, had he *tried*—I'm not suggesting that he was ever going to get 50 percent of the African American vote—I do think that he could have been far more successful than he was. But there was a psychological block in his head to the notion that he could effectively reach out to that community and win them over.

Fred Siegel   There's no question that the campaign was aimed against Koch, but that's not why he lost. Remember, this is his first political campaign; it's a huge learning curve: he takes positions on social issues. He never *had* positions on social issues and he took positions he hadn't thought about much because he hadn't been much interested in them, so he wasn't the fully formed figure we know from the mid '90s.

David Dinkins   He was certainly no pushover. He and his people did a good job in preparing him, but they probably underestimated me, notwithstanding the closeness of the race. Keep in mind that I had gone through a whole primary and that's a long time for a primary and a general election—one ran right into the other. Given that I had run three times for borough president before I succeeded and I could very easily have been reelected borough president, I put everything on the line to run for mayor.

Ed Koch   I don't know whether I would have beaten him or not. You should know that I'm very proud of my record in this area. Rudy is a difficult man, a very good campaigner. And he can be very charming, and, in my judgment, very cruel. That's just *Rudy*. The *Village Voice* had an article that when he thought he was going to run against *me*, he commissioned somebody to follow me, and I called David Garth when Rudy asked me to support him in '93 and I said, "Did you read that article?" And he had read the article and he said, "Why don't you call him up and ask him?" So I called him up and I said, "Rudy, I just read that you had this guy follow me, that you were looking into my sex life"—that's what the article said. "Oh," he said—my recollection is it was something like: he did it on his own; when I found out about it, I stopped it. Maybe. *Maybe*. Who knows?

The Lauder Factor

Fran Reiter Giuliani is very much the political neophyte: he has to face Ron Lauder [a former U.S. ambassador to Austria and the son of cosmetics legend Estée Lauder] in a Republican primary. He's in this battle with Al D'Amato. D'Amato gets Lauder to run; Lauder puts up $13 million to run a primary he's not going to win, but do as much damage to Giuliani as possible. And it is ultimately the Lauder candidacy, and the lateness of Giuliani's recovery from it, that loses him the election in '89. I think that Giuliani would have won were it not for that and also that he would have won had the election been two weeks later, that he had come back enormously from this pit he had fallen into during the campaign. What happened—it goes to the notion of fusion [the cooperation among various political parties most notable in the elections of Fiorello La Guardia, in 1933, and John Vliet Lindsay, more than three decades later]—is that the Liberal Party and Giuliani were still feeling one another out in that '89 campaign. Giuliani became convinced by political consultants that he had hired—two guys from Washington who had been high-ups in George Bush the First's presidential operation but didn't really know New York politics, didn't really understand fusion— that he couldn't ignore Lauder, that he really had to win the Republican primary *big*, by a huge percentage.

Winning a Republican primary by a huge percentage is meaningless to the people you need in this general election; you've got to convince Democrats to vote for you. The more you look like a Republican, the less they're going to want to vote for you. So, in fact, it was counterproductive: he ran a real primary campaign against Lauder rather than ignoring him and he used up a lot of resources. All he had to do was beat Lauder by one percentage point. Instead, he goes head-to-head, gets into this big primary fight. In turn, the media pays a lot of attention to it and the primary gets far more attention in everybody's minds than it should have. His numbers go way down and he's now in a hole that he has to climb out of in a relatively short period of time—there's seven weeks between primary day and election day. Late in August, he finally realizes he's in trouble and he brings in Peter Powers, his closest friend, a very smart guy with political instincts, and he brings the Liberal Party to the table in a big way. Now, seven weeks out, he's fifteen or twenty points down in the polls. When there is a black candidate in a race like this, people lie to the pollsters. So, two weeks before, we were still down by fifteen points according to every poll. He didn't make the same mistakes in '93. He now understood what fusion really meant—that you've got to win the general election and not pay that kind of attention to the primary. It was a big lesson learned.

On November 7, 1989, Rudy Giuliani lost to David N. Dinkins by less than three percentage points—the smallest margin of loss in a New York City mayoral race since 1905.

Henry Stern, member, Liberal Party; former commissioner, New York City Department of Parks and Recreation   He lost because many people wanted to give Dinkins a chance, to make Dinkins the city's first black mayor. Even so, he [Dinkins] won by only three points, although the polls had him ahead by ten points. Many people were surprised that Giuliani came so close. That contributed to Dinkins's bitterness, anger, and resentment at white voters. Dinkins felt that in so Democratic a city as New York, running against someone like Giuliani, who was making his first race for public office, he, as the Democratic candidate, should have received 70 to 80 percent of the vote. Instead of taking the attitude, As a black man, I have been elected, he took the position, because I am black, I was almost defeated.

David Dinkins   Given the large Democratic enrollment over Republican, given that there hadn't been a Republican mayor for some time, and even if Rudy were Superman, nobody knew it at that time, the question was: How did I manage to win by only fifty or sixty thousand votes out of 1.9 million votes cast? A larger question is: How come he did so well? Why didn't I overwhelm him? And so reporters used to ask me, "Why do you think that's so? Do you think it's because you're black?" And I would simply respond, "Why do you *ask*?" And I say to this day, "Why do you *ask*?" How does one figure? Whatever frailties, whatever shortcomings I had were certainly not evident at that point and whatever greatness there was in Rudy had not yet been revealed. So how come 1.9 million votes and I win by the skin of my teeth? Keep in mind that if the margin were sixty thousand, it means that thirty thousand would have altered the outcome.

Frank Luntz   On election night even the exit polls had Dinkins winning by nine points and Rudy only lost by two and a half. But my survey had him losing by 5 percent; I had the closest survey to the actual result and he never forgot that. What was happening at that point was that you still had white fear: you had interviewers with black-sounding voices calling into white neighborhoods, asking who you were going to vote for. And so people said that they were going to vote for Dinkins because they didn't know who they were talking to. What happened in that election was that nobody really focused on Dinkins and so he got a free ride until the last couple of weeks, when some of his business dealings came into play. And even though Rudy was known as a tough prosecutor, his image had not been filled out. They had a good impression of him but not a *deeply felt* impression of him. And it was not a good year for Republicans, either. He wasn't going to win that first race, even if he thought he was going to win.

Did Giuliani Really Lose the 1989 Election?

Rudy Washington   It was a common fact, probably even right into the U.S. Attorney's Office, that in Brooklyn and Queens, the dead would vote. And let's face it: New York City prior to Mayor Giuliani was a Democratic bastion—from the presidential races on down. It was: New York City will deliver the Democratic vote and, for that matter, translate it to New York State—that a person running for president would count on New York State being Democratic. For the person running for mayor of New York City, the election was settled in *September,* not in November. And the registration was five-to-one, Democrat to Republican, so by all rights, Rudy shouldn't have been in this race at all, just on *the numbers*. So, knowing that we were going up against the county organizations that controlled the apparatus that over the years—not in ancient history, in *recent* years—had had cases brought against it for ballot tampering and all those types of things, we knew we had to do ballot security. We knew that people would vote two or three times, be registered in a couple of different locations. And if you understand the apparatus of the Board of Elections and how people get appointed to the Board of Elections and, at that time, who appointed them—you've got a whole history of county leaders, the Donald Maneses, the Stanley Friedmans, and all the rest, who have appointed the people at the Central Board of Elections—they control everything and you now have to cut through that for any kind of challenge. You would have to cut through twenty-five or thirty years of people constantly appointing Democrats to these operations. And within the black community, you had the black representative sitting at the Board of Elections; within the Italian community you had the Italian; and you had the Jewish. It was a well-organized machine where everybody had a little piece of the action and Mayor Giuliani came along and said, "Okay, now I'm here and we're going to penetrate this and take on this apparatus." So we knew we were fighting this apparatus from the lowest guy on the totem pole to the mayor.

Raoul Felder   It was stolen from him: there were districts where he didn't get one vote in New York City, which is almost impossible. There were multiple voting questions; there was at least one case of more people [voting] than were in the election district—crazy stuff. I remember saying to him afterwards, in a telephone conversation, "Why don't you take it to the courts?" And he said, "It's not the right thing to do for New York." I thought that was a very responsible comment. I was impressed: here's a man who probably could have been elected through the courts and he felt it was *wrong*. And maybe in his mind it would have inflamed the racial situation. I don't think too many people who had that desire to be a high elected official would have done that.

Frank Luntz   They stole about a percent. So whatever the numbers were, he didn't really lose by two and a half, he probably lost by one and a half. In '93, buses with fifty people on them would go from polling place to polling place; there were machines that would break; machines that would record more people voting than actually lived in the precinct—all sorts of political shenanigans that happen in places like New York, Los Angeles, and Chicago happened in this race. One of the untold stories in '93 was the effort by Peter Powers and the Republican Party to prevent that from happening again and they really made an incredible effort. But Rudy in '89 was not the Rudy of '93. He was not as well-rounded a public figure. And, also, New York had not sunk to the depth that it hit in 1992.

Rudy Washington   Rudy knew all about the games—what could happen in terms of stealing the election—and we did everything we could for ballot security. Rudy made a determination that night: he wasn't going to challenge the 2 percent. He told everybody at campaign headquarters, "I'm not going to do it"—that he would accept the defeat and move on. I respected that; *he* was the candidate. If he had challenged it, I would have stood with him and we would have slugged it out in court.

On November 7, 1989, Was Rudy Already Planning His Next Campaign?

Rudy Washington   Six months later he contacted me again and said, "Rudy, I'm thinking about going again. Would you sign back up?" I said,

"You *know* I will." So he put me on his fund-raising committee. I never had envisioned being part of that mechanism. I saw myself as a street operator—able to make things happen—but I never saw myself as being on the money side.

Raoul Felder　He lived on 86th Street and I was visiting my niece on 86th Street and I saw him. He's coming from the supermarket, carrying two bags. He's going home and I thought, Fortunes change like this; this fellow was going to be mayor—a national figure—and he's taking home groceries. And he seemed very jolly. I think he understood that he was going to run again.

Fran Reiter　There was no question he was going to run again. He spent that four years going to school, if you will, and going to school in the way that I think has served him extremely well and also says a lot about who he is, because this is not an ideologue. It's very hard to characterize Rudy Giuliani as a Conservative or a Liberal. In fact, it's impossible to describe him that way, which, I think, is a big part of his success as a Republican becoming mayor of the City of New York and really giving truth to the notion of being a fusion mayor.

Brother Peter Bonventre　I don't think that kind of personality likes to lose: I've lost, *so what*? I'll go on to something else. It probably was very tough to lose to Dinkins and more of a challenge for him to move ahead.

Henry Stern　In the winter of 1991, accompanied by Bobby Wagner [the late Robert F. Wagner Jr.—he would die on November 15, 1993, at the age of 49—a city councilman, deputy mayor, and chairman of the Board of Education], I was walking my dog, Boomer, in Carl Schurz Park and we ran into Rudy Giuliani and his son, Andrew, who was about five at the time. Andrew wanted to take Boomer's leash. But when he took the leash, Boomer moved forward and Andrew fell on the ice. When he got up, he said, "Daddy, I want a dog." Rudy answered, "When we get to Gracie Mansion you can have a dog." When I heard him say that I wondered, How could he know that?

Chapter 7

ACT TWO, SCENE ONE: RUDY THE WINNER

If I had his record, I'd be kind of
embarrassed to show my face.

—Rudy Giuliani, speaking of Mayor David Dinkins,
quoted in the *New York Post*, April 8, 1999

To say that Rudy Giuliani learned from his many mistakes in the 1989 campaign would be an understatement; his learning curve was becoming decidedly vertical, and while continuing his unabashed boosterism of his beloved city, which had sunk deeper and deeper into crime and racial strife during the Dinkins regime, he realized the need for a tough-talking, take-no-victims strategist. He found his man in media maven David Garth, the creator of Ed Koch's brash "How Am I Doing?" persona. In fact, Mayor Koch attended a series of lunches with Rudy Giuliani.

Ed Koch   I don't remember whether David Garth asked me to meet with him or not. But I would have whether he had recommended it or had stayed silent. There was no animosity between us. My position on meeting with people—irrespective of whether they were Republicans or Democrats or [members of] any other party—was so long as they were mainstream in their philosophy, I would meet with anybody who wanted my advice. I always believed that the education I received as a public official and as a candidate obliged me to give advice when asked. And it was clear that he wanted advice. I had three lunches with him and at the end of the third one he *did* ask me for support.

I said [to David Garth] I had doubts about Rudy's performance, which arose from two cases: the stockbrokerage case and the daughter of Justice

Gabel. He said, "Why don't you ask him about it?" And so I said, "Rudy, I'll tell you what bothers me about the stockbrokers' case, where you had the three brokers taken out in handcuffs" and he said, "I had nothing to do with that; that was a decision made by the U.S. marshal. When he sought to get them to leave their offices, they refused to do it and so he put hand-cuffs on them. But I didn't *direct* him to do that." To this day, I don't know whether that's true or not. And I said, "Rudy, I'm distressed that you would use the daughter of Judge Gabel to tape her mother on the phone for the purposes of a criminal indictment. It's just not *right* to use a daughter that way." And he said, "I didn't do that, *either*. That resulted from an accident on the daughter's part; she pushed the wrong button and she *herself* taped her mother." To this day I don't know whether *that's* true or not.

Rudy announced his second mayoral bid on May 28, 1993, his forty-ninth birthday. He brought on as his press aide the intense, dark-haired and dark eyed twenty-eight-year-old Cristyne Lategano, who as a young girl had written the future mayor an adoring political mash letter but would emerge as the Lady Macbeth of the Giuliani administration. Adding sizzle to the steak, Rudy placed Donna Hanover front and center as a key adviser—at least until Lategano got the upper berth.

Armed with a five-inch-thick "vulnerability study" that dealt with antic-ipated embarrassing questions concerning his personal and professional lives, among them the fact that his marriage to Regina Peruggi had been annulled on the grounds that they were cousins, Rudy, on Garth's advice, ran on a fusion ticket with two Democrats, Herman Badillo and Susan Alter, the candidates for comptroller and public advocate, respectively.

Herman Badillo   The meeting [Badillo's first substantive encounter with the fusion candidate] was arranged by my partner, Rick Fischbein—my law firm is Fischbein Badillo Wagner Harding. Rick arranged for me to meet with Giuliani at his home at 893 Park Avenue. Ray Harding and Peter Powers were also there, as was David Garth. At that time, I was consider-ing running for mayor myself and we began to talk about issues like the future of New York City and about what we felt needed to be done. We had several such meetings. And eventually they got around to my view that Dinkins had done a very poor job in anticipating the problems of the city, that he had been an abysmal mayor, and that the city was going downhill. My view, then and now, is that the city is governable and that whatever the problems of the city are, they can be resolved. We discussed the issue of crime, for example, and I pointed out to him that the policy of Mayor Dinkins at that time was that the average policeman would not be allowed to make arrests on the street, that it had to be a special squad that made arrests for drug dealing. I told Giuliani that every ten-year-old knew who was selling drugs, that if you asked a ten-year-old, "Who's selling drugs in the street?" he'd say, "That guy over there."

The problem was that the drug leaders were very sophisticated and they knew when the special squad was going to come in, so when the special squad would come in, say, to 138th Street, they would disappear. I pointed out to him that I'd been told by my sources in the Dominican community that the drug dealers were franchising corners in New York City, for example, that they had sold the corner of 165th Street for several hundred thousand dollars and they guarded that corner with machine guns, and only the people who had paid for that corner were allowed to sell drugs. And that was an important corner because people would come in from New Jersey to 165th Street, get drugs, and then go back to New Jersey. And I found out that there was a corner at 138th Street and Park Avenue where they were selling seven different kinds of crack. And, again, it was a franchise—like McDonald's. We all laughed about it, but it was grim. And so Rudy promised, and he did emphasize [that] after he got elected, that average policemen could make arrests—that they didn't have to wait for a special squad.

After several such meetings, we found that we got along quite well together. And I got along well with Peter Powers and, of course, I had worked with Dave Garth long before—he had been the press guy for John Lindsay and I had worked with him during the Lindsay years. So I decided to run with Rudy, for comptroller, and we campaigned all over the city.

Fran Reiter He took that four years and he consulted with think tanks, journalists, political scientists, and a host of experts representing a wide array of public policy areas, from all ends of the ideological spectrum. So he wouldn't just talk to someone at the Manhattan Institute [a think tank funded by wealthy, right-wing foundations] on the Conservative side about welfare policy; he would talk to people on the other side. And this process served him enormously well. He brought on board Richard Schwartz—he was an issues/policy kind of guy—who had had government experience working in the Parks Department with Henry Stern. Henry was an early supporter of Giuliani's and suggested that he work with Richard, and Richard spent a good deal of time educating Rudy but also setting up the schedule of meetings throughout that four-year period with all of the various people and organizations that Rudy met with. The result was that by the time he got ready to gear up for the '93 election, this was a very different candidate: this was a candidate that could speak more than intelligently and with great knowledge, having given great thought to a whole host of issues beyond the obvious crime and quality of life issues, which were central to his candidacy, his mayoralty, and, frankly, to who he is as a human being. This was a candidate in '93 that was very ready to be mayor.

Henry Stern   Bobby Wagner and I became advisers. Giuliani would have seminars at his law office at 666 Third Avenue on topics such as city history and city government and he made an enormous effort to educate himself.

Gene Russianoff   I got to brief Giuliani. He was personable and attentive and the thing that struck me was that he was smart. He took notes and I was impressed that he actually listened; with most politicians, you could watch it go in one ear and out the other. Maybe that was happening; it was just that he was writing while it was going in one ear and out the other. We pitched to him the fact that we believed that one of the flaws of the Dinkins administration was their view on incineration. Dinkins's first deputy mayor was Norman Steisel, the former transportation commissioner, and they wanted to build incinerators. We, for environmental reasons, disagreed. We said to Giuliani, "Both because of the substance and the politics—look at the Staten Island Fresh Kills Landfill—you should do something on incineration." He *got* it; he made a hallmark of his administration the closing of the Fresh Kills Landfill and the end of incineration in New York and so it's hard to characterize him because, in our view, that was the progressive position.

The view of the Dinkins administration was what I call the "development Democratic view." We had submitted a questionnaire to him and to Dinkins. We were troubled during the Dinkins era that all the MTA [Metropolitan Transit Authority] board members owed their jobs to the mayor and could not exercise independent judgment. So one of our questions was, "Would you appoint people from your staff?" Giuliani said, "No, I would look for independent people" but he went ahead and he chose people from his staff—John Dyson and Joe Lhota. That was particularly galling to us because he chose a deputy mayor and his chief of staff.

While Garth did not succeed entirely in transforming his candidate's rough edges—Rudy still appeared to be both combative and insecure, his Dickensian visage and comb-over haircut accentuating the negative— he was definitely on mission, exclaiming, "We have a city to save!" He took on murderers, rapists, narcotics dealers, pimps, and even the greasy rag-bearing "squeegee men" who roamed the city's congested streets, forcing their services on hapless motorists and demanding cash in return. And he declared, "Color lines and racial lines and gender lines and ethnic lines and religious lines have nothing to do with what we're about." That message would resonate with New Yorkers traumatized by racial divisions that had intensified following an episode that would come to be known simply as "Crown Heights" and likely cost David Dinkins the 1993 election.

Joining the Campaign

Frank Luntz   Well into the campaign, certainly no earlier than April, David Garth found me working for the [New York] *Daily News.* Giuliani had said to Garth a couple of weeks before, "Remember the guy who got it so right for the *New York Post* in '89? I want him to do my polling in '93." He didn't remember my name, but he knew *the pollster* and so Garth called and asked if I'd be willing to do it. I had to quit the *Daily News*—I lost money; the *Daily News* did not pay me what it owed me because I had quit.

They set up a meeting with Rudy. There was no one else in the room. It was about a forty-five-minute meeting and it went about fifteen minutes longer than I expected. They had these big, blowup pictures of him and that's what triggered my questions. I had two: first, "Why would you want to be mayor of this godforsaken city?" And second, "Don't you want to know a little bit about how I poll?" He answered the first question. He believed that it was phony compassion to give people everything they asked for and not to ask for anything in return. Even back then he was talking about responsibility and accountability. I don't remember if he specifically referred to Wilson's "Broken Windows" theory [James Q. Wilson and George L. Kelling of Harvard University's Kennedy School of Government had written the original article on which Kelling and another colleague, Catherine M. Coles, based their book, *Fixing Broken Windows,* their thesis being that when dealing with crime, if smaller problems, i.e., broken windows, are corrected, then larger problems will be more easily remedied]. But he did talk about the decline in quality of life and the importance of holding people accountable for what they do. There was that sense of responsibility and accountability that permeated all of his conversations and his philosophy. On the second question, he said he had made up his mind even before I had walked in. He never asked me about my polling capabilities; he never asked me about my knowledge of New York. He spent thirty minutes telling me what he was going to do as mayor and fifteen minutes telling me what the Yankees needed to do to win a championship. I love politics and baseball, so I loved the meeting.

On the Campaign Trail

Fran Reiter   He was much more comfortable as a public person—he was stiff in '89; his speeches were not as smooth, not as natural sounding. Now he knows what he's talking about and it helps to really understand the subject matter you're being asked questions and making speeches about. He had become an expert on welfare reform; he had done an enormous amount of work in economic development; he had done a lot of work in educational issues. This was somebody you could ask a question of about almost any aspect of city governance and he knew the answer. He literally went to graduate school over that four-year period. That translated into his being a much better public speaker who could afford to be more relaxed in public and not constantly on guard. This is a crack litigator—Rudy has the communications skills of an exceptional lawyer—and when he's in a milieu where he's comfortable, it's a lot easier for the lighter side of his personality to show.

Herman Badillo   Every day he was out on his "ice cream truck," as they called it. He campaigned very hard till late at night. We covered every part of the city, and wherever we went, the response was quite good—people were telling him, especially in middle-class areas, that he had to win because otherwise they would leave the city. There was an enormous amount of dissatisfaction with Mayor Dinkins on the part of a huge number of people. I know from campaigning with him that he *loves* pizza. I had enough pizza in the time I was campaigning with him to last me the rest of my life, although there are interesting pizza places—there's a place in Staten Island that has pizza with vodka that I'd never heard of. And he loves a place like Patsy's, in East Harlem. I think he can go through life eating nothing but *pizza*, every day.

Did Donna Play a Major Role in the Campaign?

Fran Reiter   A *big* role; she was a regular part of the campaign, in a lot of meetings, a close adviser to her husband. It was never my sense that Donna was particularly involved in media- or press-related issues. She was there much more on public policy issues, political strategy issues, and as a general adviser to Rudy. She was *very* much a presence and *very* much a campaigner.

Herman Badillo   Donna campaigned with us every day; she was with us in high heels and she went everywhere and, in fact, sometimes she brought the kids too, so she was very much a part of the campaign and very important to the campaign—she was a hundred percent part of the campaign, seven days a week.

Fred Siegel   I don't think her influence was big one way or another. The argument is that Garth's ads, with Donna and his mother, softened him. If they did, they didn't mean many votes.

Raoul Felder   I was traveling with her. It's been overrated; she was not involved for the heavy lifting, really. I did a fund-raiser. She came down and enjoyed it. She was an actress and these people don't like to see other people in the spotlight. It may have been as simple as that.

Frank Luntz   I felt she did. She was the first person to ever use a four-letter word in my presence, in her response to something David Garth had said. David Garth intimidated me; I found his yelling and his bravado frightening. I'm a suburban kid; I was new to the world of rough-and-tumble New York politics. Today I may sound like a bus driver; back then, I had a pretty clean way of articulating and I did not use four-letter words. In one of the meetings, she let Garth *have it!* And I was so excited about it because I felt she was right on and I didn't have the guts to do it myself—not in '93; my confidence and outspokenness did not happen until after the election. But she told him exactly how she felt, in words that you could not air on network television.

Ed Koch's Endorsement of Giuliani

Ed Koch   People were very supportive of me although I had been out of office for four years. Now when I speak around the country, I always tell the story that when at that particular moment in '93 when people were fed up with the choice that they had between Rudy and David Dinkins, they would say to me five to ten times a day, "Oh, Mayor, you must run again!" And my response, which was not carefully thought out—it was an immediate response on the first occasion, but it was such a good one that I used it thereafter—was, "No. The people threw me out and the people must be punished!" People loved that response. And *I* did too, to tell you the truth.

Rudy still had a big problem, however, in connecting with the electorate: his bad temper. He would get so angry that he would kick the television set in his headquarters whenever Dinkins's image appeared on screen. And the incumbent candidate exploited Rudy's ire, goading him to explode in public by stating to reporters, "He doesn't have the temperament to be the mayor of New York City." Garth went into action, presenting New Yorkers with a kinder, gentler Rudy—the Rudy who cared about giving kids a chance through education; a determined Rudy—the Rudy who got rid of the squeegee wielders and waged war on the pimps and drug dealers. Garth's strategy worked. After trailing Dinkins for a time, Rudy surged ahead and on November 2, 1993, carrying four of the city's five boroughs, he was elected New York's 107th mayor. His margin of victory was nearly 45,000 votes.

Did Giuliani Win in 1993 Because People Were Favorably Disposed toward Him or Because They Were Fed Up with Dinkins?

Ruth Messinger It was some of both. Dinkins suffered from a combination of heightened expectations by being the first black mayor and of beating Ed Koch coming out of racial strife in several communities. The disappointment in David was heightened by the gap between expectations and reality, only some of which was his fault. Then there was Giuliani's image from the Wall Street prosecutions. I thought it was unfair that Dinkins never got credit for the demonstrable fact that crime had started going down. Sometime in '90 or '91, the statistics started improving, which was partly from the increase in community policing, a strategy that worked, which Giuliani *un*did. And there were urban crises in that campaign year that just heightened the difference between the considered way in which

David approached most issues and the image of Giuliani as coming down on a white horse and being able to solve all problems.

Fred Siegel   Dinkins himself asked the question of whether New York could survive and [Senator Patrick] Moynihan [D-NY, 1977–2001] said, looking at the out-of-wedlock birthrate, "The city's future is foreclosed for three decades." There was tremendous pessimism. And even though in '93 Giuliani had a whole raft of thoughtful proposals, the polar frost of pessimism was so thick, so deep, nothing penetrated. Even his supporters didn't think much could be done. That was the assumption all around.

David Dinkins   If Mario Cuomo and the speaker of the Assembly at that time, Mel Miller, had not permitted the Staten Island secession issue to have been on the ballot, you would not have gotten the turnout you got in Staten Island, and Rudy came out of Staten Island forty thousand votes ahead of me. Well, if the margin is fifty, sixty, or seventy thousand, Staten Island alone made the difference. And Rudy was by no means perfect, but they ran a good race and they won. Some people said if it hadn't been for Crown Heights, I might have won—that it made a difference. I don't agree. I have responses, but, obviously, they didn't mean too much to the general media and the public at the time. All that notwithstanding, the margin was very, very thin.

Two Defining Incidents of the Dinkins Administration: The Korean Grocers Boycott and Crown Heights

The long, racially inspired boycott of a Korean grocer in the Flatbush section of Brooklyn by African Americans began in January 1990, following an incident at a Red Apple market. Giselaine Felissaint, a Haitian immigrant, was rushed from the store in an ambulance after claiming to have been injured. The Korean grocer claimed that the customer had fallen to the floor after refusing to pay full price for several limes.

David Dinkins   There were at least two other cases at around the same time involving a Korean grocer and a black consumer that were resolved within a day or a day and a half by the very same people on our staff that were handling the Korean boycott in Brooklyn. They included Bill Lynch. They employed the same methods but there were people in Brooklyn, in this particular case, who did not *want* a resolution. There would sometimes be three pickets out there and when they heard that a meeting was going to take place or the press was coming, then the picket line would swell to twenty-five to fifty. At one point, the court said the pickets should be at a certain distance. The city appealed that. When there's an appeal, there is an automatic stay. Our detractors chose to say that we were violating the court order, which is just *not true*. We took a heavy hit for that.

———————

On the evening of August 19, 1991, the running over of a seven-year-old African American child, Gavin Cato, by a driver in the motorcade of Grand Rabbi Menachem Schneerson set off major rioting. A bystander, Yankel Rosenbaum, a bearded Australian rabbinical student, was stabbed to death by black youths shouting, "Let's get a Jew!"

Ed Koch   I decided that David Dinkins did not deserve a second term and that I could not under *any* circumstances support him. I like him. I don't think he's a racist, or anti-Semitic—he's very supportive of Jewish concerns—but I thought that he didn't fulfill his responsibilities. A report was issued by Governor Cuomo that gives it day-by-day and the thing that most affected me was that [highly respected and successful public relations strategist] Howard Rubenstein, who was a good friend of his—it took great courage on the part of Howard to do this—is reported to have called the mayor at Gracie Mansion and told him what was happening and that, nevertheless, the mayor allowed the rioting, where Jews were beaten up simply because they were Jews, recognizable in their caftans in that Orthodox Hassidic area, to continue for three days without intervening.

Herman Badillo   Bill Lynch and his crew were unprepared because they had not taken into account the potential for a riot at any given time. I mentioned that to Rudy and he made notes of it. And then when *he* became mayor, he *made sure* that a community action unit was aware of all of the areas of the city where there could be a problem at any time, because New York City is really not so much a melting pot as it is a *boiling* pot. And if you understand the city, you know that the potential always exists for an explosion at any given time; usually having to do with the police or with someone being killed.

Albert O'Leary   The average cop feels that Dinkins laid back and let it get out of control—that action should have been taken in the very beginning. Any time you're doing enforcement activities against a minority, someone can say "racism." But if you're "on the side of the angels"—a Bill Bratton quote—let them say what they want. *Do* it.

The Mayor-Elect

Ruth Messinger   In December he paid a call on most elected officials who were in the government. Obviously my position is biased—I had supported Dinkins's reelection—but I remember thinking that it was really all for show, that he wasn't paying any attention to the issues that I was pretty serious about, and have remained serious about. That was not a huge surprise given both that he was a Republican and a brand-new mayor.

Raoul Felder   There was an event at Park East Synagogue and Giuliani and Dinkins were the speakers. There was a question about Rodney King [an African American motorist whose beating at the hands Los Angeles police officers on March 3, 1991, was videotaped by a bystander, a case in which the four police officers identified as the assailants were acquitted in California on April 29, 1992, leading to rioting in Los Angeles later that day]. Rudy praised the mayor for being able to prevent a riot here. It was nonsense because nine-tenths of cities in America didn't have riots, but he was being gracious.

Mark Green   I put in for a meeting with him since he was the mayor-elect and I was the public advocate–elect, and I thought it important that we try to get along. We met in his campaign office. It was an absolutely delightful conversation, half political BS and half how we would work together. I made one substantial suggestion: that we should work together on the problem of the mob control of the garbage industry. I had gone after them for years as the consumer commissioner and he had gone after the mob generally as the U.S. attorney and I thought this was an area where even though we were of different parties we could work together toward. He heartily agreed. And, in fact, the only substantial thing we really did well together was when, a few years later, we collaborated on a bill that became law that did get the mob out of carting. He would [normally] have had the press alerted to show that he was bringing the city together. Only later did I realize that the press had not been alerted that we were meeting. Looking back on it, I assume he kept *ours* private because he didn't want to highlight *me* in any way. The relationship went significantly, and steeply, downhill immediately after we were both sworn in. And it stayed an unproductive relationship for the entire eight years.

PART V

The First Term: January 2, 1994 – December 31, 1997

Chapter 8

GETTING THE GIULIANI
ADMINISTRATION UP AND RUNNING

*By New Year's Eve, almost every one of the fifty-plus
top commissioners were ready to be sworn in. . . .
The next day, we hit the ground running.*

—Rudy Giuliani, from *Leadership*, on the staffing
of his first administration

The Transition

Rudy Washington   I joined the transition committee. It started the week before Christmas. I was involved in interviewing and hiring 40 percent of Rudy's government. He had several committees, each made up of about five members. And every night, from the time he won the election in November to December, we would meet from four to ten or eleven o'clock at night, sometimes till midnight, and we would go through résumés and interview people for various positions. Rudy wanted three names for each position. We had *thousands* of résumés. But by the time the day staff would vet out the real ones, we had twenty-five or thirty for *every* position. We would come to him once a week and make a presentation on why we thought these people were the best three people for this one job. Rudy would listen to the presentation and then he would pare it down again. If it was really serious, he would bring in all three himself, or, just based upon the presentation, he would make a decision on one person then and say, "I want to see this person." I slowly became team leader and I'm sitting there with Bill Diamond [who would become Giuliani's general services commissioner] and [New York City real estate executive] Bernie Mendik, and a few other heavy hitters, all millionaires or billionaires—I'm the only minority person and the youngest—and all of a sudden, I'm doing all the talking. The five of us would go meet with Rudy once a week and do a presentation. They would say, "Rudy, do the presentation," and I would do it. It took me until the second meeting to realize that he was more interested in the dynamics—he probably doesn't even remember this, but I can read people—and at one point, I realized: he's just looking around the room and I'm trying to give this presentation. Why is he doing this? Then it dawned on me; he's sitting there saying to himself, How is this happening? How is this guy leading these guys? How is it that they're following *his* lead? I think he was more interested in the dynamics of our relationship, and how it developed, than what I was saying at the time.

Reaching Out to Koch Administration Personnel

Henry Stern   I know that both Ed Koch and Bobby Wagner spoke to Giuliani about me and I assumed I would be part of the administration. A panel was appointed to examine candidates for positions. These panels normally consist of socialites, people with little political experience, and the jobs in Parks and in Cultural Affairs normally went to limousine liberals. I don't know how well I did with the panels, but eventually I was appointed.

Lilliam Barrios-Paoli   I was then the executive director of a not-for-profit and I've always been a Democrat and I had worked for Ed Koch for ten years. But those were the days of a coalition government and I had been asked to help with the transition. I assumed it was more a courtesy thing than anything else.

Rudy Washington   There was a reaching out. I called Randy [Mastro] and said, "Look, send me some résumés." People were still sending résumés into City Hall; they were looking for jobs. There were people that the transition [team] had identified as potential managers. I didn't have people in my back pocket that I wanted to put in, and as I began to see people, I saw people I could work with and I said, "Great! This is the kind of individual I need."

The New Mayor's Swearing-In

On the morning of January 2, 1994, as Rudy Giuliani's nearly eight-year-old son, Andrew, standing at his father's right, mugged shamelessly, repeating his father's words, his wife, Donna, and daughter, Caroline, four and a half, looked on, the new mayor stood in front of City Hall and delivered his inaugural address.

Mark Green   I was told I could give a ten-minute speech at our swearings-in. I'm a writer and a lecturer and a lawyer, so I wrote something and I delivered ten minutes of it. The thought had never really occurred to me then that I might someday run for mayor and I was not competing with Rudy Giuliani for anything; *he* was the mayor and I was very happy to be the public advocate. Immediately after giving the speech, I got a call from Peter Powers, who said, "The mayor didn't like your speech." I went, "Why *not?*" He said, "He thought it was too *mayoral.*" I said, "You know, I'm always interested to hear the mayor's and your editorial opinions of my speeches and I welcome them. I don't work for you"—I'm independently elected—"Thank you for your views."

It's one thing if in the third year of an administration you realize that a citywide official, or a commissioner, is thinking of running against you and you take appropriate political action. To take it after I'd been in office literally three hours and when, in point of fact, I had no concept that I would ever run against him—and, of course, *didn't*—tells much more about *him* than about me.

Staffing the New Administration

A crucial appointment was that of police commissioner. Mayor Giuliani would during his two terms in office appoint three men to fill that post: William Bratton, who served from January 1994 until his forced resignation on March 26, 1996; Howard Safir, a close friend of Rudy's—who, like Rudy, would suffer from prostate cancer—who held the post from March 28, 1996, until his resignation in April 2000; and, lastly, police detective Bernard Kerik, Rudy's bodyguard and driver during the 1993 campaign, and later his commissioner of corrections, who would be appointed police commissioner despite never having served as a borough commander or a deputy commissioner. Kerik's appointment to the top police post was announced on April 17, 2000. He had been chosen over a thirty-one-year police veteran, Chief of Department Joe Dunne, the highest-ranking uniformed officer in the NYPD.

Regarding the new mayor's first appointment, although he had considered reappointing Ray Kelly, who had served in that post in outgoing mayor

David Dinkins's administration, he instead selected out-of-towner Bratton, whose "Broken Windows" approach to healing the city had caught his attention. A no-nonsense Bostonian from a working-class background, Bratton was a tough "cop's cop," yet fond of Churchillian prose. He would announce at his first press briefing, "We will fight for every house in the city. We will fight for every street. We will fight for every borough. And we will win."

Fred Siegel   Giuliani wants someone who's an innovator and manager. And it's an inspired choice. Ray Kelly is a very good man, a very good police chief, but he's not Bratton in terms of his ability to introduce new approaches—he's not an innovator.

Eric Adams   His [Bratton's] coming back to New York City as the commissioner of the New York City Police Department was a first; normally it doesn't happen that you leave the Transit Police to run the New York City Police Department. He and I met when he was planning on returning—we had lunch—and we spoke of the problems we had had while he was the Transit chief. He had a vision, with which I agreed. Bratton, in my opinion, changed America. Many people take credit for what he has done, but Bratton put a concept in place of policing. Prior to Bratton, the police thought that the police had nothing to do with decreasing crime until Bratton came in and applied the "Broken Windows" concept. I thought it was a brilliant move on Giuliani's part of bringing Bratton on board and we're seeing the result of that. If anyone should receive a Nobel Peace Prize, Commissioner Bratton should; he saved countless lives. It's unbelievable when you look at the records prior to his arrival. Safir did a great job after Bratton; Kerik did a great job; and even Kelly did a great job. Crime never returned to the levels of those criminal periods because of the plan that Bratton put in place. Everyone used the plan and took credit for it. I said over and over again: "Giuliani should leave Bratton alone and let him do his job; he knows how to deal with the issue of crime."

Albert O'Leary   Bill and Ray went head-to-head under the Dinkins administration when Lee Brown stepped down because his wife was ill and Ray Kelly got the job at that point. The day we found out, Bill called me—he was the police commissioner in Boston at the time—to say, "We gave it the old college try." He was disappointed and I said, "If Dinkins doesn't win reelection, the new mayor is not going to keep Ray Kelly"—mayors want their own, a guy who's beholden to them. So I told Bill, "They just did you the biggest favor they could; you'll be the first one considered in the next go-round for police commissioner." And he was. It was obvious it was going to happen.

Ruth Messinger   It's just typical that Giuliani would have to go with Bratton because it was different and new. I mean, Ray Kelly has not yet gotten the credit he deserves. He had done some other things in between and having returned to the job, he had demonstrated pretty incredible longevity and staying power and thoughtfulness about which style the police would use. Now I have a lot to say that's good about Bill Bratton, but I'm not surprised that Giuliani felt he had to switch to someone new and then literally sort of suck the oxygen out of the Police Department press effort and claim it all for himself. That was *typical* of him.

Edward Reuss   You've got a political situation: you have the police commissioner under a Democratic mayor, Mayor Dinkins. You've had the unfortunate incident in Crown Heights and you've had the grocer incident. And now Giuliani is running and his whole issue is of the breakdown of law and order: you have demonstrations at City Hall of all the police officers who back him, so he creates the image that he's going to be a pro-police mayor. He had lost an election and now he wins, so now he has to pick his commissioner. Ray Kelly has excellent credentials, but he's connected to an administration that has had a lot of problems—Crown Heights, the Korean grocer incident, a lot of other incidents.

Giuliani's interviewing the different candidates and he selects Bratton. Bratton comes on and I love his inaugural speech there. It's almost like Winston Churchill: "We'll take back every house . . ." The cops loved that. They believed that. These are men—they're not Boy Scouts—that have seen death and destruction every day. They need someone to lead them and you don't lead police officers—just like you don't lead troops—by telling them: "Go take the hill!" You have to say: "Follow *me*." You've got to *lead* them to the hill, right? They saw in Bratton that type of a leader.

Ruth Messinger   I knew Bratton and I knew John Miller [an NBC reporter who later served as Bratton's press aide] and they were people who were able to listen to other people. Bratton, like most people in New York City government, went out of his way to meet other people, to not worry about whether people endorsed him or believed in everything; he made friends and connections. Everybody thought that Bratton was a really great appointment, with a very big ego, but also with very big plans.

Herman Badillo   I was appointed to the panel that was selecting the police commissioner. We interviewed people and got down to Bratton or Kelly. And in the closing arguments, [Guy] Molinari [member, U.S. House of Representatives (R-NY), 1981–1990; borough president of Staten Island, 1990–2001] was pushing Kelly and I was pushing Bratton because Kelly had been the police commissioner and we'd had an election, which obviously calls for change. Secondly, I felt that Bratton had a different philosophy about the approach to policing. And Bratton, although he had come from Boston, had experience in New York because he had been head of the Transit Police, so he knew the subway system and he understood the different parts of the city and the tension between blacks, Jews, Latinos, Italians, and Irish people.

Bringing in Peter Powers, Rudy's Closest Childhood Friend, as Deputy Mayor

Henry Stern   Peter Powers was Giuliani's alter ego. He was appointed deputy mayor, but then Giuliani decided he didn't want to have a first deputy mayor; he didn't want to have just one person reporting to him. So he ended up with four or five deputies. He had formed important bonds in the U.S. Attorney's Office and what was most notable was that people who worked with him there, or who had maintained their friendship over the years, dropped their other careers to work in his campaign and administration—people like Denny Young, Michael Hess, and Randy Mastro—and he had great loyalty to the people who served him.

Selecting Rudy Washington as a Commissioner

Rudy Washington   I had no plans of coming into government. I had everything wired; I had other plans. I had a new circle of friends that were very powerful—I had already made friends with people like Bernie Mendik and had met Jerry [I.] Speyer of Tishman Speyer—so I couldn't ask for more. And I had a relationship with the incoming mayor, with whom I share the same name—he would never forget my name. So I had a lot of things going for me and I wasn't thinking about government. At that time in my life, if there was ever a time that I had it all working well, it was *then*. In construction, a big thing for a minority contractor was to have a credit line and to have business, and I was probably the only minority contractor in the city that had all those pieces working. And I had a couple of million dollars' worth of work, so the last thing I was looking for was a job.

The week before Christmas, on a Saturday, he calls me up. "Rudy, I have to see you." I said, "Okay, what time do you want to see me?" He said, "Can you come in at one o'clock?" I said, "Okay, I'll be there." I get there at one o'clock and he says, "Rudy, you've got to come in." "Come in *where?*" "You've got to come into the government." I said, "I can't do that, Rudy." I resisted him that week. Monday, he calls me again. "Rudy, can we talk?" We did this dance five times. Finally, the fifth time, he had Peter Powers in on the meeting and both of them ganged up on me and I said, "Rudy, whatever you want." He said, "Here, here's the Green Book [the official directory of the City of New York]; what do you want to do?" I said, "I don't want to do *anything*, Rudy. You don't understand. I can't do this." I finally folded. We got up and we all shook hands and I said, "Well, if I'm going to do something, it should be in the area of business, maybe small business." Peter's going through the Green Book and he says, "PBS. We don't have a commissioner. Rudy, you'll take that job, right?" I reluctantly said okay. We get up and Rudy darts out of the room. Peter goes to leave and I grab him and I say, "Peter, what do I *do*? Is there a commissioner's school, or an orientation?" Peter looks at me—it's like they got what they wanted; Rudy's off to something else. Peter says, "You're bright; you'll figure it out," and walks out! I say, "Peter, this is *next week*! What do I *do*?" And he walks off and leaves me hanging.

The next thing, they call me up. "We've got a press conference; we're going to announce you." They announce me and, you know, once again, nobody tells me anything, and I call Randy [Mastro]—I call up various people, and everybody's in their own world; everybody's trying to figure things out. We've got so many hours to get this thing going; we've got an inauguration to do and it's just chaos—I didn't even know where my office was. What do I *do*? Fortunately, for me, the agency contacted me and said, "Would you like to see the office?" And that's how I figured it out and I walked in and said, "Okay, I'm here now."

Selecting the Director of Personnel

Lilliam Barrios-Paoli   I met with Giuliani in early December. I wasn't looking for a job. Giuliani said to me, "You could be commissioner of *anything*" and I started laughing and said, "I don't think sanitation or police or fire would be terribly appropriate, but management is management."

When I left that day, he said to me, "I want you to be one of my commissioners." I thanked him very much and I thought, Great! Commissioners! That's like from the sublime to the ridiculous!

I met Peter Powers that day, as well, and I went to talk to Randy Mastro, who was the only one I knew a little bit and I said to him, "Look, I don't just want to be commissioner of *whatever*; I love government, but I don't love it so much that I'd be happy to be just *anywhere*. I've been around social services and health, and that's where I'd be interested." At that point, it was between HRA and personnel and I said to him, "I don't want to do city personnel." I knew city personnel very well because I had been the head of personnel for both HRA and HHC. "It's not a very thrilling job. You could put any dead person there; it could go on automatic pilot." They were very keen on doing civil service reform and I said to him, "Look, if you're serious about your making a lot of changes, I'll *think* about it, but I'm not sure."

We went back and forth about what it would be till December 20. I'm from Mexico originally [Barrios-Paoli became a U.S. citizen in 1978]. My family lives in Mexico and that was the first Christmas after my father had died. I had made a commitment to be with my sister and the family and we were all going to meet in Lake Tahoe, and so I said to them, "I'm out of town tomorrow morning, so we either do it today or we *don't* do it." I had basically decided at that point that I didn't really want to do it. Then I got a call that night from Stan Brezenoff [a deputy mayor in the Koch administration], who's been as close to a mentor as I'll have—he was somebody I really, really respected and cared for a great deal—and he said to me, "You belong in government; you should go back to government—you know, personnel." So I accepted at eleven o'clock at night. There was a press conference the next morning in which Giuliani announced that I had gotten the position and I left like that afternoon. Everyone was going to be sworn in on the thirty-first at a big thing at the museum and I was the only commissioner that wasn't there. Maybe that was an omen as to how things were going to evolve.

"I learned during my friendship with the Giulianis that they were from Brooklyn."—JOHN O'LEARY, FORMERLY BROTHER ALOYSIUS KEVIN

The house, right, at 419 Hawthorne Street, in Brooklyn, New York, owned by Rudy Giuliani's maternal grandmother, Adelina D'Avanzo, where Helen and Harold Giuliani brought Rudy—baptized Rudolph William Louis—to live following his birth on May 28, 1944.

"Bishop Loughlin was a scholarship school, so all of the students were very bright and they were there because they wanted to learn."—JOHN O'LEARY, FORMERLY BROTHER ALOYSIUS KEVIN

The main entrance of Bishop Loughlin Memorial High School.

"He would come in here [to the assistant principal's office] on occasion. He was a very vivacious personality, full of spirit, a lively individual who got into the life of the school. And whatever talents he had, he used those talents."
—Brother Peter Bonventre

Rudy's famous for many things, like holding the presidency of 126, founding Loughlin's Opera Society, bothering Long Island Rail Road passengers, being the highest batter in 1960 softball intramurals, managing the white party's campaign, and telling everyone how wonderful JFK is.

Rudy is really the all around (har!) type person, since, besides the above accomplishments, he's a La Salle Club Representative, Cathechist, and committeeman of several past Loughlin dances.

St. Raphael's Parish, East Meadow, doesn't — nay, couldn't! — know what a gem they possess in Rudy, who plans to study medicine in Manhattan.

RUDY GUILIANI

While the then-heftier and more hirsute Rudy Giuliani's many accomplishments brought him to the attention of his high school newspaper, the *Jamesonian*, that publication's columnist missed the boat regarding both Rudy's future profession and the correct spelling of his name.

"The impression that I retain from our first encounter . . . was of a very sharp and highly motivated, able lawyer of whom we all expected great things."
—RICHARD THORNBURGH

Rudy Giuliani, at the podium, addresses a white-collar-crime news conference on January 31, 1989, as Attorney General Richard Thornburgh looks on.

"This was a candidate in '93 that was very ready to be mayor."
—FRAN REITER

Mayor-elect Giuliani and first-lady-to-be Donna Hanover embrace as their children, Caroline, four, and Andrew, seven, right, and Rudy's mother, Helen Giuliani, left, enjoy the moment following his oath-taking at campaign headquarters on Tuesday, December 28, 1993. Giuliani would assume office at one minute after midnight on New Year's Day.

"Bratton is remarkably like Giuliani—quick mind, tough, fearless. They're both ramrods, type A leaders who were competing."—FRED SIEGEL

Mayor Giuliani, second from left, confers with Police Commissioner William Bratton, far right, in 1995, as other officials look on.

"When you stood at that podium to speak and you looked down, past City Hall, down Broadway, it was filled with humanity as far as you could see."
—SANFORD RUBENSTEIN

The Reverend Al Sharpton, front row, fifth from left, in suit and tie, links arms with Sanford Rubenstein ("Brother Rubenstein") as they and other community activists protest amid many signs reflecting the demonstrators' feelings about Mayor Giuliani during the March for Truth and Justice for Abner Louima, August 19, 1997.

"It was huge: over twenty-five thousand people were crossing . . . and we closed the Brooklyn Bridge. We went to Federal Plaza; everybody made a statement."
—SAIKOU DIALLO

Saikou Diallo and former mayor David Dinkins flank the Reverend Al Sharpton, front row, fourth from right, on April 15, 1999, as they and other activists cross the Brooklyn Bridge toward City Hall in the demonstration for justice for Amadou Diallo.

"People wanted to take the coffin and walk all the way from the funeral home to City Hall. But, of course, we could not let that happen because we had to bury him. . . . My main focus was to bury my brother the way he needed to be buried, correctly. And he went out like a real trouper."—MARIE DORISMOND

Reverend Al Sharpton and Sanford Rubenstein, front row, right, on March 25, 1999, during the massive demonstration en route to the church for Patrick Dorismond's funeral. Anti-Giuliani feeling was at a fever pitch; witness the sign directly behind Sharpton bearing the legend ARREST GIULIANI!

"He had this infectious smile. . . . It's obvious from his public life that he enjoys the limelight."—BROTHER PETER BONVENTRE

"I was surprised at how he really, truly loved New York City. He believed that New York was worth fighting for."—FRANK LUNTZ

An ebullient Mayor Giuliani presses the flesh near the new state-of-the-art minor league KeySpan stadium in Coney Island on June 25, 2001, during the parade celebrating the return of baseball to Brooklyn with the establishment of the Cyclones.

"I'm sure he wanted to go back down to South America, where he was a guide on a glacier in Patagonia. . . . I said to him, 'Christian, you could fall off a mountain in the wilds of South America and no one could ever find you.' It was a terrible, cruel irony that he was safer in the wilds of Patagonia than he was in his own city."—SALLY REGENHARD

"If you had had a truly integrated response where the police helicopters told the Fire Department what they were seeing overhead, things would have been different."—GLENN CORBETT

"Probie" firefighter Christian Regenhard participates in a training exercise.

"The press clearly made Giuliani the hero of 9/11 in New York and that resonated throughout the country."
—SANFORD RUBENSTEIN

"Let's give Rudy credit: he knew that not just the people of the City of New York were going to watch his every move and listen to his every word, but that the entire world was going to be looking to him for guidance, for updates, for information, and Rudy rose to the occasion."—BENJAMIN BRAFMAN

The morning of September 11, 2001: Mayor Giuliani, his grief etched on his features, speaks to the United States and the world outside St. Vincent's Hospital, in Manhattan, moments after the collapse of the World Trade Center towers.

Chapter 9

ADMINISTRATIVE STYLE

*There isn't a Democratic or Republican way to run
New York. When cities have such complex problems,
they need the freedom to select the best solutions.*

—Rudy Giuliani, quoted in *The Economist*, March 22, 1997

What Was It Like to Work for Mayor Giuliani?

Lilliam Barrios-Paoli Early on, he used to have meetings on Sunday evenings at Gracie Mansion, around pizza, and talk general policy issues. He really believed that people should work in exchange for a grant—that able-bodied men and women had no business getting money and doing nothing in exchange for it, and that you had to end that state of affairs; and that there was a lot of fraud going on—a lot of people working either under the table or double-dipping. He believed they were the scum of the earth living off the system and that that had to be ended.

Fred Siegel The people who had to be held to account were at the eight o'clock [morning] meeting. People were expected to be prepared and people were supposed to be held accountable.

Lilliam Barrios-Paoli He is very much a boy's boy and he loved sports, any kind of sports. Meetings would begin with talk about baseball so if you were not into sports, for the first twenty minutes, you'd be totally out of it.

Rudy Washington We used to talk about what happened last night, what's going to happen today, and what's going to happen tomorrow. And

Rudy would weigh in on every one of those decisions. At that table were the deputy mayors, general counsel, budget director, press, DOI, which basically covered all the government. I had a big portfolio and I used to joke about it because when I became the new kid on the block, my portfolio was made up of everybody that people couldn't control. Peter Powers got rid of his headaches, Fran got rid of her headaches—they were all trying to fire Henry Stern; nobody could deal with him—every headache in government they dumped into my portfolio. But, at the end of the day, I had one of the most effective portfolios. Henry Stern was almost a genius; I would bring him in and say, "Henry, I want to get somebody on the payroll, but these people are blocking me. How do you do that?" Henry's been knocking around government for thirty years; I began to use Henry as a resource. All of a sudden, Henry began to see the value of me: he said, "Wow! This guy listens to me!"

Henry Stern   The mayor was there to settle disputes between the commissioners and the deputy mayors. He was fair-minded and I think he was surprised at how much of his time was taken up in settling disputes within his government. Giuliani made decisions on the merits. He always tried to reach a just result. Koch was more collegial than Giuliani, but people knew that if they disagreed with Koch they would pay a price. In Giuliani's case, he often sided with me, even in disputes with people who were much closer to him than I was. I worked closely with deputy mayors Fran Reiter and Rudy Washington. I had known Fran Reiter for many years—we were both in the Liberal Party. Fran was very assertive. Since she was my deputy mayor, in a normal relationship, she would supervise me, provide oversight, and help me. But she wanted to dictate, to do things that were improper. When she tried to bring me up on trial before Peter Powers [Giuliani's alter ego], he just laughed. Here were two people from the Liberal Party attacking each other. Rudy Washington was a wonderful deputy mayor, an excellent deputy mayor. He helped us in all kinds of ways. He saved me many times from enemies who came after me. The contrast with Reiter was like night and day.

Rudy Washington   The mayor used to enjoy blood sport, for lack of a better term, and I'd been known to offer up some big battles. Henry Stern got into a pitched battle over City Hall Park. I was the construction guy; I handled it right out of my office and another deputy mayor was on the other side of the fence, saying, "Parks [Department] shouldn't control this;

they don't know what they're doing." But despite things getting so bad in front of the mayor, he wouldn't stop them. We convene a meeting, it mushrooms—it gets so big that we're not going to meet in the Blue Room, we're going to meet in a big room. I thought, Okay, maybe somebody is using the Blue Room. I get to the meeting and there are fifty people there—cops, the Fire Department—to see this fight! I feel like a Roman gladiator. Henry and I are sitting there and Henry jumps up and says, "I feel like a giant amongst midgets!" Some of those battles were epic and I know Rudy got a kick out of them. It was [press secretary to Mayor Giuliani, 1995–1999] Colleen [A.] Roche's birthday and we were going to give her a surprise party. We're upstairs and the mayor goes down to get Colleen. She says, "What's the matter, Mr. Mayor?" He says, "It's round two of Levine and Washington," and she comes running!

Carol Bellamy   He was honest, which I consider to be very important. While you have to be tough and strong as mayor, I don't think you have to be quite as pugnacious. I thought he picked many too many fights. There's a difference between being strong and fighting all the time. It seemed that if you could pick a fight or not pick a fight, he picked a fight.

Fran Reiter   I served in the first term. It was exhausting, but he was fabulous to work for. He was engaged in ways that shocked a lot of people. The budget is an example. It's generally done by the professionals at the Office of Management and Budget and the mayor usually comes to it towards the end of the process. But this mayor was involved in the budget process from *day one*. And I learned really early on that he who controls the budget controls everything—that if there was something I wanted and was going to fight for and wanted to make sure was part of that budget, I went to *every* budget meeting—I didn't care if it was three o'clock in the morning. Because if you didn't show up, somebody would steal your money from you.

If you can understand the budget process, then you can effectively govern. He was *unbelievably* engaged in the budget. That's where a lot of these debates played out: you'd have two deputy mayors who were at odds with one another who had to debate in front him. One won and one lost. There was a lot of that, so that we were, as deputy mayors, allowed to be really *fully* engaged in governing with him, which was great! You win some, you lose some. And when you lose, you've got to get out there and support the mayor's position. And if you do that and he trusts you, then he's going to invest a lot of authority in you. And he *did*.

Fred Siegel   When Giuliani came into office, the city was completely broke. He and Peter Vallone [speaker of the City Council] did not panic; they did not want the Financial Control Board coming in. They controlled the situation and together they very quietly pulled the city back from the brink of bankruptcy.

Henry Stern   Giuliani gave his budget presentations with facts and figures and without referring to notes. It was spectacular. It was amazing to watch him, like [watching] a ballplayer making an impossible catch.

Mark Green   He tried to cut the budget by something like three-fourths, but Speaker Peter Vallone wouldn't allow it to happen. Subsequently Vallone told me that Giuliani had completed the entire city budget and then said, "One more thing; I want Green's budget whacked." Peter said no and Giuliani started shouting. Why he was that personally antagonistic, I can't say. As soon as I detected it, I didn't wait for a second opportunity to be surprised; I criticized him, based on my investigations, and sued him, based on my sense of the laws. He couldn't bully me because I didn't care what he thought.

Rudy's Relationships with Female Staff Members

Fran Reiter   Rudy became in that first term very close—put aside the personal; I'm talking about a *working* relationship—to Cristyne and me. I became much more influential than most of those boys thought I was going to become; Cristyne became much more influential than anybody thought she was going to become. Rudy thought that was great; he had no problem with it. I've never seen a sexist bone in that man's body. I don't know how he deals with girlfriends or wives, I can only tell you as somebody who worked with him, that this was a nonissue for him.

Lilliam Barrios-Paoli   He was very paternalistic. My father was a lovely man to women, too, as long as they were *his* women—that little possessive adjective. He [Giuliani] was certainly not unkind *at all* and he was a gentleman and warm. But it was from a very paternalistic point of view. I'm not saying that he couldn't deal with women, but he felt much more comfortable with the guys. At the end of the day, the women in his administration were *his* women. Fran was the big exception in that inner circle—Fran always deferred to him—but it was always a power relationship that was never negotiable: it was very clear who numero uno was and everybody else was assigned a number.

The Mayor and the Media

Perhaps the most controversial member of the Giuliani administration was communications director Cristyne Lategano. Her high-handed tactics in the campaign were said to have upset advisers, most notably David Garth. And she would go on to alienate many of the journalists assigned to cover City Hall during the Giuliani era.

Did Lategano Get a Bad Rap?

Raoul Felder   She's an extremely competent person and she's dedicated to whatever she does. I, personally, have never seen one iota of real proof of any of those accusations. In fact, everybody involved denied it. I've had secretaries like that, gatekeepers; they'd lay down and die before they'd let somebody in who's not supposed to be in here. You don't see many these days, but you used to see them all the time.

Lilliam Barrios-Paoli   Cristyne was very, very young; in her twenties; a *kid*. She adored Rudy. It was hero worship all the way: she believed he was the greatest thing in the universe and wanted to do what was best for him, was intensely loyal, and worked twenty-four hours a day—if there were twenty-seven, she'd work that, too. Did she lack the experience to get the amount of responsibility that she got? Yes. But you know what? She wasn't alone; so did a lot of other people. And that's not unusual in government. And that is, in essence, one of the most vital things about government—that if you're very young and quite inexperienced, and they give you a lot of responsibilities, if you manage to survive, you contribute a lot and it's wonderful. It's not unusual that young people get big jobs and struggle and grow. In the climate of City Hall, where everybody wanted to be the mayor's favorite child, the fact that *he* clearly liked her very much did not help her *at all*, because everybody else *disliked* her—it was almost like a visceral reaction. I think she got a horrendous bum rap. Whatever her relationship was with Rudy, it's neither here nor there, nor do I care, but as a *professional*, she was not in any way, shape, or form the monster that people painted her to be. It was easy to take Cristyne on in their minds because she was a woman, she was younger, and she was more vulnerable. And then, when the personal things began to emerge—clearly, a lot of people liked Donna—that was a *real* problem.

Fran Reiter   Rudy's a big boy and, ultimately, whatever advice Cristyne may have been giving him—and she *was* giving him advice; so was *I*, so was *everybody*—ultimately, the decisions rested with Rudy Giuliani. So the notion that you're going to blame Cristyne Lategano, a very smart young woman, but at the time with very limited political experience, for the decisions of a forty-five-year-old man who's had the life experience of Giuliani, is just ridiculous! Do I think she became a scapegoat? Yes, to a great extent. Do I think all the advice that Cristyne gave him was good? No, not always; I think she fed into certain fears of his a little too much.

On the other hand, where she was incredibly successful on his behalf, even though it demonized *her*, was in controlling Giuliani's message to the greatest extent possible. The things he was trying to do in New York City were huge—this is a city where nothing's changed for a hundred years, certainly in the post–World War II period, where we are mired in a bureaucracy and a social welfare system and a policing system. He tried to radically change all these things. Do I think that all the advice Cristyne gave him was good? No. I'm not sure all the advice *I* gave him was good. Do I think that he probably allowed her to be too influential? There probably were times when that was the case. But, on the other hand, he's the man! He's got to make these decisions. And she was incredibly loyal; she worked hours that no human being should ever be expected to work. Ultimately, the only person you can hold responsible is Rudy, not Cristyne Lategano. And I also think people were jealous.

Albert O'Leary   There are certain ways to do media when you're doing a political campaign and a very different way of representing government. But she never shifted gears; she never got out of campaign mode. It was always: you're either *for* Rudy or you're *against* Rudy; there was never an understanding that the mayor is different from the politician on the stump. And that's why she would continue to do in City Hall what she did during the campaign: I didn't like your story; I'm not talking to you. Well, guess what? You work for the government: you don't have *the right* to say, "I'm not talking to a reporter from the [*New York*] *Daily News* or a reporter from *Newsday*." You *talk to the reporter*. They represent the public; you're getting paid by the public; your agencies are *getting paid* by the public. And they never seemed to get that if you're using tax dollars to do something, then you have to be accountable for those tax dollars.

Stanley Friedman   Nobody was allowed to talk to the press; if anyone did, they got fired. Aside from the police commissioner and the fire commissioner, nobody knew the names of the commissioners under Giuliani. He ran that office like a prosecutor's office, like there's a grand jury inquest. It was not an open government. How many Freedom of Information requests were made during the Giuliani years? I'm sure it's a huge number, which means that the information was not given out to the press and therefore the public was never aware of it.

David Dinkins   Rudy was seen as vindictive: If you defy me and you anger me, then I will deny you access. If there's a storm coming, each network, each news outlet, will lead the news with predictions of how much snow is going to come; predictions of what it will cost—the rule of thumb is a million dollars an inch—how much sand and how many snowplows are operative, and things of that sort. This is an exaggeration, but it's like if the [*New York*] *Post* called, they were told, "We have so much sand and so much money in our budget for overtime," and if somebody who's been less favorable to the administration called, they would be told, "File a Freedom of Information request."

Albert O'Leary   You'd file the Freedom of Information request; you'd get an acknowledgment that your request was received and that it would be considered; and then you'd get a second acknowledgment later on. But you'd wait *a year*, if you got a response at all, and then when you got the information. the *important* information would be redacted. The Giuliani days represented a dramatic change in how government dealt with the media. And while it was effective, I think it was *wrong*. It was a very difficult time to be a press officer in city government.

Fred Siegel   It became too much of an adversarial game There were plenty of people in the press corps who were just simpleminded liberals, but there were people who were trying to do their job and were serious and hardworking. He never distinguished, so Lategano became the object of opprobrium. And she had vast power she didn't enjoy. She said to me, "I'm just a press girl." And that's exactly right: she was just the *voice*, the press secretary. She wasn't making any substantive policy. She had a very tough job.

Rudy's Small Inner Circle

Henry Stern   Every mayor has his inner circle. I wouldn't have had any success in inserting myself into the Giuliani circle. I tried to steer clear of it. I just wanted to do my job well.

Lilliam Barrios-Paoli   Early on, it was very clear that few would be chosen. The people who had been with him through the years were the inner circle and then there were the rest of us, some more liked than others, that were useful, but never totally trusted, especially those of us who had been Democrats. If they asked, "Why did you do that?" and you told them, it was always assumed that that was not the complete agenda, that you were *hiding* something. I'm not like that, so it was like: Why would I lie to you? I mean, in this town, where everybody knows everybody's *underwear*, why would I even *go* there? It was very cloak and dagger out there and so I stayed away from City Hall as much as I could.

Rudy Washington   He doesn't let you into his inner circle easily. I suspect that comes from his upbringing in terms of the U.S. Attorney's Office: you keep a closed circle and control the flow of information. You just didn't walk into Rudy's world and the next day you're a player. No, you had to *earn* your seat at that table. It could take a year or two. I really didn't get a seat at that table until after '96.

Frank Luntz   You understand from the personal stories what makes a human being tick. You understand not just what makes them laugh but also what makes them cry. You understand at what point they reveal their human persona instead of their public persona. And for me, it wasn't until '97 that I started to see the other part of him. He doesn't show it to many people.

Fred Siegel   Socially it was a tight group of people—"Rudy and the Rudettes." But they were much more open to ideas than the Koch people, so they were more closed and more open at the same time. And they were open to argument and debate: you made a good argument and they'd hear it, not just Giuliani but the people around him. It was when they came to an agreement on something that they closed ranks.

Fran Reiter   He expected loyalty, and once he made a decision, we all had to get on board. What I loved about working for him was that before he reached that decision—or even if he'd reached a decision and you disagreed with him—he gave you ample opportunity to try to change his mind. This was not someone who was ideologically driven. He certainly had things that he believed in, but on most issues if you disagreed with him you were given a *lot* of opportunity if you wanted to take him on. He was tough—I believe *x*; if you want to get me to believe *y*, you're really going to have to work for it. But you *could* change his mind on pretty much any issue.

Rudy never dictated or examined how you were going about doing your work. So if I had a serious policy initiative that was assigned to me, or a problem that I had to solve, my inclination was to reach out to a lot of different people and get their input—not unlike what Giuliani did when he was educating himself—and then come to a conclusion and go back to the mayor and say, "This is my recommendation." Giuliani was trying to do a lot of things in this city that were so radical: he was taking on welfare in New York—unheard of! He was taking over the police. That inner circle stayed very tight. The rationale behind it was that in the taking on of these really tough issues, if you let the advocates in, they'll tell you what they think; they'll *look* supportive; you'll end up making a decision they don't like; and the next minute, you've got a demonstration going on outside. Why bother? The only way I can do this is if I keep control over it. He was not totally wrong but, on the other hand, there were certainly times when it appeared to be extreme.

Access

Ruth Messinger   If you didn't have a relationship with Peter Powers, you didn't have access to the mayor. You could talk to Peter, but many, many people in the first Giuliani administration were best at pushing you away, ridiculing your ideas, not wanting to work with you on issues. I never gave up; I had lots of big fights with the mayor, but I also had a lot of work to do on behalf of the borough and so I would contact Peter Powers. Fran Reiter and, occasionally, Rudy would even be on the same side [of an issue]. But there was never much acknowledgment or support from the people around him that you were actually working on something with them. And there was never any respect from *him*.

Lilliam Barrios-Paoli   In any administration you always go through somebody at City Hall, whether you report to a deputy mayor or a special adviser. It was very rare that any commissioner would pick up the phone and call the mayor directly. It's just not the protocol. That being said, when I was commissioner of Personnel, Giuliani did indeed call me a number of times. I never had that in Housing; Fran was the person I reported to then. She's great; she probably had the best sense of the whole group of how government worked—that it was give-and-take—and she was a very good horse trader.

Crossing Swords with Rudy

Among those with whom the mayor crossed swords was Public Advocate Mark Green. The two would be referred to as the "Muhammad Ali and Joe Frazier of New York."

Mark Green   I don't want to be the sweet naïf, but I remember thinking that our meeting in his campaign office after we both won was a good, positive, substantive meeting. But it went downhill right after my swearing-in and it stayed in the valley for what we now know are the obvious reasons. I was about the first person to say that with Giuliani, his style is: "It's either my way or the highway." He is intolerant of criticism, contemptuous of people who are liberal, and has an impulse toward interpersonal imperialism and destruction to a level I've never seen in public life before or since.

Gene Russianoff   We [the New York Public Interest Research Group] have what I would call a "Wile. E. Coyote–Road Runner" relationship with the various mayors, and we've had our run-ins with Koch and with Dinkins and with Giuliani and now with Bloomberg, so we're not exactly the most popular people on the planet with City Hall. There's a natural friction and tension, but I would say that it was particularly tough during the Giuliani years. I do two issue areas: subways and buses and a lot of good government work. And we had our encounters with the former mayor.

Ruth Messinger   That administration looked regularly to pick fights with people about whom they didn't think anything good, so we had several big, and somewhat public, fights, several of which I won *on paper*. At some point during the budget crisis, the Borough Board, which I chaired, was able to hold a hearing. We invited commissioners. All of them accepted. The administration then found out because some commissioner told them that they were coming to testify before the Borough Board. They *forbade* their commissioners to come. And not only *that*, but they said something in the press about that they were within their rights—that the agencies did not have to testify—and that was clearly not *true*.

Herman Badillo   He's a prosecutor by temperament and prosecutors tend to do outrageous things. I've been a defense attorney and the difference is that prosecutors believe that *everybody* is guilty beyond a reasonable doubt and defense attorneys believe that *nobody's* guilty beyond a reasonable doubt. Prosecutors tend to be very mean and do things that are inexcusable. Certainly Rudy was one of the ones who went to great excess, and it was reflected in his personality because he had been a prosecutor for many, many years before he got to be mayor.

Lilliam Barrios-Paoli   Ed Koch once said to me, "What is the difference between Giuliani and me? If you get up in the morning and you say to your advisers, 'I want to kill all twelve-year-olds,' I can think of ten people who would say, 'Please get a life! What, are you, *crazy*? *No way!*' And there'd be a big argument and at the end of the day, somebody's judgment would prevail." And, with Ed Koch, even if you became stubborn and did what you wanted to do, there was always room for people saying, "I'm not working on this one," and it wasn't the end of the world. If Rudy would say, "Let's kill twelve-year-olds," there would be deep silence in the room and then somebody would say, "That's *brilliant!*" And then somebody else would say, "Have you thought of *thirteen-year-olds*, too?" And then it would escalate: who could outdo themselves, so the mayor would be more pleased with them. And there would always be three or four people in the room going, "Oh God! Oh my God!" but were very afraid of saying anything because not only the mayor but everybody else would gang up on you.

Mark Green   Giuliani wants all the oxygen in the room, or the city, and everybody now knows that. He would withdraw contracts from bidders who were Democrats who supported Dinkins; he would not appear on a stage with a public official who had ever criticized him. There was a pattern of bullying retaliation that was like in a Fourth World country. I'm a little surprised that the press never much discussed it. Why? First, it's hard to document because the people being bullied don't want to acknowledge it. And second, a mayor who does that to enemies can do it to *you* as a reporter or an assignment editor or an editor. Giuliani constantly said that *The Godfather* is his favorite movie and, of course, after he won the election, he insisted that all his commissioners and he watch the movie for the umpteenth time. Of course, the credo of Machiavelli [quoted] in *The God-father* is "[It is] better to be feared than loved." And you'd have to say that's *his* [Giuliani's] credo.

Ruth Messinger   Once he said that I wasn't a lawyer, so I couldn't understand the city documents. And once he called me "hysterical"—this was *before* I was running against him. If you crossed him, you got whatever available insult or put-down was around and in several of those instances, he was *wrong*. Sometimes we could prove that he was wrong; sometimes he could win with his wrongness because he was just powerful enough.

Removing Troublemakers "Giuliani's Way": Forced Resignations

Raoul Felder   I was sitting with him in Gracie Mansion and somebody came in and told him a certain person had resigned and he said, "Well, I was going to have to let him go and he must have sensed it." I sense some relief there, but I think he'd be able to square with an employee and say, "Look, it's not working out." I know of two cases where he just discharged people—highly appointed people. They just couldn't do the job. And both people were supporters; he *liked* them.

Lilliam Barrios-Paoli   By the time I left, it would have been totally expected. It wasn't just *one event*; there were a number of things that played out. Clearly I was not on agenda with them. But I decided that I was going to do what I was going to do and that was it! I didn't do anything behind their backs; it was a very public agenda. But there were things that they wanted implemented that I said I simply wouldn't do because I didn't agree with them. Every Friday I met with Tony Coles—there were a lot of people there—and it was very contentious. I became convinced that I'd be totally out, and in November, the day after the election, I submitted my letter of resignation. I got a call from Beth Petrone [one of the mayor's three executive assistants], saying, "The mayor doesn't want you to resign." I said, "Thank you; that's very nice," and I called Randy Mastro and I said, "Okay, so the mayor doesn't want me to resign. I don't think the mayor wants me to stay at HRA, either, so what are we going to do?" He said, "It's too early. Let's all think about it."

In mid-December, I walked into a staff meeting and Randy Mastro came over to me and put his arm around me. He had tears in his eyes, and said, "Things happened during the weekend and the mayor wants a change at HRA." I said, "Okay, I'm fine with that. Let's just figure out the timing." And he said, "It's going to move quickly." And he then said, "You know, there may be possibilities at the Health and Hospitals Corporation." The commissioner of HRA is an ex officio member of the board of HHC; the chair of the board of HHC is somebody I've known thirty-some years and I had worked at HHC, so I knew the people very well, and I had gone to all their board meetings, and I said, "There's no position at HHC right now." He said, "Well, talk to [Dr.] Rosa [M. Gil, chair, Health and Hospitals Corporation]." Then he said, "We have to start the meeting." I sat next to two colleagues, one of whom I'm still very close to, and I said to her, "I was just screwed." I went to my office after the meeting, called Rosa, and said, "Do you have any secret?" and she said, "I have no idea what's going on, but whatever we can do . . ." The only person that I knew was leaving was Donna Lynn, who was in the same position that I had been in fifteen years before—there's backwards and then there's *backwards*—and I talked to her and then I went to another friend's agency for lunch. Afterward I was in her office when she got a call from Ninfa Segarra [a deputy mayor and a member of the Board of Education in the Giuliani administration], telling her that I had been let go. And this is supposed to still be a secret. I laughed and I said, "Oh, God! Now it's going to *really* hit the fan!"

I had a meeting at Health and Hospitals that afternoon at two o'clock—this began happening at nine—and as we're sitting there, Donna Lynn comes in and says to Liz Michaels, the president of HHC, and me, "Come, come, come." Randy's on the phone and says, "Somebody leaked it to the press." And I say, "Leaked *what*?" And he says, "That you're going to go to Lincoln Hospital [in the Bronx]." I said, "Randy, there *is* a president of Lincoln Hospital. What's going to happen to *him*?" Liz is sitting there like the deer caught in the headlights. Apparently, the guy from Lincoln heard it on the radio; nobody had told him he was fired, so he was as surprised as *I* was. I went to Lincoln and the people were beyond shell-shocked; this guy had been there seven years and everybody loved him. I sat down and I said to them, "We all had the same choice in this one. Let's try to see what we're going to do with it." Actually, it was a very good eight months.

Rudy made some comment about the fact that the reason for the change was that I wasn't on agenda with him and I didn't agree, blah, blah, blah. And then the [*New York*] *Times* had an editorial that said that I was really let go because of my integrity. To some degree, both are true: I was faithful to what I saw as my integrity and I wasn't on agenda with him. It was hard the way it was all done publicly, on the radio. But I wasn't of him; I was never *his* creature, so I'm sure that at the end of the day I was a total disappointment.

On October 15, 1995, following months of escalating and debilitating friction with the Giuliani administration, Ramón Cortines, a highly intelligent, but in the eyes of his major critic—the mayor—an ineffectual and insubordinate schools chancellor, resigned his post.

Ruth Messinger   There are many mayors—and Giuliani certainly fits into this universe—who can't stand the fact that the schools chancellor is not appointed by them and totally immediate to them, so it's a thorn in the side because to be the chancellor of the New York City schools, you really have to be a strong person yourself, with a lot of ideas. And you have the prerogative, which no other commissioner has, of being able to demand your own budget, so there's public disagreement with the mayor, and Giuliani just couldn't stand that—particularly that Cortines was not sufficiently deferential.

And everything about them was opposite: Cortines is Latino, not macho, and he was clearly developing his own style, which, we know from some of Giuliani's remarks, he [Giuliani] ridiculed as being sort of effeminate. Also, Cortines was becoming really popular, and the word was spreading that as hard as everybody knew it was to improve the New York City schools, here was a chancellor who *cared*—people felt he was listening and trying. He was building up some independent base of support and the mayor was ready to take his head off.

Raoul Felder   One of the things Rudy wanted to do was get his arms around that whole education business. It took up a lot of his time. I know that. It was very difficult, with the teachers union and all this business; it was very hard to deal with all those things.

Fran Reiter   This is one of those monumental undertakings: Rudy was trying to radically change the way the Board of Education worked and trying to get control of education policy and governance. And he didn't have the legal right to do it back then; that wouldn't happen until Mike Bloomberg became mayor. But Giuliani certainly wanted a chancellor who was going to be supportive of the kinds of change that were necessary—changes in the bureaucracy; changes in the budgeting; changes in where the resources were going—that he believed were necessary to start remaking the system and improving public education. But Ray Cortines clearly wasn't prepared to do that. There were meetings where Cortines would apparently say yes and be very gentlemanly and the mayor would think they had reached an agreement, and then Cortines would walk out of his office and hold a press conference and blow the whole thing up, which infuriated the mayor. And I don't blame him!

Those of us who, apart from governing types and policy types, also wore political hats were very concerned about how this was playing out: it was ugly and it hurt Giuliani politically, *big-time*. Giuliani's poll numbers were dropping and he never looked like a bigger bully. This wasn't Bratton he was fighting—big, tough Bill Bratton—this was *Ray Cortines* he was fighting, a nice guy. While it hurt Giuliani politically, it was one of those things where he just believed it was too important, and if he had to lose politically, it didn't matter; he was going to keep going.

Herman Badillo   I got involved in the issue of education because he asked Chancellor Cortines what he had done with the $8 billion he had received from the city and Cortines said, "I don't know." He says, "What do you mean, you don't know?" and Cortines says, "There are incompatible computers and I never know which is which." So he [Giuliani] said, "Look, you let me appoint a deputy chancellor; we'll figure out what to do, or else I'm going to appoint my friend Herman Badillo, who is a CPA as well as a lawyer, who understands budgets and who understands education, to figure out the budget. I'll give you twenty-four hours." And in twenty-four hours Cortines didn't respond, so he appointed me special counsel for the fiscal side of education. Cortines resigned. But Mario Cuomo, who was then governor, got him back on.

I went to see Cortines and said, "Is it true you have incompatible computers?" And he says, "Yes." But he says, "I'm working on it." "So good, so we'll have the answer in a few weeks?" He says, "No, no. It's going to take me three years." I said, "Listen, we don't *have* three years." So I talked to Rudy and got some CPA friends of mine from Coopers & Lybrand and within *four months* we figured out the budget and we presented it to Cortines. And when he saw that there were very serious discrepancies, he announced he would resign. And he left two weeks later.

Ed Koch   What he [Mayor Giuliani] did in driving him out I thought was terrible. And I said so. Ray Cortines was the best chancellor since Frank Macchiarola [chancellor from 1978 to 1983]; I thought he was wonderful. Rudy destroyed him. He summoned him at midnight to Gracie Mansion. I talked to Cortines after he decided he was leaving, and I said to him: "Why did you *go*?" "Well, the mayor called me." I said, "And you didn't *bring* anybody! It's *crazy*! You go to the mayor's office, I understand that.

You bring somebody with you—your counsel, your deputy. And then when the mayor says to you, 'You have to fire these people'"—I think he told him two people who had to be fired—"What you should have said is 'That's fine, Mayor, and what I'm asking is that you fire two people in *your* administration, and we'll fire all four at the same time.' How *dare* he tell you whom to fire? You're not his commissioner; you're independently selected."

———————

Little more than two weeks into the new mayor's first term, the January 16, 1994, edition of the *New York Daily News*, one of the city's two tabloid newspapers, had good things to say about his newly appointed police commissioner, Bill Bratton. Therein may lie the first seeds of Giuliani's resentment against him. Two years later, in January 1996, a cover story on Bratton in *Time* magazine—Bratton was pictured in a telephone booth, wearing a fashionable and expensive trench coat—cemented Giuliani's resentment. Two months later, on March 26, 1996, Bratton announced his resignation.

Eric Adams   Jack Maple [an aide to Commisioner Bratton] and I had dinner at Elaine's [an Upper East Side celebrity haunt] and I said, "You guys are doing a great job; crime is decreasing." And I'll never forget Jack Maple saying, "Eric, Giuliani will fire us tomorrow if we don't get less press." I said, "You've got to be out of your mind. You guys are doing a number one job and there's *no way* he'll let you guys go."

It speaks volumes about Giuliani's personality that because his ego was bruised, he was willing to throw us back into the period of criminality by getting rid of a commissioner at the peak of his plan: he was willing to say, You know what? You got that article. I'm the top person; I'm the person who should have been in *Time* magazine; I'm the person that people should have stood up and clapped for. It was: *Me! Me! Me! Me!* Giuliani was so egotistical that he was willing to remove our success in crime; he was willing to remove the person who had the plan, right in the middle. We had yet to reach all those records that we eventually reached. But he was willing to risk that because his ego was bruised. When Jack told me, "Eric, he'll fire us tomorrow," I said, "Nobody would be foolish enough to take that risk." Nobody would be that foolish to throw our city back to that."

Fred Siegel   It was the biggest mistake of the Giuliani years. The problem was that they're the same person. Bratton is remarkably like Giuliani— quick mind, tough, fearless. They're both ramrods, type A leaders who were competing: while Giuliani was handing out [David] Osborne's [and Ted

Gaebler's] *Reinventing Government* [which promoted the privatization of health care and garbage collection, thus removing them from union domination and going against liberal ideology], Bratton was handing out [James] Champy's *Reengineering the Corporation* [coauthored by Michael Hammer]. They were both used to being the number one and they stepped on each other's toes in that regard. There wasn't room for two of these guys in the administration and that was unfortunate. It wasn't just the personal; they operated so similarly: if Giuliani had an eight o'clock meeting in the morning that ran the day [meaning the agenda for the day was established], Bratton had a nine o'clock meeting. When the two of them were in a room, there wasn't enough space for anyone else to breathe. It was unfortunate. Giuliani should have transcended that. There were social tensions between them—stylistically they were very different, but it was an inspired choice.

Albert O'Leary I'm interviewing with Cristyne Lategano for deputy commissioner of public information under Bill Bratton. A guy from David Garth's office who worked on the Giuliani campaign, Denny Young, asks me, "Does Bill Bratton require any special media handling?" I remember thinking, Here comes the question I didn't want to get. And I told him, "Bill Bratton likes to use the press to his advantage, but he takes advice from his staff and he understands that he can't be jumping in front of every TV camera that comes along. He was very, very willing to let me make the judgment calls on those things and it worked well for us." Denny Young just looked at the other two and said, "That's all *I've* got to hear." They knew Giuliani's penchant for getting all of the press for himself.

Fran Reiter Bill Bratton had enormous success—the Department had enormous success—and I think his ego became enormously swelled and he became a celebrity in his own right and forgot that he worked for the mayor.

Raoul Felder I don't think it was as simple a question as ego. At one point, Bratton, who I like, was out of control; he wanted to have a parade on his birthday! Did you ever hear of that? And Bratton was basically holding court every night in Elaine's. There's nothing wrong with that—I go to Elaine's too—but a lot of that stuff Rudy may have viewed as inappropriate.

Henry Stern A commissioner is a subordinate and a commissioner should not build up a personal agenda. He was establishing himself as a society figure. He appeared to be burnishing his credentials for a race for mayor.

Lilliam Barrios-Paoli   I like Bill Bratton a lot. Bratton has a very healthy ego—so does Giuliani—and I think that Giuliani had the sense that the only person who should get credit in the administration is the mayor. Bratton had done a lot of good things in the Transit Police and in the Boston Police. But history gets rewritten by the people who win. Rudy wanted it to be *his* win, but Bratton wanted it to be *his* win, and that was the big clash. Look, the mayor is elected and the police commissioner is *appointed*. Clearly, he should defer. I don't know that Bratton really *got* that.

Fran Reiter   I'm a real believer that we serve at the pleasure of the mayor; *they're* the ones who've been elected; *they're* the ones who answer to the people, not me, as a deputy mayor, and not Bill Bratton, a police commissioner. We serve at the pleasure of the mayor. And this was not a mayor, despite what some of his people who don't like him will say, who always had to hog the spotlight. That's just not true. I can't even *begin* to remember how many major projects my office was involved in where when we got ready to announce them, I stood up there with the mayor, at a press conference in the Blue Room, and *I* did most of the talking. There was never a question with Rudy Giuliani about sharing credit.

Albert O'Leary   It comes down to not having the staff there who saw the warning signs and could react and tell him and say, "Hey, Bill, we've got to cool this a little bit; we've got to step back and think about this and improve our relationship with the Mayor's Office before it gets out of hand." I firmly believe that if he had had somebody with experience there who understood the relationship he could have lasted for the whole Giuliani administration. Bill is very smart. Bill is very, very willing to give credit. He's the first one to say the mayor was the guy who got us the resources and the cops are the ones who did the job. And he also recognizes that, in doing that, *he* gets credit—*he's* the guy saying it: it wasn't me; it was the *mayor*. Nobody understands that better than Bill Bratton. It's just that nobody read the warning signs at that point. And Giuliani's a guy who likes his press, you know.

Raoul Felder   Bratton was sailing on his own dime, to mix metaphors; he was taking bows all over the place. It was a difficult situation because he had Jack Maple, who was really like an idiot savant—he used to walk around in spats. He was the real brains behind all of that. I know for a fact that Rudy was warned—a friend of mine was the one who warned him—

before he hired Bratton that there would be problems with him, but he hired him anyway because he felt he was the right man for the job.

Albert O'Leary   It wasn't entirely between Giuliani and Bratton. There were people who worked for Bill Bratton who had poured some salt on wounds, people who were very gung ho but nobody with any experience in city government who really understood the relationship between the Mayor's Office and the Police Commissioner's Office. Everybody working in the Police Commissioner's Office, including Jack Maple and John Miller, felt they were made of steel wrapped in Kevlar. Well, they forgot they had a boss: *the mayor*. Instead of recognizing that the really hyped publicity was creating a problem with the mayor and then toning that down, they went full speed ahead: The hell with it! Let's do the *New York* magazine cover!

Mark Green   Something went terribly wrong. Bratton once said to me, "You know, I'm a focused person who *likes* people; I don't enjoy *hating* people. But, I've got to admit, I hate *Rudy Giuliani*."

Chapter 10

HIZZONER THE MAYOR: SAINT RUDY OR MUSSOLINI ON THE HUDSON?

Stand up to bullies. . . . Under-promise and
over-deliver. Don't assume a damn thing.
—Rudy Giuliani, *Leadership*

His career as a tough prosecutor prepared Rudy well to be an even tougher mayor: during his two terms in office he made New York's streets safe again, bringing down the overall crime rate by 57 percent and the murder rate by 65 percent. While doing so, however, he made an initial blunder, incurring the wrath of New York's major African American officials, when he refused to meet for the first five years of his mayoralty with State Comptroller Carl McCall and strung along Manhattan Borough President Virginia Fields, the highest-ranking African American officials in state and city government, respectively. The mayor would later ignite some of the worst racial strife in the city's history by minimizing the excesses of his police department at the expense of the city's African American and black immigrant communities.

Giuliani and Bratton's Racially Tinged Baptism of Fire Power

On Sunday afternoon, January 9, 1994, little more than a week into Giuliani's first term as mayor, two African American police officers, responding to a 911 call reporting a robbery in progress at Muhammad's Mosque Number 7, Nation of Islam leader Louis Farrakhan's New York headquarters, located above a grocery store on 125th Street, in the heart of Harlem, arrived at the site. Dashing up the stairs and into the mosque, the police officers engaged in a fierce fight with the mosque's security guards, during which they were injured and their guns were taken from them. That incident escalated into a full-fledged riot. As Bratton attempted to deal with the situation, Mayor Giuliani, infuriated by the treatment meted out to the investigating officers, intervened numerous times by telephone, screaming at his newly appointed police commissioner, "I want arrests!"

Edward Reuss   It was a setup job to embarrass the new mayor and his police commissioner. Bratton [who would assume his new position at midnight that very Sunday] handled it well. That's *leadership*.

Eric Adams   Bratton would have been able to bring in the Muslims of the mosque to have a meeting to resolve the issue. Because of his previous relationships with all fringes of society, it was his mind-set that no matter what fringes of society you are involved in, even the far left or the far right, we exist together and we have to exist in this city in a peaceful manner. That was not the belief of his boss. Giuliani told him that he couldn't have the meeting.

That incident would prove to be but the first of the many difficulties that would come to bedevil the mayor's relationship with his police commissioner.

The Mayor's Initial Refusal to Meet with African American Leaders

David Dinkins   Not only did he refuse to meet with them; he refused to meet with them on the occasion of the riotous situation at the mosque in Harlem.

Rudy Washington   Rudy is *Rudy*. Rudy doesn't believe in consorting with the enemy. He understands the fundamental way they used to do business and that was: I'll call you all kinds of names and then when we get behind closed doors, we'll cut a deal. Rudy didn't play that game: you don't call me a racist, Al Sharpton, and then expect to meet me and work out a deal. You declare me your enemy, *fine*. I'm going to be *your* enemy.

Ruth Messinger   I don't think Rudy wanted to meet with very many people; he was pretty sure *he* had the answers and he knew where he was headed and what he wanted to do. And right through to the end of his mayoralty he certainly lumped together all blacks, all Hispanics, and all Democrats. And unless they proved to the *contrary* by endorsing him, he had nothing to share with them. Then there's Giuliani's obsessive notion of one strategy fits all: you don't have to listen to different ethnic groups; you don't have to listen to different neighborhoods; it's all the same. That is an absurd take on New York or on *any* place.

Fred Siegel   That's just nonsense; he met with all sorts of people. He would not truckle under; he did not operate under the model that in order to do something in Harlem, you had to get permission from Charlie Rangel [Member, U.S. House of Representatives, D-NY], who says one [positive] thing [about an individual] to the media and then goes out and issues a statement denouncing you. Charlie Rangel can say the most outrageously stupid things—to him, interracial adoption is like the Holocaust—and he's never held to account.

––––––––––

In fact, according to an official who declined to speak for attribution, when Virginia Fields, a prominent Democrat running for the post of borough president, was locked in a tight race with Deborah Glick, the mayor did oblige when asked to help her. Two weeks before the election, Fields called the authors' source, saying, "I can win this race for borough president. I need $100,000 to do one more mailing. You can raise that money for me," to which her potential savior replied, "Okay, Virginia, I possibly could do this for you. However, I've got to go to Rudy [Giuliani]; I can't do this for you behind Rudy's back." Fields at first demurred but finally acquiesced, saying, "Okay, go to Rudy." The authors' source did, saying, "Rudy, it comes down to this: pick your poison, Deborah Glick or Virginia Fields. We can make the difference, not to mention that we'll get a big IOU." The mayor reportedly replied, "Okay, you can do it." When told the good news, Fields reportedly asked, "What's this going to cost me?" The authors' source replied, "All we ever wanted from you is to deal *fairly* with us. We don't want anything else; Rudy didn't put any conditions on it." Fields went on to win the election.

Mark Green   To come to his defense, he was partly an equal opportunity angry man: he didn't like meeting with me, *either*. He saw no governmental need or political gain in meeting with people who disagreed with him, whether they were white *or* black. But it didn't take a genius to realize that when he refused to meet the state comptroller, the Manhattan borough president, and others of that rank, who all were black, it was wrong. And so when the police incidents happened [the attack on Abner Louima and the killings of Amadou Diallo and Patrick Dorismond], he had no reservoir of relationships or goodwill in the black community to draw on.

Carol Bellamy   Racial issues are never easy—something this country has not absorbed as much as we'd like to think we have, certainly in a city like New York, where there is such diversity. Nevertheless, if you are the mayor of a city with as much diversity as New York, you've got to work at it. There were some incidents that were beyond his control but I don't think he worked as hard at it as he might have. This isn't a partisan issue; Democrats have to work at evenness in race as much as Republicans have to.

Ed Koch   I said to him, "Why don't you meet with them?" He said, "I don't agree with them." And I said, "Rudy, you only meet with people you *agree* with? That's crazy!" Then he told me that Peter Vallone had arranged a meeting. That's *Rudy*. He did a lot of good things but, on balance, bad because of the spirit that was created in the city. This city is two-thirds minority, approximately, and they were outraged. Now that doesn't mean it's easy if you're white to get along in a position of authority in a city that's roughly two-thirds minority. And the reason that any white mayor, myself included, had, and would have, problems is that when a city has fiscal problems and you have to reduce the delivery of services to the poor, who are overwhelmingly black and Hispanic, they don't want to understand and explanations don't suffice. The middle class will grumble and then they'll go to the Hamptons. The rich, if they don't like what's taking place, will buy the services for themselves or they'll leave town. But the poor are mired here so it's very difficult and you have to understand that.

Fran Reiter   He didn't really feel he could get anywhere with them, that they would always be taking potshots at him; that they would never support anything that he was doing. I think he was wrong, and there were those of us in the administration who tried to convince him that he was wrong, but we never really succeeded. I think he could have been successful, at least on some issues. He ended up having a better relationship with Virginia Fields. Would it have been better had he done the outreach? We'll never know.

Rudy Washington I've lost track of the number of times that I brought Rudy into the community. I brought him to a number of the churches in Southeast Queens. And I've got to say that never, in any of those visits, was I ashamed. I think Rudy is his own best kind of ambassador. When people give him a moment and really *listen* he's able to penetrate; he's able to reach past people's predisposition toward him. I watched him on a number of occasions do that. When my sister died, Rudy came and spoke at the funeral. He had probably already visited my church twice before my sister's funeral in April of '96 and every time he would go, it was never the same crowd. And at my sister's funeral, it was a lot of her old friends, people who were not part of my church, who had never seen the mayor before and the only thing they knew of him was the verbal stuff that resonates in a community and passes around, that he's just *evil*. And he's given fund-raisers at my house. It took a number of years; Rudy doesn't trust easily.

A Debate: Is Giuliani or Is He Not a Racist?

David Dinkins I don't call him a racist. I have always taken the position that you can describe behavior, and I can say I find it unacceptable, but to characterize it, that's another thing. I can't think of a time when I called anybody a racist; I just don't use that kind of language because to call someone a racist, then you have to defend your accusation. So I choose not to use that kind of language because it doesn't serve my interests.

The Reverend Al Sharpton, president, National Action Network I don't know anyone that knows him well enough to make that determination. Whether he himself sits around and plots against people of different races, I don't know. But I definitely think he plays on racial hysteria and racial divisiveness. I know that he has the achievement of polarizing this city. I think it was an intentional strategy; whether it was political or whether it spoke of who he was, I have no idea. And it really doesn't matter to those that were victimized. I can't remember *any* issue—whether it was police brutality or community empowerment or education—that the African American community or the Latino community pursued that he supported. And that takes effort in a city like this. He had not calculated that he was going against the African American man and that he would have a reasonable portion of that race and just write them off and continue to write them off and try to exacerbate the numbers on the other side, in the Staten Islands and the Queenses of the world. You would think that at some point he would grow beyond that kind of politics and say: If I'm going to have a legacy, I want to have a legacy of bringing people together.

Herman Badillo   He never reached out to Al Sharpton. Let's face it, Al Sharpton in the Diallo case was conducting day-to-day confrontations in front of police headquarters, urging the Bronx district attorney to indict the four policemen, which is really trying to interfere with the judicial process. But that wasn't the worst of it. If you look closely behind Al Sharpton, there were placards that said NEW YORK POLICE = KKK! That was *outrageous*! The message behind it was really disgusting. If I was Rudy Giuliani, I would be attacking Al Sharpton, too, because it's one thing to disagree with the police, or to say that that they have acted improperly, but to say that they equal KKK is beyond the bounds of reasonable debate.

The Reverend Al Sharpton   He'd make the point of saying, "I don't talk to Al Sharpton." He was purposely sending a signal. I've never asked for a meeting; I've never invited him to come up to my headquarters because he made it clear he was not going to come, and I did not want to trivialize what we were doing by associating with a man who was turning down an invitation when everyone else was there—most of the U.S. senators and everybody of importance in the city. Why would I want to overshadow a memorial to King on whether or not the mayor came? And the mayor not only did not come; he didn't let anybody else come. He didn't go *anywhere* unless it was a sole cheering squad for him. And that not only suggests to me a policy, it suggests a very insecure, fragile ego. He probably enhanced us by *not* dealing with us because he made us the object of his wrath. Fred Siegel takes the position that he ignored us and, therefore, that was good. Well, good for *whom*? The city was polarized.

Fred Siegel   Sharpton had in 1992 run for the Senate with the implicit support of Mario Cuomo. He had already been an instigator in Crown Heights and had been hanging around with [Nation of Islam leader Louis] Farrakhan and never been held to account. If you want to hold someone to account for Sharpton, look at New York 1: it became the Sharpton News Network. Look at the other news stations; look at the press, which never held him to account for *anything* and treated him as good copy.

Gerald Lefcourt   The first time I heard the name Al Sharpton was in the early 1980s when I represented Matthew Ianniello. Sharpton was talked about as a witness for Giuliani, who had threatened him with prosecution. Later, they certainly fed off each other. Sharpton was good for Giuliani's supporters, who loved anything that was anti-Dinkins, anti-black, and anti-squeegee. I don't think that Giuliani has a hatred of blacks. He is part of that cop world that at the highest levels is not friendly and not involved in the black and Latino worlds. I think Rudy's views come from a time and place that are not sympathetic to these groups.

Henry Stern   He wasn't anti-black. Just like in the McCarthy period, when people were smeared as communists, today people are smeared as racists so that anyone who adopts a policy that adversely affects members of one racial group are viewed as entering into a conspiracy to injure that racial group. It's completely unfair, has led to lawsuits, and is ridiculous. Rudy Giuliani treats all people alike and race is not a factor. You can never do as much as extremists want who take the position that since blacks comprise a third of the city's population, therefore, a third of the commissioners should be black; and since the majority of people on welfare are black, the welfare commissioner should be black.

Eric Adams   When you use a term so often, you dilute its effectiveness. "Isms" are rooted in one's ignorance or lack of understanding. I believe that much of Rudy Giuliani's problem is rooted in not understanding other races. Giuliani was uncomfortable around blacks unless it was a black like Rudy Washington, who was completely loyal to him. He was not comfortable around blacks who in any way disagreed with him. He interpreted that as a lack of loyalty. Throughout his eight years as mayor of this city, he made a conscious effort to write off black people, particularly black male youth. Our policing policies under that administration—all the experts were saying we were going too far—were to introduce more juveniles to the criminal justice system than ever before. The behavior of juveniles normally associated with youthfulness was turned into *criminal* behavior. And now these young people have married a police record and no matter where they go in life, when they go to American Express and compete with their counterpart across town, for whom the same policing policies were *not* in place, they have to say, Yes, I was arrested. No one is going to go back and look and say, Okay, that was during the Giuliani period, when they were arresting kids for riding their bikes on the sidewalk or not having a bell on their bike. No one is going to analyze that. All they want to know is that this is a black child whose normal, youthful, mischievous behavior was criminal. And that's going to stymie their ability to move through life normally. Some of these kids will never be teachers; never be cops; never be firemen. Thousands and thousands and thousands of kids' lives have been altered, and eventually they're going to become part of the segment of society that never will feel like they're part of society, so they'll become the ills of society. That is the legacy of Giuliani. So was he a racist? I think it's far more than that. Racism is not the term to use. I felt that he was dangerous, that he allowed people to be comfortable with some of the ills and bad aspects that we have as human beings.

Ed Koch   The greatest thing that Bloomberg brought to the city was racial peace: the minute he was elected, the tenor of city debate changed. One of the first things he did was to see Al Sharpton; he went over and shook his hand. Rudy could never do anything like that! Shaking hands is a social grace, it's not an imprimatur that I agree with you, or that we're close personal friends. Rudy is *not* a racist. I would always tell blacks who complained to me—they'd say, "Rudy is a racist; he's insulted us"; they were absolutely livid with him, the black leadership, and others—I walked around a lot and talked to a lot of people, and I would always say, "That's not true. He's not a racist; he's nasty to *everybody*."

Eric Adams   Giuliani pitted New Yorker against New Yorker; he made us comfortable with some of the ugly parts of us. We all have biases and dislikes. Giuliani made us comfortable with bringing those dislikes to the forefront: it was all right for the guy in Bensonhurst to say: "We don't want any niggers on our block"; it was all right for the guy in Bedford-Stuyvesant to say: "We don't want any crackers around here"; it was all right for the Italian guy to say: "We don't want any Jews." You walked the streets and saw some of the fights and the confrontations: someone cuts someone off and it's: Nigger! Watch where you're driving! Or someone doesn't hold the door: Damn spics! Everybody was comfortable with being divisive; it was a normal part of life for eight years. As a police officer, you saw the different New York; my New York was not the [*New York*] *Daily News*; it was seeing the stories before they got to the *Daily News*. This was a divided city.

And he did something that I felt was insulting: he insulted the Jewish community. Giuliani understood the fears of the Jewish community and he played on those fears. And he will continue to ride those fears even to the White House. There's a danger with people who play on the fears of people. It's almost like saying, You've got to let the cops do what they want because if they don't, those spics and niggers are going to move into your neighborhood and the property is going to go down because all of us have values; all of us want our kids to go to safe schools; we want our homes to be safe. And if people play on those things that scare the hell out of us, even if we are decent individuals, we have a tendency to start thinking, Oh my God! If we allow anybody into our neighborhood, those pedophiles will get our kids; if we open our schools up to anybody, they're going to start playing *their music*—that hip-hop stuff—in our community; our daughters are actually going to be having intercourse with those people! He played on all those fears.

Malcolm Hoenlein   Giuliani *did not* pander to the Jewish community. The Jews got a fair shake. There were many agencies in earlier periods where Jews couldn't get jobs. We used to get complaints all the time about it and it's very hard to make the case because you can't prove it in most cases. But Giuliani put Jews in visible positions—he tried to put different kinds of people in visible positions.

Eric Adams   I saw him do it over and over again. Giuliani and I used to go at it all the time because I saw him for what he was. It wasn't that I disagreed with him politically; it just reached the point that someone had to go on record. I guarantee you, when scholars look back over the period of the Giuliani reign, which is far from over, we're going to say to ourselves, How did we stand by and allow this to happen?

Other First-Term Issues

Mark Green   An event occurred which illuminated how the relationship would go for eight years. My job is to monitor city services, and I did an early investigation and discovered that the Police Department was doing its own repair of police vehicles and cleanup of its own buildings and I thought: this is an area that should be privatized. Normally that word is associated with Republicans. But I, a Democrat, thought that it would be cost-effective for the Police Department to stick to *policing* and to have some car jockey fix cars and a cleaning company to clean buildings. I did a rather boring study but a useful one; I released it after getting an indication from Commissioner Bratton that he supported it. I was amazed when at two o'clock that day—I had released it that morning—Giuliani attacks me for my naive proposals because terrorists (this is in 1994, after the first World Trade Center bombing but well before the big one) could put bombs in police vehicles. And I was thinking: why is the *mayor* responding to a ho-hum study of the Police Department where I never mentioned his name? I then discovered that the Secret Service and the FBI contract out auto repair and made the obvious point that a terrorist would have to work real hard to take over a repair company in the hope that *they* would get the contract and then someday *maybe* put a bomb in a vehicle. It's absurd!

The story doesn't end. At six o'clock that day, the mayor himself is on the phone with the reporters writing the story, spinning them on why I was an idiot! I then realized: this is the way he plays. Fine, here we go. And it didn't let up for eight years. He picked on the wrong guy to try to intimidate. I had my jurisdiction, he had his; he was a very skilled guy in what *he* did, I was skilled.

I will not psychoanalyze why he was so antagonistic. I'm sure he could cite some public action I took or some private thing I said to justify it. I will tell you that while he's a proud Republican and I'm a proud Democrat, and under the city charter people of different parties held the two top offices, I didn't approach him in a partisan way. In fact, I remember thinking for a while that it was likely Dinkins would win and that I would have to be a watchdog over *him*. Trust me, I would have released the exact same report on privatizing police vehicle repair and cleanup of police buildings whether Dinkins or Giuliani were mayor.

Rudy on Mission: Declaring War on Mobsters, Murderers, Squeegee Men, Rapists, Dealers, and Pimps

Sanford Rubenstein, attorney; represented Abner Louima and his family   That whole thing about the squeegee men was used by the Giuliani administration as an example of how Giuliani was going to "clean up the city," an example of what they promised to do when they were running for election. It certainly didn't—in my view—affect the overall fight against crime. But it was a tangible change that people could see, of what he had promised in his campaign. And now he was mayor and he was *delivering*.

Jay Goldberg   When you used to get off the Willis Avenue Bridge [linking the Bronx and Manhattan], there would be ten to fifteen squeegee people there. I remember a lady who didn't want to pay; they took her windshield wipers and broke them. There are no squeegee people there now. That's a minor quality of life issue, but this is a different city.

And Times Square was a cesspool: there were hookers and sex movie places, and it was a place to be avoided. If you go up and down Times Square now, you don't have to worry about being mugged. The place is beautiful. I travel and on many occasions I ask people about New York and they all know Giuliani and that the city is a safe place to go. The FBI has released a report on the number of crimes in the largest cities of the nation and New York is next to last. I represent a big Broadway producer; he says Times Square around the theater district is now considered safe and wonderful. Everybody gives that credit to Giuliani.

Steven Brill When it comes to stuff like the squeegee guys, a lot of New Yorkers like me thought, It's not good. As a policy matter, it's not the right approach; it's a civil liberties matter. But thank God *somebody* is doing it.

Fred Siegel Giuliani is at his very best in moments of crisis, when he comes into office and the city is about to fold. He governed against the grain. Does that mean his operatic personality didn't sometimes overwhelm the situation? Absolutely! When he goes after the vendors in the second term and on some of the traffic issues, he goes over the top.

The Fulton Fish Market

Located in Lower Manhattan, near the South Street Seaport Museum, the sprawling Fulton Fish Market had for 175 years been the major supplier of fish and seafood to the city's five boroughs. Over the years, the Mafia had infiltrated the market, and one year into his first administration, Mayor Giuliani had had enough. On February 1, 1995, the mayor declared war on the Mafia, making known his intention to remove its stranglehold on the market by removing six Mob-connected unloading firms. Just as America's Founding Fathers had secured independence for a new nation, a latter-day Washington would lead the charge.

Rudy Washington The mayor said to Randy and me, "We're going to deal with this fish market." I knew I was going into a war zone. I looked at the team I had and I said, "It's just not going to work." I'm at City Hall: I redeployed half those people; some of them I just had to move on. I put together my own team because I knew I was going to battle. Randy Mastro was actively involved in writing the legislation. We did it and basically announced that I'm going to bounce twenty-three guys out of the market. When Rudy announced the legislation, I was his point guy. The press was fascinated by the fact: wait a minute, he's not out of the U.S. Attorney's Office; he's not a cop; he's not this; he's not that, Mr. Mayor. And Rudy stood up in front of a press conference and said, "I have the utmost confidence in him." But what the press probably didn't realize then was that while Rudy knew about it [fighting organized crime], I had had running wars with the Mob years earlier, not from a law enforcement point of view, but I had put my gun on and stood watch at my jobs and basically told the guys: "I'm here! You want to kill me? Come on out here!" It got so bad at one point that the Port Authority Police called me and said, "Look, Mr. Washington, we picked up a wiretap; these guys are going to hurt you." And they offered me protection. I look back on it now and say to myself, Rudy, you had rocks in your head; you and your little six-shooter! You think you're going to fight the world! When you're young, you do stupid stuff. I had that history and I halfway understood the mentality of some of these characters. And a lot of that was what I brought to the table at the Fulton Fish Market.

The legislation passed, prompting the Mob to retaliate by staging a fire at the market. Washington and Mastro were at a luncheon at the residence of the South African ambassador to the United Nations during negotiations in early 1994 in advance of a visit to New York by South Africa's president, Nelson Mandela, when their host remarked, "There's a big fire downtown."

Rudy Washington   We look out the window and see the smoke coming up. It's a big fire, but we think nothing of it; we think it's just some factory burning. Then my beeper goes off and there's a message. Before I can get to it, Randy's beeper goes off. This is not good! The message is, "Your Fish Market is on fire!" Randy and I run out of the place, down to the Fish Market. The mayor was there; *everybody* was there. And the press was like: Wow! Need I say Rudy was not happy? He was spitting fire. But I got the market up and running that same night: even though we lost the building, we didn't lose *one day*. The Fire Department determined very quickly that it was arson—they saw the gas cans and the gas trail.

People around me were saying, "You've got to be careful. These guys may put a hit out on you!" I had a lot of threats. They got hold of my phone number; they called my house every hour, on the hour, to make sure I didn't sleep; they appeared in my neighborhood; and they showed up at one of our town hall meetings, at St. John's University. Rudy's speaking and

I whisper to him, "We've got some organized crime guys in the audience." Rudy's eyes widen and he continues to speak and then I slip a note to Randy, who's sitting on the other side of him, "Fulton Fish Market guys are here" and Randy's like, "Where, where?" Now we're slipping notes *all over the place* and intel [plainclothes police] finally gets one of the notes. Because I spend nights down there [at the market], I'm the only guy who knows these guys by name *and* face, and now, without trying to create a disturbance, we're trying to put an intel cop on every single one of them and they're spread around in the audience. Now it's time to leave. I'm in the parking lot—they don't realize that I'm being shadowed by intel—and we have this big showdown and they say: "Oh, we just wanted to *talk*." We really didn't have anything to arrest them on because they didn't have any weapons and they hadn't assaulted me. These were the kinds of things that just never hit the papers.

Washington went into the market on the first night of the action with Chief Wilbur Chapman, a distinguished African American police officer. They were accompanied by sixty members of the force to deal with twenty-three troublemakers.

Rudy Washington   We figured we could control the situation. We brought the cops with nightsticks up; we were going to physically take them out. The next thing I know, the whole market turns against us: we're surrounded by six hundred guys with hooks. It was like *The Showdown at the O.K. Corral*. Everybody knew this was going to happen and the press was there.

The task force was rookies for the most part. It's two thirty in the morning and these guys are closing the circle around us. I get Randy on the phone. "Randy, this is going south *quick*!" He can hear the guys yelling. "Rudy, what's the matter?" "A whole lot of people are going to die tonight." He's saying, "Rudy, don't *talk* like that!" and Chapman is yelling, "Rudy! What are we going to do? I'm too old to take a hook!" Randy is listening to us and trying to get us to stop. And I'm like, "Randy! Stop *what*? I'm just going to let these people *hook* me?" And he says, "Rudy, let me get the mayor!"

When Chapman and I unholstered our weapons and those young kids saw what we did, they started putting their hands on *their* guns. I think that they [the market workers] looked at those young boys and girls and saw the fear in their eyes and that they were shaking, and these guys with the hooks were thinking, This is going to be *bad*. The last thing they wanted was young kids with shaking hands and guns in their hands, and they parted the way for us—it was like God parting the Red Sea for Moses. It's four thirty in the morning and we back out of the market and the press is taking pictures.

Chapman and I drive up to this local diner to get coffee to steady our nerves. I say, "I've got to go confront the mayor; he's not going to be happy that we had to retreat." When we got to City Hall, the sun was just coming up. Rudy was livid; he was spitting fire! He couldn't wait to hold a press conference. He held it at ten o'clock and went ballistic: I'll close that whole market down; there won't be any fish in New York! He finished the press conference and called Bill Bratton and said, "You get Chapman whatever he needs!" Chapman said, "I want five hundred cops; we're going to match them man for man." Bratton almost choked. But the mayor had already said he'd give us whatever we needed to fight this battle.

Washington, Chapman, and their huge force went back into the market the following evening only to incur the further wrath of their adversaries. They dragged all twenty-three of the troublemakers from the market. Returning the following night, they were confronted by a wildcat strike. Washington then engaged in an act of very risky brinksmanship that would result in the resolution of the issue during the Giuliani administration.

A decade later, the Fulton Fish Market would still be making headlines. Among the issues in the fall of 2005 was the possibility of infiltration by organized crime personalities at the market's designated new location in the Bronx. The lawyer for Laro Services Systems, the company that had taken over the market in 1995, was Randy Mastro.

The Harlem Empowerment Zone

On July 20, 2001, former president Bill Clinton would establish offices on 125th Street, the nerve center of Harlem. His decision to do so had its roots in the creation in the early years of the Giuliani administration of the Harlem Empowerment Zone, which would lead to the controversial ridding of that neighborhood of its street vendors.

Rudy Washington   There were skirmishes that the public didn't see. A lot of people were running around, taking credit, but it was this process, played out in the first three or four months Rudy was in office back in June of '94 that made it possible for Bill Clinton to come in. When Rudy was elected in 1992, he had announced he was doing the Empowerment Zone. I wrote the application and became chairman of the Empowerment Zone. Charlie Rangel was one of the architects of the legislation and David Dinkins had designated Harlem being in the Empowerment Zone. When Rudy really looked closely at the legislation, he started thinking, Why should it all go to Harlem? That's not the only community in need. He said, "The South Bronx [a depressed area of abandoned buildings] should share in this." Charlie Rangel said no. From day one we were at war with Charlie Rangel. But we controlled a hundred million dollars; we controlled the application and Charlie Rangel was down there in Washington. The mayor was like, Let's go ahead. You want a hundred million dollars? God bless you! Now Charlie is blowing fire up in Harlem. Freddie Ferrer [Bronx Borough president] figures out that Rudy says, "The South Bronx." Freddie comes in, he's going to be unreasonable—he wants 50 percent. Charlie goes crazy—this might be some of the bad blood today. I meet with Freddie Ferrer and try to reason with him; I meet with the congressman and try to reason with *him*, and if you know Charlie, that's like reasoning with a shark. But I begin to make some headway and the borough president of the Bronx realizes that 20 percent is better than no percent. I can tell you now that Rudy was getting to the point of blowing this whole thing off. Here he is, trying to help, and he's being attacked in the papers constantly. I finally got the two of them to agree and I was able to write the application. It was the size of a phone book. It had to be submitted in June of '94 and we were awarded in October of '94. But the Giuliani administration never got any credit for it.

Fred Siegel   When Giuliani has to clean up 125th Street, the guy who does it is Rudy Washington, who got no credit. Rudy Washington has to go up to Harlem and force demagogues, like Rangel, to essentially promise, in writing, that while they're cleaning up 125th Street, there won't be demagogues up there because the merchants are dying up there. The street has been taken over by these street merchants; there are feces on the street; there are rats—it's a Third World situation.

Rudy Washington   I took Rudy up there in '93, before the election, and we couldn't walk down the sidewalk. The sidewalks are twenty-five feet wide, or wider, up there, within three blocks on 125th Street, but the vendors—there were thirteen hundred; we did a census count—had both sides of the street and there was only *a path* to walk down the sidewalk. Chief Ward whispered in my ear about how bad it was and about how the cops had retreated under Dinkins and it had gotten worse.

While I'm in the middle of this war in the Fish Market, I'm taking pressure from community boards and business organizations in Harlem, saying, We couldn't get the previous administration to do it; unless somebody deals with this, we're going to stop paying taxes. This is crazy! I go up to a meeting there one night and say to them, "I'll get rid of the vendors." I walk out and an elderly gentleman, a statesman up there, a businessman there for many years named Eugene Webb, says, "Sir, either you're the most naive man I know or you've got to be walking with God. Nobody's been able to get rid of these vendors." And there was an inspector at the meeting who said, "If you get rid of those vendors, I'm going to build a monument to you." I see him today and I say to him, "Where's my *monument*?" and he bursts out laughing.

Fred Siegel   In order to get into Harlem, Giuliani had to pay off Rangel. At key moments he had people who helped him. Peter Vallone was of enormous help. And Pataki was helpful in breaking the control of the Harlem Urban Development Corporation. The guy who's the leader of the street merchants on 125th Street is an escaped mental patient by the name of Morris Powell [a street vendor who headed the Buy Black committee of Al Sharpton's National Action Network and was described by Mr. Siegel in a *New York Post* article in September 2001 as "An escaped mental patient who had thrice been accused of attempted murder"], who also makes money shaking down merchants, particularly Koreans.

Rudy Washington   I knew that Rudy was going to be painted as some kind of racist up in Harlem when we moved on the vendors, so I devised a strategy. It was simple: I wanted every elected official to write to the mayor and to me and ask that we remove the vendors. I went to the business organizations: "Send the mayor a letter." Usually the mayor just signs letters and the secretaries farm them out to the appropriate agencies and tell *them* to take care of it. But these letters were *particular*: I had the Harlem Business Alliance, the Harlem Business Development Corporation, the ministers, and all the civic groups write, asking me to remove the vendors.

I got 90 percent of the elected officials to write to me, including Virginia Fields. I must have had twenty or thirty letters—from every organization up there, every potentate you could think of. But the mayor was still somewhat nervous about it because he knew what was going to happen—that the moment I went up there, he was going to be vilified: he's a racist mayor depriving people of their livelihood and all that sort of stuff. I gave Rudy the plan: I'm going to create a vendor's market. I'm not going to shut these guys down; I'm going to put them in a location. Rudy liked it and I got everybody to sign off.

On the eve of the action, the mayor was having second thoughts concerning the operation. Mindful of the political damage that would ensue, nervous, and seeking reassurance, he summoned Washington and Chapman to Gracie Mansion.

Rudy Washington   He called at nine P.M. I was just getting ready to go home—we were going to do this at four o'clock in the morning. He says, "Rudy, take me through this again. Are you *sure* you've got this plan together?" His last words to Chapman and me [that morning] were, "Rudy, my mayoralty is in *your* hands." We walked out of Gracie Mansion, looked at each other, and Chapman said, "What did we just commit to?" Then the gravity of the situation hit us. We reconvene at four A.M. There's nobody on 125th Street. At daybreak, we put the cops out there. At seven thirty, people start hitting the street and see all these cops. By ten o'clock, Charlie Rangel is holding a press conference and blasting us: "My community looks like a prison camp, blah blah blah!" But there are no vendors. Eleven o'clock, *still* no vendors. Twelve o'clock comes and we're sitting down on the river—we have our command center down there—and we shake hands and say, "Well, we pulled *this one* off; this is a ground ball."

The radio traffic picks up. It's an inspector, a big tall Irish guy named Collins. He's calling for his arrest team and I'm like, Oh, my God! Chapman says, "It's on! Rudy, come on, let's go!" We get out there and we're in full-scale, hand-to-hand combat with the street vendors. The first day we arrested twenty-eight; the next day we had to arrest something like twenty-three.

The next thing I know, I'm on the front page of the *New York Times*. And every newspaper, every network, is vilifying "Rudy and Rudy." Charlie Rangel was the only one out there saying, "This is a police state!" And some congressman—I can't remember who he was—said, "Hey, if Charlie Rangel doesn't want those cops, send them to *my* community!"

Fred Siegel   Giuliani brings new stores to 125th Street and in the political life of Harlem, Giuliani is evil. Well, the reason for this is straightforward: politics in New York is dominated by people who live off the public sector. They treat poverty as an industry. We sell our poverty to Washington and we get our matching funds back. To the extent that Giuliani broke with that, he was a threat to their livelihoods, and so he was demonized from the get-go. Poverty should be a passing phase on the way to something better, and compassion shouldn't be an excuse for turning poverty into a vast employment sector for the city so people can be kept poor permanently.

Rudy Washington   They took a picture of the market and it was of a lone vendor sitting there. Just *one*; nobody else would go into it. After about a week there were five vendors and then ten vendors. Then, when I hit a critical mass, the mayor and I went up there and held a press conference and announced that we were going to get the tour buses to come through and support them and help them. At Christmastime they put up lights and do promotional programs. Then we were able to do some real policing up there and get crime under control. We started funding new businesses coming up there, like Starbucks, the Magic Johnson movie theater [Magic Johnson Theatres at Harlem USA], and Gap. The mayor's insistence turned Harlem around and today Rudy gets zero credit for it. The hypocrisy of it! People up there know *better*.

Fred Siegel   When Morris Powell no longer has those street merchants to lead, he looks for another gig and then we get Freddie's Fire. [In the fall of 1995, Al Sharpton organized a series of demonstrations against Fred Harari, a Jew and the owner of Freddie's Fashion Mart, located on 125th Street. Harari had been in a dispute with an African American tenant over commercial space he owned. On December 8, 1995, Abugunde Mulocko, aka Roland J. Smith Jr., a reputed member of the Black Liberation Army, entered Freddie's Fashion Mart, shot three white people and a Pakistani, and then set the store afire. Seven employees—five Hispanics, a Guyanese, and an African American—died of smoke inhalation and Mulocko apparently took his own life.] He and Sharpton turn a landlord-tenant dispute into a racial dispute, seven people are killed, and Sharpton's never even mildly held to account, nothing. Not *one* person is killed; *seven* people are killed. No one is held to account. It takes place diagonally across the street from Charlie Rangel's office; Charlie is very, very angry at Giuliani about this.

Rudy Takes On the Board of Education, Fellow Republicans, and Arafat

The mayor ignited a series of flash points of a very different sort by taking on—and making enemies of—such diverse adversaries as the New York City Board of Education; two fellow Republicans; his early mentor, Senator Alphonse D'Amato; and George Pataki, the Party's 1994 gubernatorial candidate, whom he betrayed by supporting the incumbent Democrat, Mario Cuomo (politics being what they are, however, Rudy would appear three years later at a fund-raiser for D'Amato and be introduced by Governor Pataki as "The great mayor, Rudy Giuliani"); and PLO chairman Yasir Arafat, who was literally kicked out of his seat at Lincoln Center by Rudy in October 1995 at the start of the gala celebrating the United Nations' fiftieth anniversary.

Herman Badillo We had serious problems with [schools chancellor Rudy] Crew, because I was—and have always been—in favor of eliminating "social promotion" and of having policemen in the schools, because there are two things that are necessary to have an educational system: standards and discipline. I met with many principals and one at a high school opened a drawer and showed me all kinds of guns and knives and said, "They were confiscated from the students." I said, "Listen, when I went to law school, having an illegal gun was a felony." That's one of the reasons why we pushed to have policemen in the schools and that was one of the things that we pushed Crew on, which he finally agreed upon.

It took us years of pushing him to eliminate "social promotion." He just didn't want to do it. When I first met with him, I said, "You're black and I'm Puerto Rican and you know that the kids who suffer the most are the black and Latino kids. And you know the main cause is 'social promotion' because if they do the work, they pass and if they don't do the work, they pass." What happens is that they end up being promoted up to the ninth grade and then they drop out, for the most part, without a high school diploma. That's true even today: 50 percent of black and Latino kids don't even graduate from high school. Crew agreed with me and he said, "Well, I'll get around to it." But he never got around to it. That's one of the things I debated Bloomberg on and now we're beginning to eliminate social promotion.

———————

On October 24, 1994, Mayor Giuliani stunned and infuriated his fellow Republicans by endorsing the incumbent governor of New York, Mario Cuomo, a Democrat, who was seeking an unprecedented fourth term, instead of his own party's candidate, a relatively unknown but highly competent Westchester County state senator named George Pataki.

Mark Green   I was asked by the Giuliani and Cuomo people: Would I have a press conference with Giuliani to attack Pataki and D'Amato? I said, "Sure." And for the third time in eight years, I sat down with him, on a Saturday morning, in a very friendly meeting where we compared notes on how we would attack Pataki and D'Amato. We then walked outside and held a joint press conference. I remember journalists looking at us like we were the lion and the lamb sleeping together. We came together because of mutual interest. When his political interest coincided with that of a rival's, he could put aside personal animosities and work together toward a common goal, like we did on Pataki-D'Amato. But in between, it was either you're a sycophant or you're an imbecile. I'm more of a humanist. I meet people I may not necessarily like, but I realize they have some good qualities and they can come up with a good idea. Not *Rudy*.

David Dinkins   The press conference was at a restaurant down at Battery Park. I stood next to them. At the time I was delighted because I was supporting Mario and I was happy to have his [Giuliani's] support. On reflection, that's part of the reason that Mario lost upstate. If Rudy had said, As mayor of New York I think it's very important that we continue Cuomo in office for the good of our city, it wouldn't have made the Republicans any happier, but it would have been palatable. Instead, he said something akin to: If D'Amato and Pataki get their hands on the state, then terrible things will happen.

Raoul Felder   Cuomo is vintage Rudy. They made him pay a price for it; for a long time after, they held it against him.

Stanley Friedman   Did Giuliani consider his political future in the Republican Party? Did he not care about his future in the party? Was he contemplating Cuomo's winning and switching to be a Democrat since most of his positions are more Democratic than they are Republican? And then there's Pataki's so-called forgiveness, even though it was very cold for eight years. To say he [Pataki] hates him is probably an understatement.

———————

On the evening of October 23, 1995, the United Nations, as part of its fiftieth anniversary celebration, held a gala concert at Lincoln Center featuring a performance by the New York Philharmonic orchestra. Observing Yasir Arafat entering the hall and moving toward a private box close to the stage, the mayor ordered that the PLO leader be told to leave.

Raoul Felder He had Bruce Teitelbaum [Mayor Giuliani's liaison to the Jewish community] go and tell them to kick the guy out and he left. The question is: What would have happened if Arafat *hadn't* left? Bruce was very polite to him. He didn't say, Get out, you bum; he said, "It's not appropriate; I don't think the mayor wants you here."

———————

A United Nations spokesman called Giuliani's action "an embarrassment to everyone connected with diplomacy," and former mayors Dinkins and Koch in a joint press conference denounced him. The mayor, accused at times of overstepping his mayoral role by pursuing his own foreign policy, retorted, "I would not invite Yasir Arafat to anything, anywhere, anytime, anyplace. I *don't* forget." The mayor was, obviously, referring to the PLO's murder in 1986 of the wheelchair-bound American tourist Leon Klinghoffer.

Herman Badillo He was always carrying things to excess, even as a prosecutor, so it's not surprising he'd be doing it as mayor. Obviously he knew he [Arafat] was a guest, but he figures the guy is *no good*, therefore, he doesn't have to show him any courtesy. That was his attitude and that's part of his personality. People want a mayor who's very aggressive, who shows anger, and takes out after people like Arafat.

Malcolm Hoenlein What he did to Arafat was a real turning point in people's assessment, a watershed. They saw that he was willing to stand up and that it wasn't for his benefit—he would get hit for it—but it was the right thing to do and he *did* it. People respected that very much.

Chapter 11

THE MAYOR AND THE NYPD

When I first came into office, having so much
experience working with police—and having so
many family members who were either firefighters
or cops—I was confident that I could run the
uniformed agencies effectively.

—Rudy Giuliani, *Leadership*

How Do Members of the NYPD Really Regard Rudy Giuliani?

Eric Adams The rank-and-file police officers dislike Giuliani because of the economic issue; they felt that they were the heroes of his administration—they dealt with the issue of crime; they saved lives—but Giuliani's position was: give them zero. They were not given raises; they were not treated fairly. If you speak to the rank-and-file police officer, you will find out that there is no love affair.

Albert O'Leary Bill Bratton said, "Everybody benefited during the boom time of the '90s." Everybody benefited, except the cops: Giuliani benefited; Bill Bratton benefited; and Wall Street benefited; the economy boomed with companies coming in and tourism flourished. The cops never shared in the wealth generated by their work. And it all goes back to Giuliani; he's the lightning rod. And that's why the cops, *to a person*, despise him today for building his career on their backs and becoming a law-and-order mayor and never, *never* taking care of the people who did the work.

He was behind us *publicly*. When he came into office, crime was at a peak in the city. But he also was the beneficiary of the fact that David Dinkins had been able to get legislation that allowed the Police Department to grow to peak numbers. It's kind of a dichotomy: he supported the police and, at the same time, he didn't take care of them even though he made his career on *their* backs. We got a five-year arbitration contract under Giuliani with two years of no raises and that's really what hurt us. We're starting to see the impact now: they can't get enough recruits and they've had to lower the standards to bring people on to the job. And when I say "lower the standards," I'm not talking about educational standards or age requirements; I'm talking about *character* standards. Where there was a time you couldn't get on this job if you had an *unpaid parking ticket*, today they're bringing people on who have been arrested for felonies—for robberies and assault—who had pleaded down to a misdemeanor.

Giuliani got elected on a law-and-order slate and he embraced the police and then he mistreated them for his whole time in office—he just *screwed* us. Before he was elected, we were among the highest-paid police officers in the nation—there are countless studies and commissions, some of them started by mayors, who believe that we *should* be, because of the complications in the jurisdiction we work in, the risks we take, and the job we do. And you shouldn't have to work a second job; if you do, it takes away your effectiveness as a police officer because you do an eight hour and thirty-five minute shift, and eight hours into that shift, you see something happening and you know if you make an arrest or take action you're going to be hung up for another eight hours doing arrest processing. So you don't do it because you need that steady, full-time second job and you say, I'll give it to the next guy who's coming in. That's not good for the cops.

Eric Adams   Cops are economically driven; they're very concerned about their lifestyle and they rate themselves by comparing themselves to their counterparts: if I'm chasing guys with guns, I should be paid more than the guy who's pulling a cat out of a tree. When they see that their counterparts are making $25,000 more than they are, they feel insulted. Giuliani gives them zeros in zeros and then he announces that he's giving himself a $40,000 raise and giving 10 to 15 percent raises to all of his commissioners. The cops can't take that. This is the police officer talking: If we all have to suffer, we suffer together; don't tell me that I have to suffer while you're rewarding yourself and your commissioners. The cops are very bitter about that.

Edward Reuss   There's a flip side to that. I say to cops, "Wait a minute, how much overtime did you make during those years?" They were making arrests left and right, so they were in court, making a lot of overtime; they were making a lot of money—not everybody, but the ones who were out there doing their job. "He may not have been able to give you a base raise, but what was your W2 at the end of the year?" I don't know what the operating budget was for Giuliani at the time. I'm sure if he could have, he would have given them the raises that they all asked for. It's not an easy ride for the head that wears the crown.

Who Was Really Responsible for the Drop in Crime?

In the spring of 2005, the *New York Times* published a letter written by Albert O'Leary in which he took issue with the view held by many New Yorkers that Rudy Giuliani had almost single-handedly put an end to the city's soaring crime rate.

Albert O'Leary   What prompted my letter to the *Times* is the feeling that Jack Maple, the fellow who is most responsible for the safety of the City of New York, hasn't gotten the recognition he deserves. He was a lieutenant in the Transit Police Department, a bit of a maverick. He was pretty typical of cops, the type of guy who understood how the criminal mind works and how easy it could be to beat them if you actually wanted to do the job and had the resources and if everybody played on the same team. He actually started CompStat [Computerized Statistics; a computer-based method of tracking crime]. It's a big marketing thing, but he actually started it in an office in midtown when he was in charge of the Central Robbery Unit for the Transit Police. He had huge maps of the subway system and he had colored pushpins. There'd be a guy doing chain snatches at the 42nd Street station, so he would put in a yellow pushpin and the times [of the chain snatchings]. And he recognized the early patterns of crimes because if you have somebody out there committing crimes, they're not just doing *one* crime, they're making their living doing crimes. If you get one person who's responsible for ten or fifteen chain snatches, that has a big impact on the crime statistics and you get that person out of circulation. Every big city has followed our lead.

Eric Adams   I'll never forget Jack Maple. Jack would drive down the block and if he saw a mugging going on, he would jump out of the car and go chase the guy. Bratton loved Maple. Maple took the brilliance of Bratton and made him survive in the big show. Bratton had the brilliance; Maple had the dream. Jack was the kid in the minor leagues—the Transit Police was considered the minor leagues; they had no respect. He knew he could play in the big leagues if they would give him a shot. Bratton gave him that shot. And with Bratton's brilliance and Maple's practicality, he [Maple] was able to become the big-league player that he wanted to be. It was remarkable what was happening in the city. The first phase was dealing with crime and the second phase was building a relationship between the police and the community. But before we could do that, Bratton and Jack Maple believed we had to be the marines and hit the beach.

The Impact of the "Broken Windows" Concept

Fred Siegel   There's an argument made that crime began to decline under Dinkins. That's true only in the marginal sense because it had nothing to do with *Dinkins*. Dinkins believed in root causes of crime; he didn't think policing could have any effect. And crime declines not in *poor* neighborhoods—where it declined more sharply under Giuliani—it declines in midtown, where a version of "broken windows" policing, in terms of the Business Improvement Districts, is already in place.

Edward Reuss   Bratton was a Boston police officer. He rose in rank and became very conversant with the people from Harvard that were talking about this idea of fixing broken windows—that if you fix the *small* problems, the quality of life problems, it will lead to a correction of bigger problems. There were police officers saying, "I'm too busy to handle derelicts in the street or graffiti or abandoned vehicles or broken windows. I'm worried about homicides; I'm worried about robberies." That makes sense. It's not that we weren't aware of it, but, apparently, these people studied this problem in depth. When you fix minor problems—broken windows, abandoned cars, graffiti—you're going to start to create a climate, a feeling, that there's order in the society. When you go into a neighborhood and you see a lot of graffiti on the walls, you see trash all over the place, derelicts sleeping in the subways—we all lived through this—you get the feeling: gee, nobody cares.

Gene Russianoff   Giuliani's smartness was that he hired Bill Bratton to be his police commissioner; he employed a lot of those theories. I went out with Bratton one night. There had been a sweep and it turned out that a big percentage of them had outstanding warrants.

Albert O'Leary   Crime didn't come down by accident; it came down because of new ways of dealing with it. They weren't coming out of City

Hall—not at all. They were coming out of the management of the Police Department, which at that time was Bill Bratton, John Timoney [the first deputy police commissioner and a top adviser to Bratton], and Jack Maple. Those guys became Bratton's boys because they were willing to think outside of the box; they didn't want to play the old-boy game with policing and they all became stars, all of them, in their own right. Bill Bratton pulled out all the guys in the NYPD who weren't team players. It was only two years, but it was a good time and we're still reaping the benefits. To say one day that police departments can't have an impact on crime and then the next day say, "Oh, yes they *can*, and *here's how*" and then demonstrate it is a miraculous transformation.

Gene Russianoff   A lot of what the mayor did in policing he has to get credit for. Over our objections, he merged the Transit Police with the New York City Police Department. He put a lot of energy into it and we put tremendous energy into *opposing* it. Now [in June 2005], some ten years later, I have to admit that it's not been a big deal. For whatever reason [crime continued to drop], from about nineteen thousand felonies to about three or four thousand felonies, and you have to give the Mayor that credit.

Albert O'Leary   The problem at that point was—not so much in the subway but especially on the street—that the crime stats were six months old before anybody saw them. That doesn't help you in your crime-fighting strategy. So Jack Maple came up with the three-pronged approach: reliable intelligence in the form of crime statistics; rapid deployment of resources—if you know a guy is working Times Square, get your cops in Times Square; if you know he's working Nevins Street, in Brooklyn, put your cops there (a combination of uniform and plainclothes); and relentless follow-up. That's what really brought CompStat into being. There's a big operations room and a precinct commander or detective commander would be brought in and, essentially, be grilled: What's happening in your area? We see that there's a lot of grand larceny of autos in your area. What are you doing about that?

The Effectiveness of CompStat

Edward Reuss   CompStat is information sharing. Each borough has their CompStat meetings in precincts and they'd be brought into the building to report on conditions in the precinct. The commanding officer is there; the exec is there; the administrative lieutenant, perhaps; the detective commander is there; you'll have the Transit Force that covers that area; the Housing Force that covers that area; you'll have people from other agencies. They'll all be there. Now, when they start discussing the problems—maybe there's a rash of fires in the Manhattan Precinct— it's amazing to watch, because they'll exchange information about people that may be connected to it, people with street names. A lot of the criminal elements have street names. You may know their given names, but if you don't know their street names, you don't know who they're talking about. All of a sudden, the Housing Force may say, "I know that guy!" And then someone may chime in from another agency; you're exchanging all this information and putting it together. It's really a wonderful system to see in action.

Albert O'Leary   It turns out that the police *can* have a real impact on crime, if they have the information, the resources, and are willing to really put the time in and hold people accountable. Bill Bratton took the information and applied it to the subway and then, when he became police commissioner of the City of New York, applied the same tactics and strategies to the street. But it was all Jack Maple, a funny little guy who used to wear a homburg and spats—a very colorful guy—and that's why I wrote the letter, because *Jack* is the guy who deserves the lion's share.

David Dinkins   There are some who do not heap all the credit on Comp-Stat. They had something akin to CompStat long ago. But he's [Giuliani's] the one who gets credit for it and so much so that some of the people under him—Bernie Kerik and others—have gone forth to advise other countries on how to fight crime, as has he. I don't know whether they know any more about it than you do, but that's what they do.

    The numbers will show that crime started to go down as early as 1991, and it's only been in recent years that Kelly is again police commissioner that some people have begun to acknowledge that that's the case. Before Ray—"the colonel" as I call him—was police commissioner under Mike [Mayor Michael Bloomberg], you didn't hear much of that, but the fact is that it did start to go down as early as 1991, certainly '92 and '93. Ed Koch says, "If a sparrow falls anywhere in the city, it's the mayor's fault and so if something good happens anywhere in the city, the mayor can get credit for it." I used to say, "If something good happens, credit my staff, those people I selected. If it's bad, I'll take the hit; blame *me*." As far as crime goes, there are many, many factors involved in its reduction, the availability of crack and cocaine among them, and where the economy stands. You have to examine other cities in the country at the same time.

Ed Koch Giuliani never gave David Dinkins any credit, and David Dinkins deserved credit for getting the legislation that permitted a special tax so the numbers of cops rose to 40,000—which is a lot from probably 30,000 or so. At one point in my administration, the NYPD, exclusive of the other two services—transit and housing—the NYPD went down to 22,000; it fell enormously because we couldn't afford it. When you have 40,000 cops, you can do a lot more than before, and David Dinkins is responsible for getting the money to do that. Crime started to fall. I wrote an article on this not very long ago, saying that, regrettably, what's happening now is that people are saying, "Oh, the sentences are too tough; we've got to get rid of mandatory sentencing and remove discretion from judges." But that's why we have reduced crime: people who commit crimes are recidivists and so long as you keep them in prison, the fewer crimes are going to be committed! Now it's, "We're keeping them in prison too long!" *Bullshit*! I would keep them in prison *longer*! We've got to fight that and it's very hard. You have the *New York Times*: Don't send them to prison; send them to *Harvard*! So it's tough. But what Rudy did was to bring Bratton, and Bratton brought in the systemic changes.

Fran Reiter It is absolutely true that crime had started to go down towards the tail end of the Dinkins administration. But it was a very small decrease and what hadn't happened at that point was any recognition of the validity of the "broken windows" theory and the quality of life approach to policing. Lee Brown had notions of community policing. They were different than what Giuliani and Bratton would ultimately move towards, but that was never communicated well to the Department and it never took hold. And then, towards the end of the Dinkins years, you have Ray Kelly, but not there long enough to really make his mark. You start to have some of the advantages of the "Safe Streets, Safe Cities Program," which started under Dinkins and was paid for by a surcharge to the real estate tax. Then, when most of it wasn't implemented, the real estate community that had signed on and was willing to pay the tax if it went to make the city safer, threatened to sue Dinkins if he didn't actually implement his own plan. So he started to implement it, but very little happened before Dinkins's term ended.

There were downturns in crime across the country starting then, although infinitesimal compared to the downturn in New York. So to suggest that you shouldn't give Giuliani or Bratton any credit because "crime went down across the country" is *absolute nonsense*, driven by dislike of Giuliani and not wanting to give *him* credit. Ultimately *the mayor* is responsible; the mayor hired Bill Bratton. If Bratton had failed as a police commissioner, then Giuliani would have been blamed for it. If Bratton succeeds, then you should give Rudy Giuliani the credit for it.

The Post-Bratton NYPD

Albert O'Leary   The cops admire Bratton a great deal. He brought a lot of pride and resources. He would ask you to do something, to go beyond what was required and then he would praise you for it, reward you, get you something you needed. He got the Transit Police 9 millimeters [pistols], which was the first time that we were ever envied in this town by other cops because he led the way in the area of equipment. But I don't think you can say the same about Howard Safir or about Bernie Kerik. John Timoney called Safir a lightweight and the entire rank-and-file believed he *was* a lightweight. Anybody who worked for Giuliani—even our *own*, even Bernie Kerik, who was a detective and who was very well-liked and had a very good working relationship with the PBA [Police Benevolent Association]—was viewed as one of Giuliani's marionettes. That's the way Giuliani *was*: he was a figure that would not tolerate somebody being "off message," as he called it.

Eric Adams   Bratton brought a level of leadership. In the climate that he created, we would not have had a person sodomized in the Seven-O Precinct and we would not have had some of the feelings that engulfed the city under Giuliani in the law enforcement area. Would you have had shootings? Yes; throughout the history of law enforcement there have been accidental discharges. But it was the level of distrust that turned those incidents into a level of mass protest. You were missing the person at One Police Plaza that took proactive steps to ensure that justice would prevail.

The Reverend Al Sharpton If Bratton had been there, he would have set a different tone. Even though he did not question Giuliani's policy, the tone Bratton set was that the police community is not going to get away with barbaric and over-the-line actions. I don't always agree with Bratton, but he had standards and the police knew it.

PART VI

Three Tragic Incidents: The Issue of Excessive Force by the NYPD

Chapter 12

LOUIMA

*I think brutality happens, but in
the late 1990s it's an aberration.*

—Rudy Giuliani, quoted in *Newsweek* magazine, April 5, 1999

In the early morning hours of Saturday, August 9, 1997, a melee occurred outside Club Rendezvous, a Flatbush, Brooklyn, watering hole frequented by members of the city's Haitian immigrant community. In the process of breaking it up, Police Officer Justin Volpe was pushed to the ground and kicked in the head. Angered, he grabbed Abner Louima, a thirty-year-old bystander, arrested him for assault and disorderly conduct, and with three other officers—Thomas Bruder, Charles Schwarz, and Thomas Wiese— took him in a squad car to the 70th Precinct. The rest is history. What took place in the precinct's bathroom that morning would come to be regarded as one of the most notorious episodes of police brutality ever to be recorded in New York City.

Edward Reuss Did the mayor create the climate for this to happen? It could have happened under anyone's administration. If this is a police thing, it would have been happening all over the place—if you're talking about a police force with forty thousand members, you'll get an incident like this. I'm active with a retirees' group and I know detectives who've been around a long time. They were amazed; they never believed that the officer who was accused, who had committed the act with the broom, had done it, because over the years, the worst incident was that someone was thrown off a rooftop or beaten savagely—these are accusations; I'm not saying that they're true. But something like this was such an extreme aberration. When he [Volpe] finally admitted it, they couldn't believe it.

The Reverend Al Sharpton　There was a tone. And the fact that something so vicious could be done by somebody like Justin Volpe in a *police station* with *other officers* there has to give you [an idea of] the mentality that the police must have had at that time, that they could get away with it. You're not just talking about a psychotic guy that brought him down under the railroad tracks in the dark, by the Belt Parkway; he did this *in the precinct* and no one turned him in, no one stopped him, no one made a *move*. And that's *frightening*.

Stephen C. Worth　I've spent almost my entire thirty-year career in criminal justice and this is a *complete* aberration. Do cops punch guys from time to time? Sure they do. But this sodomy thing is off the charts. In my experience, it's that much of an aberration. And I find it offensive that the government would allege that two people did this. If one cop was crazy enough, as Volpe was, to want to do this, and he goes to any other cop and says, Look, I want to sodomize this Haitian with a stick; give me a hand, virtually every cop I ever met would say, No thanks; you're on your own. On ten levels of fairness, compassion, it being repulsive, any other cop would say: You want to do *what*? You're on your own; I want no part of this.

The Street Altercation That Precipitated the Bathroom Assault

Robert Volpe, captain, New York City Police Department (retired); father of Police Officer Justin Volpe　Justin arrived on the scene that night to save a man's life; that's how the call came over. He was the first one on the scene because nobody liked the sergeant who was calling for help, which in itself was sad, that you put your personal opinion before duty. I brought my son up to not be a victim and to help people, and he put duty before his personal feelings for this man and helped him. In the process of doing that, Justin was assaulted. There was no innocence on the street that night—this is Mr. Louima's testimony, not mine. That night started off by someone's doing the right thing. Then the good guy became the bad guy because he retaliated, which you're not supposed to do. Justin found himself alone and it took twenty minutes—that is the court testimony of others, not my son—before he found a friendly face. In the meantime, they were yelling, "Kill the pig!"

An off-duty corrections officer there was flashing a badge and my son knew that his sergeant, who went by the book, would have had that man arrested for being drunk and disorderly. The guy takes his gun out and my son sees it. Now, if he had shot him at that point, he would have been covered. My son sees him pass the gun to his brother and he could have locked both of them up because now you have an unlicensed man in possession of a gun; you could lock him up for passing a weapon while being intoxicated. My son said, Get the fuck out of here! What Mr. Louima saw was a young cop trying to be compassionate and understanding and forgiving, maybe when he shouldn't have been, and Mr. Louima started yelling, "We won't be treated like that." Oh, excuse me! If you were in Haiti and you pulled that, you would have been executed on the spot. My son would never have arrested Mr. Louima, except for the exchange of punches. The next morning, he was going on vacation with his [then] fiancée, Susie, who, coincidentally, was a woman of color. Their biggest decision was whether to get on their Harley-Davidson or drive in his car across country, something she had never done. You can ask any police officer: the last thing they want to do is make an arrest [on the eve of a vacation].

Stephen C. Worth   Quite frankly, at this point in history, whether it was actually Abner Louima who punched Justin Volpe or Abner Louima's cousin who punched him doesn't really matter. Volpe to this day insists that it was Louima himself, but my view is that it's a minor detail of the case.

Was the Assault an Aberration?

Alan Vinegrad   Justin Volpe mistakenly believed that Abner Louima had punched him in the head, knocking him to the ground. Without that precipitating event, would this have happened the next week, to some other person that Justin Volpe had some interaction with? You'd have to get into the psychology of Justin Volpe to know that.

Stephen C. Worth   The reason that Volpe got to that [point]—this is my opinion; he's not my client, so he didn't confide in me—was that he was on steroids and it came out of 'roid rage. I understood this case a lot better the day I visited the Seven-O Precinct. It's a shambles and should have been condemned when *La Guardia* was mayor. Next door is what used to be its garage and they've turned it into a gym. After I looked around the precinct, I went next door to the gym. It has mirrors everywhere, brand-new gray carpet, chrome free weights, and Nautilus equipment. And there were many, many young men there with thick necks and built-up biceps, asking one another, How much do you bench? How much do you lift? There's a whole culture of bodybuilding that I think Volpe was part of and part of that culture is steroid use.

Sanford Rubenstein   It was not just Volpe; *four* police officers were involved. The fact that this happened in a police precinct house bathroom was demonstrative of the fact that the police at that time believed they could do whatever they wanted to do with *impunity*. I think that exemplifies the mentality that existed at the time.

Learning of the Assault

Robert Volpe   You prepare yourself for the knock on the door, but not *this kind of knock*; it's totally something you're not prepared for. My son came home that morning and I was waiting for him, like I did every night. People said, "You have two sons on different shifts now, so when do you sleep?" If I wasn't a parent who was deep undercover—I worked the streets—it would have meant nothing to me. But I knew how dangerous the streets were. That morning, he was going to get in a couple of hours of sleep and he and Susie were going to get cleaned up and get on the bike. When he walks in, I go to hug him as I always did—we always give each other a bear hug—and he pulls back. I say, "What's the matter?" And he says, "Pop, I'm sorry." I look at the side of his head and it's all swollen. I say, "What happened?" He says, "Pop, don't even *ask* me. Last night, this stupid . . ." And he goes on to say what took place. "It's just stupidity." And he wasn't just talking about what happened to him; he was talking about the conduct of other people, including officers. He said, "I got blindsided. I went down; they sent me to the hospital. I can't even frigging think; my head is all screwed up." Then he went to sleep. He never went on vacation. When he got up, we were having a gathering of fifty people because someone was leaving and I threw a party for them. And as people are coming in, the news is breaking on television and he's sitting there. I'm looking [at the television screen] and all of a sudden I see my son's face. I said, "What's *that*?" And he said something as if nothing had happened. And I said, "Did anything happen?" My son has always been so brutally honest—you know, kids come home and you say, "Where were you?" and they tell you and you'd wish they *hadn't*—but he was brutally honest; he didn't know any other way. He said,

"Nothing happened. That's the guy that hit me; that's the guy I was in a fight with. Yeah, I punched him, but, you know . . ." Now the psychologists all say he *blanked* it. Children who are abused as children blank that; I know people who have survived the Trade Center—some of them are basket cases. They were never *there*. They *blanked* it.

Alan Vinegrad   At the time, I was the deputy chief of the Criminal Division of the U.S. Attorney's Office in Brooklyn, the number two person in the division of all the criminal prosecutors at the office. I was home, recovering from a tonsillectomy, when on Thursday, August 14, 1997, I first read the name Abner Louima in the *New York Times*. My initial reaction was disbelief. Not that I didn't believe what he was claiming, but I couldn't believe that something like this could have happened.

Stephen C. Worth   I was in private practice and would do conflict work for the PBA. Years before the Louima case, I had represented Officer Schwarz on a minor matter, something that had happened on St. Patrick's Day. When the Louima matter broke, the PBA's counsel got a number of outside lawyers to represent the cops and I was assigned to Chuck Schwarz. In fact, before we formed this partnership, my present partner, Stu [Stuart] London, was assigned to represent Tom Bruder. I had the same reaction most people did—utter disbelief. I certainly knew that it was not in Chuck Schwarz's character because I knew him pretty well. And once I talked to him, I was even surer that this was just utterly out of character.

The Reverend Al Sharpton   I was called by Abner's cousin [Harold Nicolas]. Then Mike McAlary, who was at the time a columnist for the *New York Daily News*, since deceased, who was no political ally, calls me at home and we talk about how this young man is lying there, handcuffed, in this condition. And he says, "Coney Island Hospital is not making a big deal, but it's *real*; you should *go*." And I went.

Sanford Rubenstein   I had represented a cousin of Louima's in the past, in an auto accident case. I got a call in the office—it may have been the day after it happened—explaining the circumstances. Having gotten that call, I sent one of the young lawyers in the office to the hospital to meet with him. Subsequently, I got a call to meet with his uncle at the church he pastors. I met with him and a day or two later, I got a call saying "Mr. Louima would like to retain you. Would you please go to the hospital to meet with him?" I met with him and he retained me.

Visiting Abner Louima at the Hospital

The Reverend Al Sharpton   When I got to the hospital and stepped out of the car, this lady fell into my arms and started crying. I later found out it was his wife. I've been in a lot of situations where I had to deal with family, and my first reaction, having heard all these horror stories from McAlary, was to try to comfort her. It was a human reaction. We finally got inside, but it was a little eerie for me because this was the same hospital I went to when I was stabbed [in the chest in 1991, during a protest rally in Brooklyn], and it was literally the first time I had gone back to Coney Island Hospital since that night. There was the controversy about whether or not we were going to see Louima because he was in custody and he was not supposed to be visited. I was not being naive enough to think that if someone like me went to the hospital—especially since I'm a candidate for mayor at the time—that they didn't call downtown to One Police Plaza. And One Police Plaza might have checked with City Hall before they would have said yea or nay. I had stood outside and held a press conference before I entered the building. They had more than enough time to have run that up the pole. Then the lawyer at the time—this was pre Johnnie Cochran's involvement—Carl [W.] Thomas, said that I was to be allowed in as his minister, so that's how they got around the rule because they couldn't deny him a ministerial visit, even in custody—just like they couldn't deny him a legal proceeding. They had no choice because they couldn't explain to the media how they had denied him a ministerial visit.

When I was finally brought into the room and saw him lying in such a pathetic position, *and handcuffed,* I was outraged. At the same time, I wanted to be disciplined: I didn't want to ask him any questions because the police were right there; I didn't ask him anything that they could later use against him, saying, "Well, you said this in the hospital." So I basically asked about his health and I told him there were a lot of people who were going to come out and support him. Then we prayed and I left. But I was determined, standing at his bedside, that we were going to do whatever we had to do to bring this case front and center.

Sanford Rubenstein   He was in intensive care. At that point his focus was to get better physically and to recover. Remember, they had to do emergency surgery and he had a colostomy bag. He knew who I was; he knew that his uncle had spoken with him about me and he wanted to meet me. He is a very bright, articulate man, extraordinarily strong physically and mentally. We spoke for a relatively short period of time, but he asked a bit about me. I had handled another police brutality case years before, [that of] Jacques Camille [a Haitian taxi driver shot to death by the NYPD in 1992], and I mentioned that case and that I was very well-known in the Haitian community: I had been back and forth to Haiti many times. I was involved in the Democracy for Haiti Movement; I had met [Jean-Bertrand] Aristide when he came to New York before the coup and I led demonstrations in the city with the consul general of Haiti after the coup. I had been involved in the election of Aristide to the extent of going with a group of Haitian Americans to Washington with Congressman [Benjamin] Gilman [R-NY], who was on the Foreign Relations Committee. And ever since the '70s, when the big influx of Haitians came into Brooklyn, I had represented Haitians. I had a storefront in Bed-Stuy [Bedford-Stuyvesant] in close proximity to where they live.

Mayor Giuliani Visits and Intervenes on Louima's Behalf

Sanford Rubenstein His uncle asked, when Giuliani came to visit with Louima in the hospital, if the handcuffs could be taken off and Giuliani had the handcuffs removed.

The Reverend Al Sharpton If McAlary hadn't broken the story, I don't think Giuliani would have done anything, but he had a mainstream columnist, a police reporter, talking about it. At the end of the day, he didn't do a whole lot other than not doing a lot of hostile things. And that had as much to do with the fact that it was an election year than anything else.

Robert Volpe There's something nobody knows about. I got this from very good sources. Before Giuliani walked in that night to see Mr. Louima, his security man, a boss in the Police Department, went into his room and, *allegedly*, when he walked in, the so-called victim and the "Dream Team" and Al Sharpton were all sitting there, laughing it up. He announced that he was with the mayor. Thirty seconds later, the mayor walks in and the whole scene is different. The individual who first told the story got afraid because it proved too big to repeat. I'm sure he was told, "Shut your mouth; you can take a lot more down with that." Why would someone come forward with that information and then go back on it? There were so many unanswered questions.

On Thursday, August 14, five days after the attack on Mr. Louima, Mayor Giuliani and Police Commissioner Safir held a press conference during which they announced a massive shakeup at the 70th Precinct. The mayor also said that any officer who failed to come forward with information about what had taken place in the precinct's bathroom would be dismissed from the NYPD.

Stephen C. Worth   Giuliani and Safir were saying, These guys are criminals; they're going to be punished. Giuliani completely backed away from the police in this case. But in his defense, the medical evidence that it had happened was overwhelming. I took Chuck Schwarz on *60 Minutes* two weeks later and they asked him, Do you think it happened? And he said yes. And then they said, Did you do it? And he said no. But there was no denying that it had happened; the medical evidence was compelling. The man had nine-inch injuries inside him; that didn't happen from anything other than exactly what he claimed.

"It's Giuliani Time!"

At the very moment the mayor was speaking to the media, Abner Louima was telling television correspondents gathered at his bedside that at one point during the assault, Volpe had yelled, "Stupid nigger. . . . This is Giuliani time. It is not Dinkins time."

Alan Vinegrad   Just to clarify, the allegation was that one or more officers had made that statement to Mr. Louima when he was being assaulted in front of the Club Rendezvous when he was initially apprehended, not in the bathroom. The evidence was that there were certain individuals who befriended, or attended to, Mr. Louima in the initial days when he was at Coney Island Hospital. One was a nurse who had a husband and he had a brother, so there were people in that family looking out for him, and the evidence was that one of those gentlemen came to Mr. Louima shortly before he gave his televised press conference and suggested that in order for people to take what he was saying seriously and so that the authorities would pay attention to this case, he make that statement. Mr. Louima, I believe, testified to that at a number of the trials that followed.

Stephen C. Worth   It was clearly fed to him by someone who knows something about sound bites and journalism, and knows that that's going to give it a theme and get it picked up, which it did. It was a very fluid time in this case. Mike McAlary is writing for the [*New York*] *Daily News* and it's getting a lot of play, but the rest of the media is trying to figure out how big a story this is. It was still the early days of community activists managing stories—something they honed much better when they did Diallo—but it was learning how to manipulate the media to spin the story.

Sanford Rubenstein   What's significant is the fact that Mr. Louima used the statement early on and that the person who told him to do it knew that statement would resonate with the public with regard to the Giuliani administration. The fact that it was made with the *perception* that it would resonate is significant. That the suggestion was made that such a statement *should* be made to call attention to the case is an example of the polarization that existed in the city at that time.

Robert Volpe   When they said that my son said that, they brought the mayor into it and they made my son the bad guy for threatening his career and his future. The man was not going to stand for that and he gave a knee-jerk reaction: find out if it's true. If that statement *hadn't* been made, Mayor Giuliani would have kept a cool head. But he got frazzled. And they counted on that happening—they *played* him. He should be angry at the people who played him with that lie. And nobody's ever been held responsible for it.

The Reverend Al Sharpton   The fact that someone would feel the slogan would be believed told me the times we were living through—that people wouldn't come up with something unless they thought it would resonate. I think it was suggested by one of his cousins because they were desperately trying to get somebody to come help them. They had called me; I had not come yet. They were trying to get media and they were trying to go with anything that would resonate, to get help and that was their justification.

Henry Stern   *Sharpton* made this up, just like [he fabricated events] in the Tawana Brawley case. [In 1987, the African American teenager from the upstate New York town of Wappingers Falls claimed that she had been abducted, held for days, and raped by two, and possibly six, men, one of whom, she alleged, had flashed a badge. The Reverend Al Sharpton took her case to the media. Eventually a grand jury declared her account a hoax.] He is a liar and a fraud.

Malcolm Hoenlein   He [Sharpton] is a very complex character. He came to see me many years ago, when I was first part of the JCRC [Jewish Community Relations Council]. People warned me that he tapes everything. He takes this briefcase and puts it on the desk between us. I say, "Excuse me, I can't see you," so he moves it to the side and then, finally, I got him to move it because I knew he was taping me. He wanted me to give him $300 to expose Jesse Jackson because he said he knew that Martin Luther King [Jr.] hated him and that for $300 he could expose him. This guy's a charlatan and a crook. He's brilliant, but he's very dangerous because he is so smart. The fact that he's now mainstreaming and mainlining himself scares me.

Robert Volpe   My son said, "I *didn't do* that. Why would I take responsibility for committing the worst of the crime, but then, when you ask me if I called him a name . . . ?" Some people have pointed out that it wasn't my son [who said it]. At least *that* came out. And Mr. Louima admitted that certain individuals thought it would be a good thing to say. But my son, who at the time was taking the blame for it, caught the wrath of Mr. Giuliani: for the first time in history, Rudy Giuliani did not stand behind a police officer. And he stood behind some police officers who, maybe, he shouldn't have stood behind.

Alan Vinegrad   There's certainly been stuff written about the Seven-O— "The Lords of Flatbush" is a name that has been around. It's the sort of community where the cops had their own rules, even if they weren't the rules of the penal code. It happens on a Saturday morning. The highest-ranking person in the station house is a sergeant [Jeffrey Fallon] who, by all public accounts, was good, conscientious, well-meaning, and diligent, not somebody who would have closed his eyes or covered his ears and winked or nodded and allowed this to happen. That's not the evidence I'm familiar with. Could it have happened somewhere else? It's possible it could have. Was it more likely to happen there because of the culture of the place, or just the circumstances in terms of who was there and *wasn't* there? I suppose that's possible too. It sounds like a bit of a jump. I think commanders would probably want to believe that something like that could never happen in their midst. I'm sure if you had asked Sergeant Fallon that question on August 1, 1997, he would have said, It never would happen in this station house; I'd never *let* it happen.

Sanford Rubenstein   You have two significant factors that existed at the time: the fact that a statement like "It's Giuliani time, not Dinkins time" could and would be used to call attention to such a horrible torture as the torture of Abner Louima and in the minds of those who suggested it and in the mind of Mr. Louima, perhaps, be something they felt would be believable; and, secondly, Giuliani's refusal to meet with Reverend Sharpton as an example of sending a signal of that policy of polarization.

Abner Louima Recants

Alan Vinegrad   The impact of the retraction was plainly a matter of concern to me as a prosecutor: not only had he made that statement, but he, as I recall, testified to it under oath during his videotaped testimony from the hospital for the state grand jury because, as you know, the state filed charges additionally and then the federal government came in with charges of its own. Mr. Louima was probably *the* most important witness in the case and he was basically admitting that he had committed perjury in the events relating to his initial assault and leading up to the sexual assault.

Robert Volpe   In any other court of the land, that witness would no longer be credible; if anybody for the defense had made a mistake like that, it would have been called perjury.

The Reverend Al Sharpton   Johnnie Cochran convened a meeting at the law offices of Barry Scheck and his colleague Peter Neufeld. I was there. They said they had come to know that the statement was not true and they didn't know what to do about it. A couple of the lawyers were just like: This is going to destroy the case, Abner Louima having to *lie*. And I came up with a strategy. I said, "I'll tell you what we'll do." Abner had a cousin who pastored this major Haitian church in Brooklyn. "Tell your cousin that we're coming to church this Sunday and I'm going to be a guest preacher and I'll preach tomorrow's sermon and you're going to admit to the congregation what you did and ask for their forgiveness and tell them you're not lying about what happened—obviously the medical records tell what happened—but you said something that didn't happen." And we did. They invited the press and Abner stood in front of the congregation and we all prayed for strength and he admitted he was wrong. It was one of those moments that could have turned the case either way. Fortunately, we got to them.

Robert Volpe   The lawyers were all excited. They said, "The guy's lied about everything he's said; he made up the thing about Giuliani and made out that his teeth were knocked out." Now, if a woman with child was assaulted and something terrible happened to them and she added, "And he also stole my candy," you'd say something is either very truthful or a big lie. Now, when that part turns out to be an *admitted* lie by the person who said it, you start doubting everything. I look back at it all now and I think that even though Mr. Louima is a multimillionaire today as a result of it [due to an $8.75 million settlement from the city], he was used, as well as my son was used.

The Public Demands Justice

On August 29, 1997, a huge march for justice for Abner Louima took place in Brooklyn.

Sanford Rubenstein   It was clear that the way that the city was polarized, the perception in the black and Hispanic community was: we have to demonstrate to stop this because if we don't, no one else is going to. That, I believe, was one of the reasons for the massive demonstration in the Louima case. It was at City Hall Park and the police said we had forty or fifty thousand but there had to be a hundred thousand people: when you stood at that podium to speak and you looked down, past City Hall, down Broadway, it was filled with humanity as far as you could see.

One of the most interesting conversations I had then was with a high-powered black executive—I'm not going to mention his name; he is extraordinarily successful financially and professionally—and he said to me, "You know, when my teenaged kid goes out in the street at night, they don't know he's *my* son; they could sodomize him like Louima. I'm demonstrating because I really believe that if we *don't* demonstrate, no one is going to stand up against what's happening in this city." And that was very telling to me, *very* telling.

Herman Badillo   Sharpton was successful because of the media. For example, for about three months he had a daily press conference in front of police headquarters and he always was good for a sound bite. And he had prominent people, like Percy Sutton and and Freddie [Ferrer], who agreed to be arrested and that, of course, made a good sound bite every day. But nobody seemed to mention those placards that were there *every single day*. And that, I thought, was absolutely outrageous—and inexcusable.

Sanford Rubenstein   I had never met the Reverend Sharpton; I had only known what I had read about him. Early on in the case, there was a question raised during a *Larry King Live* interview [on the cable channel CNN] with Reverend Sharpton and the police commissioner [Howard Safir]. Larry King was baiting Reverend Sharpton to go after me, the new white lawyer in the case, and Reverend Sharpton said, "You mean Brother Rubenstein?" He knew [of] my involvement, not only in the Haitian community, but also in terms of the respect the Brooklyn political establishment, which was black at the time—it *is* black—had for me. A friend of mine called me and told me about that. So at the big march for justice for Louima when I saw him, I walked over to him and said, "Reverend Sharpton, I'd like to introduce myself . . ." And he said, "Ah, *Brother Rubenstein*" and we linked arms and led the demonstration. We spent about three or four hours together and developed a relationship to the extent that I'm now his personal attorney. And I've traveled all over the world with him.

As Abner Louima began his slow and painful physical recovery, the assault charge against him that had brought him to the 70th Precinct early that August morning was dropped.

Sanford Rubenstein   Ultimately, it was dropped by the Kings County district attorney, [Charles J.] Joe Hynes. Obviously, in the eyes of the public—the community which demonstrated for justice for Louima— those niceties weren't enough to make up for the status of race relations in the city at the time, and the fact that police officers believed they could do to Louima what they did with impunity.

Going on the Offensive to Redeem a Tarnished Image

Sanford Rubenstein   There were allegations early on that Louima was a homosexual and that this [Officer Volpe's assault] had happened because of a homosexual act. It was almost like he was being raped *again*, with these horrible allegations coming out of the woodwork and whispered, perhaps, by defense counsel to the press. Of course, as a lawyer, you deny the allegations, but simply saying, "He's *not* a homosexual" is not enough; you have to show the man for what he is and I knew he *wasn't*. We put his wife on a show, one of the very few appearances she made—it may have been *20/20*—and the question was asked directly of her: "What about these allegations about your husband being a homosexual?" And her spontaneous response was: "*Look* at me! *Look* at me! How can he be a *homosexual*?" By putting the wife on, and his children, I also made an intense effort to make sure the press knew that we were working to get his daughter here from Haiti—he had had her in Haiti by a woman he had been with before he married his wife here—but it was tied up in red tape. Congressman [Edolphus] Towns [D-NY, who represented a district in Brooklyn, New York] helped us break through that red tape, and the child came here. To me it was important, not just for a human interest story, that his daughter finally got here from Haiti—she had every right to be here by the laws that existed at the time. But for me it was more than just that; it was subtly showing that the man was a *family* man, that the man had children, had a wife who said, "*Look* at me! *Look* at me! How can he be . . . ?" All these things went to demonstrate how blatantly false this homosexual story was.

Making Volpe's Prosecution a Federal Case

Stephen C. Worth   The Brooklyn D.A.'s Office had the case first. Usually what happens in that situation is that the federal government decides that they want to exercise jurisdiction. The federal penalties are more serious and more onerous for denial of civil rights by this kind of force and, also, the rules of evidence are more relaxed in federal court than they are in state court. The feds took it over for those two reasons and also because there was this great hue and cry that the state prosecutors worked too closely with police officers and they would tend to protect them. Zachary Carter, who was the U.S. attorney at the time, happened to be black, and many community leaders felt that he would give this all a fairer shot than Joe Hynes.

Robert Volpe   I received a call from a friend in the media who said, "Bob, this is your *son*! Get him out of the country. Whether he's guilty or innocent, he's going to prison. You don't understand what's happening. Janet Reno is going to come out and make a statement." I said, "*Janet*

Reno? Why?" And they said, "She's going to make an example of your son; Charlie Hynes is not taking the case." Charlie Hynes would have fought tooth and nail for this case, but I was told, "Chuck Hynes is going to make a run for governor." I said, "Wait, my son got in trouble. What does this have to do with Janet Reno?" What do I have to do with Janet Reno? My son went to work the other night and all of a sudden, my family is national news. Something was *wrong*. The FBI was trying to get a foothold in local law enforcement across the country. If they could get it in New York, they'd have it in the whole country—federal overseers. And if that doesn't sound ominous, *it should*. It's a terrible, terrible thing. Our Constitution, our Founding Fathers were smart enough to realize we should not have that kind of overseer. But this case was going to be *it*. That's why Janet Reno got involved. I'm not blaming each and every [FBI] agent, because they go where they're *told* to go by the attorney general and by the director. But *three hundred* FBI agents in New York City? Our demise was being planned. And, as an American, I say what a waste of resources!

Alan Vinegrad   I got involved in the case after the charges were brought, right around the time that the date was set for the first trial. We had actually picked the jury for what was going to be the fifth trial and I participated in all of the trials. I absolutely did not know I would be involved in the case. I had actually left the U.S. Attorney's Office about two months after that [first reading of the assault on Mr. Louima], in October of 1997, to go into private practice and was not involved in the initial stages of the investigation of the case at all. About a year later, I returned to the U.S. Attorney's Office for my second stint there in the capacity of the chief of the Criminal Division.

The most difficult case you can bring is against people from an organization with whom you actually *work*, collectively and jointly, on many of your other cases—it's uncomfortable; it's a strain. And it's a more difficult case to prove because juries don't want to believe that the people who are sworn to protect them could betray the oath of their office and the trust that we repose in them in the egregious way that happened in this case. There were charges involving perjury and obstruction of justice in this case. People don't want to believe that sworn police officers engage in that kind of conduct. You treat a case like that with the highest degree of attention and importance and significance that you can, because it's so obviously important and significant for a whole variety of reasons, not just what happened and the public attention that's being paid.

Robert Volpe   Mr. Vinegrad, in all his theatrics, told Mr. [Robert] Draper [who interviewed Robert Volpe for an article that appeared in *GQ—Gentlemen's Quarterly*] that it was just another case to him. This was another case to him like breathing your next breath! This was his *career*. He had left the prosecutor's office, gone into private practice, miserably failed, and had to return, which I don't demean a man for. But then you don't come back with a vengeance and build your future on another man's demise. It should never have been a federal case; there was nothing *federal* about it. And there was not *one word* of a civil rights violation mentioned, or racism. It just took a life of its own. And, sadly, so many other things were going on. Now we all understand August: it's the driest month for media. I've been involved with the media—fifteen hundred articles have been done about me and my career and I have close friends in the media —so I have no ax to grind there. But I also understand that August is the slowest month and that they were fighting for a story. The story that was going to be headlined the next day was also a sad one, because another man's career was going to be made public, Mr. Giuliani's. His scandal [the allegation, published by *Vanity Fair*, that he had conducted an adulterous relationship with Cristyne Lategano] was about to break that day.

The Trials

There were four trials as well as a fifth scheduled proceeding that would not take place. The initial trial involved two incidents: the assault on Patrick Antoine several blocks from Club Rendezvous by Officer Volpe in the course of his pursuit of the person who had punched him, and the sodomizing of Mr. Louima in the bathroom of the 70th Precinct. There was also a charge against Sergeant Michael Bellomo, who was supervising the police officers on the street that morning that he had covered up the attack on Mr. Louima in the squad car. Officer Bellomo would be acquitted.

Justin Volpe was represented by Marvyn Kornberg, who in his questioning of Mr. Louima and another officer, Eric Turetsky, attempted to sow confusion by implying that Officer Schwarz had been the second man in the bathroom.

Volpe Stuns the Court by Pleading Guilty Midtrial

Alan Vinegrad   One of the more memorable parts of that trial was that Justin Volpe ended up pleading guilty in the middle of the trial, after we had presented a number of witnesses against him. One of the more dramatic ones was the sergeant to whom Volpe had confessed what he had done several hours after the assault. From all appearances, Justin Volpe did not anticipate that this gentleman would actually be a witness and I think it came as somewhat of a surprise to him and, certainly, to his lawyer, gauging from the reaction in the court at the time that that man testified.

Robert Volpe   My son and I were making eye contact during the whole trial and we knew who was lying, who was rehearsed in testimony, and who was just confused. Then Patrick Antoine says something and I watch my son's body language change—I can't talk to him; he's sitting in the courtroom—I see his whole demeanor change. He almost melts in the chair, but he looks relieved. We get a break after that and he says to me, "He was telling the truth." I said, "*Who?*" And he said, "The fellow about the cross and God, and all." I said, "Yeah?" He said, "Why would I say that if nothing happened?" Now, it hits him—it's his moment of reality. Right after Mr. Louima was taken to the bathroom, Patrick Antoine asked to be taken—this is after the alleged assault. My son comes out and takes him, which tells me already that something isn't right—he's blanked whatever took place; he takes the next man in. Patrick Antoine is wearing a cross. My son looks at Antoine and says to him, "Do you believe in Jesus Christ?" Patrick Antoine says, "Yes, I do." And my son says, "So do I. I think I've lost my mind." This is what Antoine is saying from the stand. You're trying to prosecute a guy but this whole thing doesn't fit. Well, they've got to pass that real quick. But my son comes to me and says, "Those are my words. I said that. Why would I say that if nothing happened?" And that was the turning point. He said that to the attorneys and they said, "What do you mean, 'something happened?'" And he pled guilty the next day.

Alan Vinegrad   Volpe just threw in the towel, which is very rare. It happens before trial sometimes, maybe even the *morning* of the trial, but not three weeks into the testimony. Volpe, without any plea deal or agreement with the government, just admitted all of the charges against him.

Robert Volpe   When my son took responsibility, I was one of the first to say, "You'll pay for this; you'll go to prison." We understood what was taking place. This was a modern-day lynching: guilt or innocence had nothing to do with it. My son would be in federal prison even if he hadn't been there that night and if he *was* innocent. And I'm not saying he is. My son is probably the first police officer to stand up and say, "Yes, I did it and I'll

take my punishment." The police got angry at him because he took responsibility. No cop ever owns up to anything—no cop ever committed a crime;
they're all innocent! And my son is hated by the feds and by the prosecutors because he came forward and told the truth. It sounds crazy: they
didn't want him to plead; they wanted this to go on and on because a lot
more careers would have been built. He didn't ask for leniency because he
wasn't going to get any. He ended it because he saw what was taking place:
too many people were building careers on lies.

Eric Adams   The system threw Volpe to the wolves when they found out
how foolish he was to *get caught* doing the act. Volpe was not penalized so
much because he sodomized Louima; he was foolish to have left the stick,
the evidence, there and get caught, to not have successfully covered his
tracks. *That's* what he was being punished for.

Robert Volpe   We knew he was going to get thirty years. From day one he
was told, We're going to make an example of you; we're going to send a
message of what we're going to do to you. And it worked. And justice was
not served. He would have been coming home now [in July 2005] if he had
served a fair sentence. Let us not forget that in America you get eight and
a half years for *murder*. And I'm not talking about a friendly murder; I'm
talking about premeditated murder. And for rape it's only five years
because it's only a *woman*; for child molestation it's two and a half years,
because it's only a *child*.

Alan Vinegrad   The whole set of specific rules that until January of this
year [2005] were actually binding on judges are not binding now anymore;
they just have to consult them. But at the time, there were these specific
rules for how you calculate a sentence and the judge had limited power to
vary from those rules. And one of the factors in that case that specifically
served to increase the sentence he faced was that he was a police officer
and the abuse of trust inherent in that, the fact that the victim was vulnerable, that he was restrained when the offense took place, all those things
actually did serve to take a serious crime in its own right and make it even
more so in the eyes of the sentencing law.

Robert Volpe   When court ended that day, my son looked at me, I looked
at him, and we smiled—a personal smile. The prosecutors then filed out
to meet the press. One of them, Kenneth Thompson, stopped, made eye
contact with me, embraced me, and said, "I'm sorry." And I said, "You did

your job." Another prosecutor, Mr. Vinegrad, filed out. And if he could have vanished at that moment, he would have, because he could not make eye contact. Somebody has to be the executioner—maybe that's why in the old days they used to wear black hoods over their heads, so we didn't see them grinning—or *crying*, because we're human. My son has gotten thirty years and Vinegrad knows his father is in the courtroom and he says, "I will take joy in knowing that each day of your productive life will be spent behind bars." When a federal prosecutor takes joy in saying, "I will take joy in knowing that each day of your productive life will be spent behind bars!" OTB—"Out with the Bastards"—because you know what? They will all meet their demise, because there is a bigger force. Oh, they'll be applauded here on Earth and they'll get elected to higher office and they'll make fortunes. But it's bigger than that: my son smiles when I go to see him and he says, "So what's thirty years if you compare it to eternity, Pop?" He's not magnanimous about it; he's a realist. And when I look at him, he's in there with 2.5 million other Americans.

Sanford Rubenstein   Alan Vinegrad did his job and did it well. He is, perhaps, more than anyone else in that case, the unsung hero of justice to Abner Louima.

The second trial concerned a charge of conspiracy to obstruct justice based on the allegation that Officers Schwarz, Bruder, and Wiese had conspired to provide false information to the federal grand jury concerning whether Schwarz had participated in the bathroom assault. All three defendants were convicted. The verdicts would be overturned by the court of appeals. Even though the jury found that there was enough evidence to convict, as a matter of law, there was insufficient evidence to do so.

The third trial was of two members of the Street Crime Unit who were in the 70th Precinct on the morning of the assault and were charged with lying about what they observed immediately following the assault on Mr. Louima. The evidence was that immediately after the assault, Officer Volpe removed Mr. Louima to a cell next door to the bathroom and the allegation was that the officers denied that it was Volpe who had done that. Officer Volpe stated, however, that it *was* he who had brought the victim, half-naked, into the cell. One of the two officers pled guilty before trial while the other one went to trial and was convicted.

The fourth trial, which took place during the summer of 2002, was of Officer Schwarz on assault and perjury charges. Previously, the court of appeals had reversed all convictions stemming from the second trial on the grounds of insufficient evidence as well as Officer Schwarz's conviction from the first trial for having participated in the bathroom assault, on the ground that Mr. Worth had had a conflict of interest in representing Mr. Schwarz as his fee had been paid by the PBA. The court of appeals maintained that despite the fact that Officer Schwarz had waived that right before the trial judge, saying "I know there's an issue here, but I waive it" that right could *not* be waived, as any rational person in his position would not do such a thing. The appeal would be argued for several hours yet not one question would be asked concerning that ground. The assault charges against Officer Schwarz were retried. A new indictment was obtained charging him with perjury for lying under oath in his own defense at the second trial—the conspiracy to obstruct justice trial. While Officer Schwarz was convicted of perjury, the jury hung, reportedly ten to two, for conviction on the assault and conspiracy to assault charge.

Did Al Sharpton Play a Central Role in the Trials?

Alan Vinegrad   It's impossible to say. The trials were really focused on the evidence. There were some fleeting references to Mr. Sharpton at one or more of the trials, particularly during the cross-examination of Abner Louima. But in terms of the evidence of the trial, he played an extremely small role. I can't possibly say whether the outcome would have been different had he not been involved and hadn't brought so much public attention to it. I would tend to think *not*. I can't fault Al Sharpton for trying to bring attention to the case. I don't endorse every means and method he used to do it, but I think he felt a genuine desire and need to bring the spotlight and attention to what happened here because it was a shocking and horrendous and egregious violation of the man's rights, in one of the most despicable ways that you could think of.

Robert Volpe   Al Sharpton shows up, like he does all the time, but that's what he *does*. You can't get angry at a rattlesnake for striking you; if you cross the path of a bee and you get stung, that's what bees *do*, okay? I'm not mad at *Al Sharpton*. In fact, there was almost dialogue coming because there was a point that he even reached out. I truly believe that if Al Sharpton could, he would reduce my son's sentence because Al Sharpton is not a *bad* man. He's an opportunist—he's *Al Sharpton*! He's a bigger-than-life character. We would watch him on TV talking about my son and Justin and

I would laugh. And we found laughter in him; we never took him seriously because he does what he *does*. He has never had the need to be employed; he lives well, does well, and when he makes mistakes, they're excused. When my son was born maybe he should have gotten a "Get Out of Jail Free" card, too.

The Civil Case

Sanford Rubenstein   Louima was clearly disappointed when the circuit court threw out the convictions of the other police officers in his civil case. We got $8.75 million—the first time in the history of this country that a police union paid damages to a victim of police brutality; we got certain equitable relief in that there's someone [an independent lawyer] the police union [the Police Benevolent Association, the PBA] is paying for, that police officers can go to, a lawyer other than their normal lawyers that do PBA work in cases of police brutality. So, ultimately, if we didn't get full justice in the criminal cases, we certainly got full justice in the civil case. What was interesting was that it was the Giuliani administration that precipitated the resolution of the matter; the ultimate settlement of the case was precipitated by Giuliani's corporation counsel reaching out to me. I had never been in the corporation counsel's office—I had only seen his name on pleadings—and I was invited there and met with him and the head of litigation for the city. They made it clear that they felt this case should be resolved civilly; it was after the criminal case had been decided. Of course, it had to be signed off on not only by Giuliani but also by [City Comptroller Alan] Hevesi. But once the settlement was reached with the corporation counsel and the comptroller's people, everyone signed off on it.

Abner Louima Today

Sanford Rubenstein   One of the reasons Louima made the decision to move to Florida with his family was to be able to be in a new environment; that it was his way of trying to start his life again. Looking back on it, it was a good decision. He's prospered in that environment: he has a lovely family—wonderful children and a good wife—and he's very happy. And there's a large Haitian community down there as well. There's always the risk of adhesions, but he has been doing well physically and he's living as normal a life as he can.

Marie Dorismond, sister of Patrick Dorismond, who was shot and killed by undercover narcotics detectives during an attempted drug bust   We've talked and we've seen each other. He's doing very well. He's healed completely. To me, he looks very fine. His family is good, and he's doing a lot of positive things here in Florida, for his country, good positive things. He's trying to reassure kids that not all officers are bad.

———————

Little more than eighteen months into Mayor Giuliani's second term, however, another young black man, Amadou Diallo, would become the victim of excessive police force—this time with a deadly outcome.

Chapter 13

DIALLO

New York is a beacon of hope to millions
around the world and here in America.
New York City has provided generations
of immigrants the opportunity to rise up.

—Rudy Giuliani, in a public comment

Amadou Diallo, a twenty-three-year-old immigrant from the African nation of Guinea, paid his portion of the rent for the apartment at 1157 Wheeler Avenue in the Bronx that he shared with three roommates by selling videotapes and socks from a stall on Fourteenth Street. Shortly after midnight on February 4, 1999, as he stood on the stoop of his building, he caught the attention of four young men—Kenneth Boss, Sean Carroll, Edward McMellon, and Richard Murphy. They were approaching in a car and noticed that Diallo was repeatedly peering up and down the street and then darting in and out of the building's vestibule. The young men were plainclothes members of the NYPD's Street Crime Unit, whose motto was "We Own the Night." Carroll and McMellon jumped out of the car. The officers later claimed that McMellon had flashed a badge and called out, "Sir, please, New York police, we need a word with you." Diallo did not respond, prompting Carroll to call out [reiterating McMellon's request]. At that point, Diallo put a hand into his pocket. McMellon called out again, and as Diallo withdrew an object, Carroll yelled, "Gun!" Then he and McMellon opened fire. As they did so, McMellon tripped and fell backward, causing Boss and Murphy to begin shooting. When the firing subsided, Diallo lay dying in the vestibule, his body riddled with nineteen of the forty-one bullets fired at him. As he writhed in pain, Carroll, removing the object from the young man's hand and realizing that it was his wallet, cried out repeatedly, "Please don't die!" And as Amadou Diallo slipped into unconsciousness, one of the other officers screamed into his radio the police jargon for an ambulance and a supervisor: "Give me a bus and a boss!"

Amadou: The Victim of an Operation
Gone Tragically Wrong

Saikou Diallo, father of Amadou Diallo   Amadou was born in Africa. When we went to Asia—I had my office in Singapore for eighteen and a half years—he was in school in Thailand. Later on, he went to Singapore, to Microsoft, for three years; he has a certificate from Microsoft and a diploma. At Microsoft, there were over fifteen hundred studying—from Australia, Japan, Southeast Asia, and elsewhere. Only Amadou was black. Every day [in Singapore], he used to leave my office and go by himself; he would go to school and he would come back. He used to ride the bus; he used to ride the train and the subway. He never complained—*not one day*. He wished to come here for about two or three years, work hard, and know the system of the country. His goal was to go back to school to complete his university [education] here and he wanted to be certified by Microsoft to work as a computer engineer. He wanted to enroll in the City College [CCNY, the City College of New York, where generations of immigrants have received a low-cost education]. That's why I am now a lifetime member of the City College. We donated a $10,000 scholarship and every year they give the award to an African [for the study of] the criminal justice system who is making 3.0 level.

The Immediate Police Investigation

Saikou Diallo   After they shot and killed my son, they went to his room. His roommates were sleeping. They woke them up and they ransacked the house—they were checking everything to see if they could find any evidence, at all, so that they could say that's why they shot him. They didn't find *anything*. And when they turned his body over, where he was lying, they didn't find any gun, or knife, *nothing*. The only things they found were his pager and his wallet; the pager was inside the wallet.

The Street Crime Unit

Albert O'Leary The theory of the Street Crime Unit was to be out there and to get the guns, because if you get the guns, you reduce robberies and homicides. And you wind up developing a cadre of police officers who can spot somebody carrying a weapon because of the way they walk or certain other actions.

Henry Stern In certain countries when you are stopped and challenged by the police, you are supposed to put your hand in your pocket and pull out your identity papers. That is what Diallo was trying to do. The police shot at Diallo forty-one times not to make sure that he was dead but because they were frightened. The media tried to depict this as the mayor's fault because he was presiding over a city with racial problems.

Stephen C. Worth They weren't ten-year veterans, but they weren't scared, rookie cops: they had made gun collars before—two of them had been in shootouts—without incident. So this was not like, Oh my God! There's a guy with a gun; we've never had this before! A confluence of things has to go wrong for tragedy to strike. You have four cops in a car who didn't normally work together; there was no supervisor in the car, and that unit was sent out there to get guns off the streets. Street crime at that point was a real issue. It might as well have been called "gun patrol" because those guys are out there looking for guys with guns.

There was a question about whether he spoke English or not. Cops come around and hassle vendors all the time and I believe that Amadou Diallo *knew* that they were police. And they felt that he knew they were police. When a guy is not complying, a cop's anxiety level goes way up. He [Diallo] makes a move that one of them feels is threatening and he [the officer] yells "Gun!"—there was an African American female witness who said she heard this—and he shoots because he believes in his heart that there *is* a gun. My guy [McMellon] starts shooting back and falls down. Now the others are *sure* there's a gun and the fusillade begins.

Robert Volpe You had an innocent man going home. But you also had four frightened police officers, young kids from Long Island, who panicked. Because they have a uniform and a gun we hold them to a higher standard. *What* higher standard? We should have greater understanding that they are at great risk and have great opportunity to screw up because they have the responsibility of life and death *every* day.

Eric Adams   I disagree. Some of the officers *are* young—there's a younger Police Department now—but I do not believe that that has anything to do with it. When you look at the history of some of these shootings, the guys weren't young. It's the mind-set that I believe is indoctrinated. It's simple arithmetic: black man in possession of a gun, or what *appears* to be a gun, equals violence. I'll never forget an officer telling me, in a very candid manner, "When I see a white person with a gun, I take precautions for him and myself, because he may be a cop; when I see a black person with a gun, I take precautions for myself." So if I'm off duty, running with a gun, chasing a bad guy and that bad guy happens to be white, then I'm in trouble, because when they see me with the gun in my hand, I'm automatically believed to be a bad guy.

The Reverend Al Sharpton   The Diallo movement got rid of the Street Crimes Unit. Clearly it had almost a cowboy mentality of just ride in and do what you want to do. Whether they were amateurs or veterans, the Street Crime Unit was set up to do exactly what it did and had no concern for civil liberties from the highest levels in this city in terms of the direction they gave to the unit's policemen. To live every day knowing that any spark could be the fire that could lead to your own harm or your own death or that of someone you love and you have no redress—who do you go to if the cops come after you?—and to live in a community where you have to be afraid of the cops *and* the robbers is certainly something I wouldn't wish on anybody.

Lilliam Barrios-Paoli   They don't live in New York City. They don't know minorities from Adam. There's a new category of liability: WWB, "walking while black." They see a big black guy and they're scared. And guess what? They assume things. If you've lived in New York, you *don't* automatically assume that if you see black kids coming towards you, they're going to mug you. But when you have a police force that works in the city but doesn't live in the city, it's a big problem.

Eric Adams   You have a handicap where your only intelligence, or "intel" as they like to say, of a particular group is what you see on TV or what you read in the newspapers. For a substantial number of police who come to the city, their first encounter with black people *in the flesh* will be answering a call. And in many of those calls, they're not seeing various groups at their best—no one is calling the cops when they're having a party; they're calling the cops when there's fighting at the party—so you automatically have a distorted view of the people you're supposed to serve and protect.

Ed Koch   I thought Giuliani handled everything very badly. My own view of the way a mayor should react when there is a charge of police brutality—particularly a killing—is that unless the facts convey something to the contrary, and the advice you get from the police commissioner is very important on the issue, you should be supportive of the cops. Their lives are on the line and if you walk away from them every time a charge of brutality is made—and there are many charges that are just *false*—there will come a point that they will say, Why should we expose ourselves? Why should we take any action if people don't support us?

Saikou Diallo Learns of His Son's Shooting

Saikou Diallo   I first learned about what had happened that same day. At around 4:30 P.M., Vietnam time, my son-in-law, who was here [in New York], called me at my home in Vietnam and said, "They shot Amadou." I said, "Who shot him?" He said, "We don't know. But they shot him and he died on the spot." I was totally demoralized. I said, "Where is he now?" He said, "He's still lying where they shot him because the police put up a blockade, so we cannot reach him, but we gave him every moral affection." In our tradition, Islamic custom, when somebody dies, we have to listen to his last words and we have to convey some benediction. I said, "Okay, let's find out what happened." I was sitting there in so much shock I didn't know what to say or do. He called again and said, "We think that the police shot him." I said, "Why? Is he involved in any criminal activity, or gang?" He said, "No. Amadou is a very nice boy, as *you* know him; he goes from his house to his working place and from his working place to his house. Sometimes we meet on Sunday, or on another occasion, or at a community activity. He was never involved in any criminal activity or gang."

Little by little, people are calling from everywhere. The media had already picked up the news so we were getting feedback all that night, Friday, and I didn't sleep. As a Muslim, you have to go to the Friday prayers and I went. I came back at two o'clock and the telephone was ringing nonstop because the news was all over the world. It looked like the police had shot him—at that time they didn't know how many shots but they saw many casualties on his body.

The Call from Mayor Giuliani

Saikou Diallo   Saturday I received a call from Mayor Giuliani in a telephone conference call through Kyle Watters [an attorney representing the Guinean Association of America], who was supposed to [arrange for] the autopsy and preparation of the body [for burial]. They came over to wash the body on that Friday, to pray over the body and to send [Amadou] back home. Giuliani sympathized and said he would do everything possible to let me come here. He said, "What do you need?" I said, "I need a visa to come to the U.S." He said, "We will assist you all the way and we'll make sure you get the visa." He did not mention the police involvement in Amadou's death.

Enter Al Sharpton

The Reverend Al Sharpton   I was in my office at the House of Justice [the headquarters of the National Action Network, a three-story building located at 125th Street and Madison Avenue, which would later be destroyed by fire] and Moses Stewart, who was on our crisis team—he was the father of Yusuf Hawkins [a young African American man from the East New York section of Brooklyn who during the summer of 1989 had ventured with friends into Bensonhurst, an Italian neighborhood, to look at a used car that had been advertised in a newspaper and was pursued by a gang and shot by a youth named Joey Fama, setting off a spasm of hatred]—told me there was a delegation from Guinea that had come to see me about a young man who had been shot over forty times the night before, in the Bronx. I said, "Moses, are you serious? *Over forty times?* Was he armed? Did he have drugs? This is outrageous, *even for me.* You'd better check." He went back to talk with them. Ironically, a policeman in Community Affairs called me—his name was Jackson; I had known him from all the marches; they'd give them orders about what to do with us—from One Police Plaza and said, "I know you heard about this shooting." I said, "No," because it had not been in the news yet. He said, "I want you to know about this shooting in the Bronx; I want you to know we're on top of it." One Police Plaza never called me under Giuliani: this was the first, and probably the last, call I got from One Police Plaza while Safir was commissioner. I called Moses back into my office and said, "There must be something to this because Jackson just called; it had to be on the order of Safir and they're concerned about this, so let me meet with these people."

They told me what happened. They had a guy that was very close to him and I agreed to go over to Amsterdam Avenue the next morning and hold a press conference with him and demand a full investigation. That's when the story broke. I called at that time for a demonstration at the residence where Amadou was shot. We expected a couple of hundred people, but over a thousand came out in the rain and packed that block.

Sharpton Preempts the Mayor

The Reverend Al Sharpton We hear on the news that Amadou's mother and father are coming in and that the father had talked to Mayor Giuliani. Our fear then was that Giuliani was going to try to get to the family and undercut the movement for justice for Amadou. I'm meeting with Guinean leaders and I'm saying, "Does anybody know the parents? Does anybody know the sister?" Somebody says, "No, and we don't know what they're going to do." I'm in my office, with New York 1 on live, and I see Mrs. Diallo land; she's brought off and the police take her and no one can get to her. They'd just about kidnapped her and we think she's probably going to denounce the demonstrations and Giuliani's going to lead the family against the community. Around four or four thirty that afternoon, a young lady comes up to the office who we call in the community "Mother Blakely" [Delores "Queen Mother" Blakely, a well known, but regarded as eccentric, personality in the African American community of Harlem], and she says, "Mrs. Diallo would like to meet you." I say, "Are you serious?" And she says, "I got to her and I brought some of her country-people and they told her what you've done for her son and we know where Giuliani's put her in a hotel and she would like us to bring you down there."

Sharpton's Meeting with Mrs. Diallo

The Reverend Al Sharpton I got into the car with my driver and rode down to the Stanhope Hotel on Fifth Avenue. There were policemen there. They wouldn't allow me into the hotel and I knew that they were going to alert Downtown [One Police Plaza] that I was there. And this lady [Ms. Blakely] said, "What do you mean, she can't see this gentleman? Mrs. Diallo's not in custody; she wants to see him." So they called upstairs and she said that she did want to see me. They reluctantly let me up to the suite and she told me she had heard from people in her land that I had come to see her and about what we were doing and that her objective was to get justice for her son. I explained to her the politics as easily as I could: that the mayor, in fact, was over the police that had killed her son and had already said that they were innocent, that he was hosting her and that if she did not want to be hosted by him, we would raise the money and provide equivalent quarters for her—and she's in a five-star hotel. She said that she would think about it, and by the end of our conversation, she said, "I'll leave with you." That's when we called one of our business supporters at the National Action Network and got her a suite at the Rihga Royal Hotel and she walked out of the hotel with me. By then the press had gathered that she had left and that Giuliani no longer had control [over] or access to her. When we got over to the other hotel, she told me, "My husband"—he was coming in the next night—"and I are separated and I'm sure the mayor will be trying to get to him." Now we've got the same concern and the same problem all over again. So, once we had her safely settled, we decided I would go to the airport to meet the husband and see if we could explain everything to him.

Saikou Diallo's Arrival at John F. Kennedy International Airport

Saikou Diallo   Giuliani's assistant, Rosemary [O'Keefe], received me at the airport. When the plane landed, they announced: "Mr. Diallo, identify yourself" and they checked me [through immigration and customs] right at the door; everything was very nice. Somebody from the Guinean embassy was outside and he told me, "All the community has waited for you here for over four hours. So has the City of New York. If you go with the city directly to the city, you are deceiving the community."

The Reverend Al Sharpton   We were not allowed into the area where he would have to come into customs. We saw the police there and they were probably going to grab him, as they did her, and shoo him past us. As fate would have it—I would say God—one of the customs officers walks over to Mr. Diallo and says, "Some of your countrymen are outside and would like to talk to you." And the police say, "No, come with us." And he says, "Oh, let me meet my countrymen." We could see, while they were talking—we were on the other side of the door—that he kept looking back and forth. It went on for about ten minutes and we had no idea what was going on.

Saikou Diallo   I told the [city's] delegation that I would not be able to go with them directly, that I must go outside to greet my community. They [the city officials] followed me outside. When I saw the crowd, I told them, "Thank you very much, but I cannot let these people down; they are here, waiting for me. From here we have to go to the crime scene where my son used to live." I took back my luggage from them and I went with the community.

The Reverend Al Sharpton   He walked over to me and hugged me and walked out with me and got into my car. We took him to the Rihga Royal and put him in a suite and that began the whole saga.

Saikou Diallo   Then they lodged me in the Grand Hyatt Hotel. I was there for the first night and then the next day they assisted me go to the Rihga Royal because my ex-wife, Amadou's mother, was there, and they told me it was better to have us in one place. Thursday evening, there were people sitting in the lobby; everybody was showing up for Amadou. I saw the media there and they told me Giuliani was there. He was on television and he said when they asked him why the police killed my son, "The police were doing their job." The right thing to say would have been: We are investigating to see how this incident happened. But he's publicly stating that the police were doing their job—that it's their right to kill.

Visiting Wheeler Avenue

Saikou Diallo   Soon we came to the crime scene, to where Amadou used to live, on Wheeler Avenue. They showed me where he was shot—all these bullets and gunshots on the wall—and people wrote condolences all over the wall. From there, we went with my son-in-law to his house. And we were there until that night, so I didn't make any statement that night to the media.

The Meeting with the Mayor That Didn't Occur

Saikou Diallo   When we were at the Rihga Royal, he sent a message he wanted to come that evening at nine—he already reserved a room there. But every thirty minutes we saw on New York 1 and every other channel that he is backing the police. And the community told us:

He's behind the police; he never tried to investigate how they shot Amadou, so you see everybody is angry. You see all the demonstrators are marching, and people are angry because this is not the first killing here; people have been killed here by the police and there has been no investigation, no judgment, no justice. If Giuliani comes here, the media will take photos of you and his [Amadou's] mother and you'll shake hands with Giuliani, and that'll be the end; there will be no justice.

So I immediately had somebody call him to tell him to postpone the talk to the next morning, Friday, at nine and he agreed. But before that hour, we saw what was going on in the city and we told him not to come at all. I canceled it; I told Kadiatou, Amadou's mother, "We canceled because either we go with Giuliani or we go with the community. The community is fighting for justice. If we will go with Giuliani, that's the end; the community will turn their backs on us." That same day Amadou's mother and I went to the funeral home to visit the body. We prayed over the body and they washed the body.

The Reverend Al Sharpton   I was there when the Guineans identified Amadou's body. The Diallos had asked me what I thought [about meeting with the mayor]. I told them it was up to *them*, to think about it, that he *was* the mayor and that he did, in my judgment, have a responsibility to deal with victims of the officers of the city. They said they would talk about it. When I left the hotel late that night—I used to stay with them all day— I was in the [Brooklyn] Battery Tunnel and my cell phone rang. It was Mrs. Diallo and she said, "Reverend Sharpton? I decided I do not want to see Mr. Giuliani. He prejudged the death of my son; there's nothing to talk about." I said, "Well, you do realize that he'll say I told you, 'Don't do this.'" She said, "You arrange an interview and I'll tell them it's *my* decision." And that's when I called Dominick Carter at WLIB [a local radio station] and asked him to arrange an exclusive interview with Mr. and Mrs. Diallo. The next morning, before the funeral, he went on live and said that the Diallos had decided not to see Rudy Giuliani.

Stephen C. Worth   Sharpton gets easier to understand and to recognize for what he is. Everybody has a role in these cases and he's the leader of the chorus. At the end of the day during the case, we'd come out to the mikes and banter a bit. One day he said, "I'm going to go easy on you today, Worth," and I said, "Well, I don't think I'm going to do the same for you." The *New York Times* reporter heard it and wrote it up the next day. He doesn't, quite frankly, give a damn about Amadou Diallo. At some level, he *does*, but it's all grist for his mill. He's forwarding an agenda and his poster boy at a given time was either Diallo or Louima or Dorismond or anybody else that was around.

The Funeral

Saikou Diallo   It was at the 96th [Street] Mosque, between Second and Third avenues. There was a huge crowd. We understand that Giuliani was *there*, attempting to go inside. But they didn't give him a chance to go inside. Up till right now, he'd been our friend—we didn't think anything *otherwise*. But we really wondered. We saw that he was always backing the police; he didn't care what they did. He was not attempting to say, Okay, we will investigate. He was with the police; we understood that he was one-sided. Otherwise, to tell you the truth, Giuliani is a good leader: he is the one who's responsible for my visa to come here. But during his time [in office] all these incidents happened—I was in Vietnam when the Abner Louima incident happened. I used to watch CNN. I didn't know at that time that Giuliani was always with the police. He never attempted to be a mediator. He was doing something really wrong.

The Reverend Al Sharpton   It must have been frightening and puzzling because they knew nothing about what was going on. They certainly didn't know the politics; they were strangers to the country—she walked out of a somewhat obscure life in Guinea and he was living in Vietnam—and all of a sudden they are in the middle of all this media hoopla and politics. It was amazing the way their whole life just flipped overnight.

The Demonstrations

Ruth Messinger   I was very involved in the protests and I thought it continued to show one of his [Giuliani's] major limitations, that there was a whole bunch of people in the city he really didn't see, which, by the way, is [also] a little bit of a problem with Bloomberg.

Ed Koch　When the Diallo case came about and people were getting arrested because the grand jury was very slow in its proceedings, I said, "I'm going to get arrested, but not to influence the grand jury, because I don't believe you should put any pressure on a grand jury to indict or not indict; it's terrible to do that." I said, "I'm so pissed that Rudy will not meet with two black leaders who have been asking for a meeting with him for about a year." And so—only in New York City can this happen—I called Al Sharpton, who was in charge of the picketing in front of [One] Police Plaza, and I said, "I want to get arrested. I have to get arrested early" because I was teaching at a college near Boston, Brandeis, and it was on a Monday, the one day I went there. "Can you arrange to get me arrested at ten o'clock?" He said, "I'll get back to you. It's a little too early, I think." He called me back and said, "I can't arrange for ten; I can get you arrested at eleven." So I said, "All right, if it has to be eleven."

I went to the gym every morning in those days and while I'm on the treadmill, I faint. We later determined it was because of a wrong dosage of a prescription drug; I had had a stroke in '87, so I took prescription drugs. I was taken to the hospital and so couldn't get arrested! Rudy visited me at the hospital—that's a very New York thing; I visited everybody who ran for mayor who was in the hospital—and when he went downstairs he said to the press, "The first thing he said to me was 'Why don't you meet with Virginia Fields and Carl McCall?'" That *was* the first question I raised with him. And he told me, "I *am* meeting with them. Peter Vallone has arranged it for next week."

Saikou Diallo　Even after we went for the burial in Guinea, for almost two months, *every day* there was a demonstration in one borough, or two, even, and he [Al Sharpton] was always leading. When we came from Guinea again, after the burial, he called for justice. On April 15, 1999, we stood at the justice building [the Bronx County Courthouse] in the Bronx, calling for justice, and after that we crossed the Brooklyn Bridge. It was huge: over twenty-five thousand people were crossing—he called all the leaders—and we closed the Brooklyn Bridge. We went to Federal Plaza; everybody made a statement. And we went to Washington, to the Department of Justice; we went to see the minister of justice [the attorney general].

Sanford Rubenstein　I didn't represent the Diallo family, but I was one of those who was in the front line of the major demonstration. People came out for Diallo to demonstrate because they believed it could have been *their* son or daughter.

Stephen C. Worth   Forgive me for being the cynic that I am—and I recognize that these people were all at some level offended by what the police did—but to the great detriment of the cops, I see an agenda beyond pure outrage. Who is getting arrested and what agenda are they forwarding? Susan Sarandon and Tim Robbins are down there—their acting careers were sagging at the time—and David Dinkins and Charlie Rangel are down there trying to stay relevant. There was no presumption of innocence for these cops; there was no: let's wait and see what happens here. You're being convicted in the court of public opinion and there's not a damn thing you can do about it.

The Indictments of the Four Officers

Stephen C. Worth   They were charged with murder. Cops generally do not plea bargain; they're all-or-nothing people because if they plead guilty, they lose their career, their honor, their respect—everything they hold dear. The PBA was assured at the time by the police commissioner, who was in close touch with the mayor, that when they had to surrender on the indictment they would not be suspended, which is normal police practice in all cases. Because everyone in the Police Department felt that these cops were right, the police commissioner said to the PBA president, "We're not going to do that." But they were betrayed: when they were indicted, they *were* suspended. You had to think that the mayor was involved because of the enormous PR effect.

Moving the Proceedings to Albany

Sanford Rubenstein   Changes of venue, which are not that frequently granted, certainly are looked upon by the public in a very circumspect way. I think that for the sake of public opinion, the case should have been tried in the jurisdiction in which the incident occurred. But that wasn't done. You can't generalize with regard to these issues. Of course defense counsel probably felt that the makeup of the jury pool was much more racially advantageous in Albany than it was here in New York and they were successful in getting the venue changed. Many believe that the reason for their verdict was the change in venue and the jury pool in Albany.

Stephen C. Worth   It played a huge role. We made the motion because the publicity was unprecedented. Diallo was the highlight of media manipulation and forwarding a racial agenda. There were the marches to One Police Plaza and the celebrity arrests, which engendered a million articles. The straw that broke the camel's back was the cover of the *New Yorker* magazine [of March 8, 1999] with the caption: "Shooting in a Shooting Gallery," like he was at a carnival: a black male was the target and the cop is smiling. When the *New Yorker* takes that kind of radical view of a situation, you're over the top; you're into a new territory. So going to the Appellate Division and being able to say, "Look at all these articles"—and we did an opinion poll, which we got for free, from a respected pollster [Warren J. Mitofsky] who found that when he polled in the Bronx and said to people, "Look, the cops shot forty-one times and the man is dead; guilty or not guilty?" people would overwhelmingly say, "They were guilty." When you asked that same question in Westchester, which was the control county, they'd say, "That doesn't mean anything in of itself. We'd have to know more facts." We cited those two things and the court then picked Albany.

We would have had, statistically speaking, a majority of minority people on a jury in the Bronx. The demonstrations on Wheeler Avenue were constant—when the grand jury was meeting on the case, they were chanting outside the window—and so the pressure would have been overwhelming and it would have been highly unlikely that we could have prevailed, either by waiving a jury and having a judge try the case or with a jury. And it had nothing to do with the facts of the case. Under the facts, the law, they were clearly not guilty of a crime. If you believe their story and you believe in the law of justification, there is no question that they weren't guilty. But the political agenda this case stood for was: we've had enough of these cops and we're not going to take it anymore. And it became a racial last stand.

Saikou Diallo   We protested; we went to the D.A.'s Office in the Bronx when we heard the news and the D.A. told us they could not do anything—that four judges had decided to send the trial to Albany. We found out that there the majority is white, so we understood that they were going to pirate the trial. So we rallied: we fought and fought. All this fighting was led by Reverend Al Sharpton. We went back to Washington again. We told them we wanted to monitor [the trial]. And after the verdict, we went back to the Justice Department *again*. We rallied seven times around the building. They said, "We will investigate. We may indict them on civil rights violations." We were not happy and we were still fighting twenty-four hours of every day and night.

We were represented by Mr. Muhamar Hammadi and Mr. [Deveraux] Cannick, our law firm here in Queens, New York. Throughout the trial we were sitting in the first row and they [the defendants] were opposite, but there was not any eye contact whatsoever. I never noticed *any* eye contact from the jury or from the prosecutor or the defendants. I was shocked. I was not able to ask anything. We just watched and listened. I was in the Crowne Plaza Hotel, near the courtroom, for the whole trial—about twenty-five days. Every day, after court, we went outside and rallied. The media was there because they saw that things were starting to change. Whenever we rallied here, he [Mayor Giuliani], the police commissioner, and the PBA would make a statement contradicting us. Our lawyers were telling us how things were turning. And every day, we met with the prosecutors from the Bronx. They told us, "We are working hard; we're presenting all the evidence; but we're not the ones who make the decision."

The Verdict

Saikou Diallo We were in shock. We already understand what they planned to do from the beginning, from the time they moved the trial from the Bronx to Albany and the picking of the jury. We understood that something was going to be wrong. But we were there just to look and listen. We understood at last, when they gave the final argument. Our lawyer and the other attorneys were very angry already because they knew what they planned to do. Almost from the beginning, even the picking of the jury, they were rushing to make it fast. They're supposed to take at least a few days or more. They never asked any of the jury to testify, to see what qualifications the person had; they just picked [the jury] in one day. In the middle, people had the energy to have seen that the prosecutor was acting very well. I mean, they were asking really tough things. But at the end, it was weakening. All the experts told us in advance that they had planned to abort the trial. We understand that the judge also was with the police because when he was charging the jury, he said they should be on the message of the police, not on the message of my son, who was killed. So that's exactly what the jury did. After the verdict, they said they had been charged to do that. We were calling for life. Maybe we would not get *life*— Abner Louima's [assailant] was getting thirty years or more. We were expecting to get at least six months, or up to five years, but we were not expecting at all total *acquittal*.

Eric Adams   We [the Grand Council of Guardians] were involved. In fact, I speak with the mother often and I interact with the dad. It's difficult to get a conviction of police officers. The difficulty increases when the victim is a person of color and increases even more when the person is an immigrant. It is as un-American as not liking apple pie to put a policeman in jail for killing an immigrant. The criminal justice system just cannot find it in their hearts to do that, so we creatively find ways to circumvent the system, circumvent the African American female judge, to get it up to Albany—the New York City version of Simi Valley [where the accused officers in the Rodney King assault were eventually tried and acquitted].

Steven Brill   That's ridiculous! Two-thirds to three-quarters of jurors are typically minority themselves; it happens all the time that cops get convicted.

Eric Adams   I believe that the federal government just decided to stay away from the case: it was [U.S. Attorney for the Southern District] Mary Jo White who made the decision not to move ahead with the civil rights charges. And remember, when Amadou Diallo was shot and killed, not one police officer, trainer, or supervisor was found to have done anything wrong. That's a terrible statement: for an innocent person to lose his or her life while standing in his or her doorway and we didn't find anything wrong with the actions of anyone involved, that was a terrible finding when we have just about taken the job away from police officers who have shot dogs.

The Aftermath

Following the acquittal of the four police officers, the Diallos sought in vain to bring federal civil rights violation charges. There was ample precedent to have done so. In the Rodney King case, the officers who had assaulted their detainee, an African American man, as he lay defenseless on the ground, were acquitted on the state charges. The federal government, however, decided to bring the civil rights violation charge and the officers were sentenced to five years' incarceration. There have been other instances of federal intervention over the years, namely in the Louima case.

In attempting to understand why federal charges were not brought against the police officers in this case, the authors sent an e-mail to Eric Holder, the deputy attorney general in the Clinton administration, who had announced the Department of Justice's decision not to do so. On July

6, 2005, Judge Holder replied by e-mail, stating, "I suggest you contact the folks who made the initial decision and who are closer to the case—the prosecutors in the Southern District of New York [Manhattan]. They'll be able to help a lot more than me."

On July 24, the authors sent an e-mail to Bill Lann Lee, head of the Clinton administration Justice Department's Criminal Division, inquiring about that decision. Responding by e-mail, Mr. Lee wrote, "Thanks for thinking of me. Unfortunately, it would be inappropriate for me to speak to you about the decision of the Department of Justice not to prosecute the officers involved in the shooting of Mr. Diallo. Best wishes." When the authors again e-mailed Mr. Lee, seeking to identify the appropriate person with whom to speak, Mr. Lee replied, "I am not sure anyone can properly speak to you about how a prosecutorial decision was made."

The authors also sent e-mails to Mary Jo White at Debevoise & Plimpton, her current law firm in New York, and spoke on the telephone with her spokesman there, Marvin Smilon, specifically concerning the decision not to bring charges against the officers. Ms. White did not reply to our inquiry.

Considering the refusal of the above-mentioned officials to comment on the issue, one can understand Saikou Diallo's frustration at not being able to achieve justice for his late son.

One also wonders whether the federal officials who had been involved in the decision not to bring charges against the police officers had in some way been seeking to protect the reputation of Mayor Giuliani, himself a former high official of the Department of Justice.

Saikou Diallo   After the trial, we went straight to Washington, to the federal court. We asked them to hold the policemen on [violation of] civil rights [charges]. Amadou's case was clearer than Abner Louima's. In Abner Louima's case, there were not so many eye-witnesses. But here the evidence was overwhelming: there were clearly forty-one shots. We were told in the Justice Ministry [Department of Justice] that they were going to investigate: first they were going to review the trial and see which way they could indict those people on the Civil [Rights] Act. And then they would come back to us *within weeks*, not *months*. We waited until January 31, 2000, before we were called to the United States Attorney's Office here. They informed us that as it was after one year they didn't see any way that they could prosecute those police officers. I responded, "I *saw* the evidence; it was clear. So if you drop the case, I'm going to do everything possible, in writing, in documenting, whatever, to highlight and to focus on this case." I spoke to Mary Jo White, who was in charge at that time of the

Attorney General's Office [U.S. Attorney's Office for the Southern District of New York]. We all think that the resistance started from the top. Giuliani was giving statements all the time to protect the police and the federal government knew very well about what happened to the case.

Stephen C. Worth   We went down to Washington and met with Eric Holder. We had submitted a big brief about why civil rights charges were not appropriate and we always knew he'd have to come to that conclusion. The reason the feds didn't come in is that you can't negligently deny somebody their civil rights. At its core, Diallo is an accident—gross negligence, recklessness, whatever level of lack of care you want to call that—but it's clearly not an *intentional* act: you can't accidentally deny somebody their civil rights; you can't even negligently deny somebody their civil rights. So it was never going to be a federal case. With all due respect to the Diallo family, the feds couldn't have taken it if they had wanted to.

Saikou Diallo   I was in South Africa during the World Conference against Racism, Racial Discrimination, Xenophobia, and Related Intolerance [in the summer of 2001; Mr. Diallo actually returned to New York on the morning of September 11]. I decided to really fight when I came back from South Africa to bring that case to light and to find some group in South Africa that was having some programs, as well. We decided on a joint effort to make it international. And we decided to go to Harlem to fight, to bring back justice. I intended to go to Geneva to make an appeal all over the world, to find international lawyers—from the United Kingdom, France, Germany, the United States, and Canada—to join the effort to bring this case to light. I doubt that any person can bring this case again because most of the police became heroes: one of them [McMellon] even joined the Fire Department. We asked the fire commissioner not to accept him, but they did. And one of them [Police Officer Kenneth Boss] had already killed somebody's son before he killed *my* son [Boss was cleared by the Brooklyn, New York, District Attorney's Office of any wrongdoing in the October 1997 shooting of Pat Bailey, who, police claimed, was threatening people with a shotgun in front of a Brooklyn apartment building] and that woman [the mother of Pat Bailey] was crying when we came here. She said, "This is the man who killed my son. He was supposed to be punished; had he been punished in my son's case, he would not have been able to kill Amadou."

Saikou Diallo's State of Mind Today

Saikou Diallo   I thought Amadou was safe because he was in the United States. My other son is in Angola, where the fighting went on for over thirty-five years; he was every day cheating death. I thought Amadou was the safer one—that *he* was in the safer place. I'm still disappointed because every now and then you see that racism is continuing. But I have faith in the system; I know that there is really justice here because I've seen so many cases after my son's death that are very well prosecuted. But it depends on who is behind the desk in the justice system. We know there are some good cops and family members; they all sympathize with us about what happened to my son. They don't talk about the case or the trial, but they talk about what happened to my son.

We have to rely on Almighty God, Allah. We have to fight for justice ourselves. I plan to stay here and, maybe, go back and forth from here to Africa. I'm still checking now [how] to get the permanent residence. I have already applied and asked a congressman, Joseph Crowley [D-NY], to introduce my petition to the Congress; I'm still waiting. We have the Amadou Diallo Educational, Humanitarian & Charity Foundation, established in 2000. Our mission statement is multiple: we have a scholarship fund; we have donated scholarships to many schools here; and we have the Amadou Diallo Basketball and Soccer Team. And I'm still fighting to purchase the house where Amadou, my son, was killed. And we are proud of the city's contribution: they have renamed a portion of Wheeler Avenue in the name of my son—they call it today Amadou Diallo Place. I will not give up because I saw so many things after my son's death—I saw that a policeman killed Patrick Dorismond. There is a long way to go.

Chapter 14

DORISMOND

*I haven't been able to communicate my message
to the African American community as well as I
should. Maybe it's my own inadequacies.*

—Rudy Giuliani, quoted in the *New York Post*, May 3, 2000

At eleven o'clock on the evening of March 15, 2000, twenty-six-year-old
Patrick Dorismond, the youngest son of a prominent Haitian immigrant
family, and his friend, Kevin Kaiser, a Hispanic who looked Caucasian, finished their eight-hour shift as security guards with 34th Street Partnership,
took off their uniforms, and headed over to the Distinguished Wakamba
Cocktail Lounge on Eighth Avenue for a nightcap before heading home to
Brooklyn. Patrick would never get there. As the two security guards tried
to hail a taxi, a man approached them and asked the young Haitian American if he had drugs for sale. Insulted at the suggestion that he could be a
pusher, he shouted and a melee ensued. When it was over, Patrick Dorismond lay mortally wounded. The would-be buyer was actually an undercover narcotics agent named Anderson Moran. As the melee escalated,
Moran called to companions standing nearby who were, in fact, plainclothes police. All three were participants in Police Commissioner Howard
Safir's recently launched undercover sting campaign, Operation Condor, to
crack down on drug criminals.

Derek Sells, attorney representing the family of Patrick Dorismond
They were looking for people who would either sell or help them procure
drugs. They had already arrested a number of people that night and placed
them in a twelve-passenger van. If they could fill that van, they would get

that much more overtime. [In an attempt to achieve balance, the authors on August 22, 2005, sent an e-mail to Phillip Karasyk, the attorney for Police Officer Anthony Vasquez, who fired the fatal shot, to which he did not reply.]

Several bystanders tried to intervene on Dorismond's behalf. According to the police, one of them shouted, "Get the gun," and Vasquez, who had emerged as the melee got under way, yelled "Police." Dorismond lunged at him, and Vasquez fired his Glock 9mm.

Derek Sells   It wasn't an accident. Police officers are trained not to pull a gun unless they intend to *use* it. You don't pull it out as a warning, so when Vasquez pulled the gun, he had the intention of *using* it.

Eric Adams   I do not believe that the police officers' account of what took place is accurate. You're approaching an unarmed person and there is no reason to have your firearm out. That was in violation of all of the department's procedures, although there is a gray area if you believe your life is in danger. But believing your life is in danger can't be merely because you see a black person; there have to be other parameters in place as to why you had your gun drawn.

Derek Sells   Officer Moran didn't approach Patrick because he saw any crime taking place; the only reason he approached him was because of the hour and because he and Kevin were standing on the street corner. When Patrick said words to the effect of: I'm not involved in drugs, Moran should have moved on. Then the fight ensued, but neither Patrick nor Kevin pulled any weapons. But Vasquez, whose history was to pull guns—he had shot a dog and he had once been in a bar fight in Pennsylvania where he pulled a gun—is quick on the trigger. So he pulls his gun and shoots Patrick—and for *what*? If you say they're fighting, okay, arrest them. But don't shoot him. There was *no reason* to shoot him.

Patrick Dorismond: The Victim of Yet Another Police Action Gone Tragically Wrong

Marie Dorismond   Patrick was twenty-six years old, born on February 19, 1974. My family is very well known in the Haitian community: my father is a singer—for a long, long time, he was considered to be the black Frank Sinatra—and my mom was a nurse whom everyone liked and called "Miss Mary." There were a lot of kids on our block and they always looked up to Patrick. He and I were raised very strictly—we couldn't go outside all the time; we were very busy with school and other activities. He was my baby brother. I'm the only girl and I'm the oldest—I have older step-brothers on my father's side of the family—and Patrick was the last of the crew; I had to remind him of that plenty of times because he was taller than I. He was a funny young man and he had two children, Infinity and Destiny—he came up with those names himself.

Patrick loved music. He was very talented. He could sit there and make music—it must be from my father. He loved sports. And he loved comedy—whenever Patrick came, the family always knew a good joke was coming. And Patrick was good-looking—he had hazel eyes. I had arguments with him because of the girls—everybody wanted a little piece of my brother! And that was the only thing we had problems with. He was cool; he didn't bother anybody; he was a fighter; he wanted to do things right on our block.

Derek Sells Patrick was once the victim of a crime. He testified and helped the D.A. get a conviction. He wanted to be a police officer and was working as a security guard in Times Square and in Hell's Kitchen at the time of his death. He didn't deserve to be mocked in the way Giuliani mocked him.

Marie Dorismond He was studying the book to become a police officer. A lot of his friends didn't like cops and he was trying to tell them that not all cops are bad. That's why he was a peace officer running around after the bad guys who were trying to break into phone booths and doing all kinds of other crimes in Times Square. He got a lot of badges for good deeds. He really wanted to become an officer and look what happened!

Learning of the Shooting

Marie Dorismond My bedroom was closest to the entrance door of the apartment. It was around four thirty in the morning when I heard a knock on the door. When I answered it, I saw two white males. They were asking to speak to "Rosemarie Dorismond" or "Marie Rose Dorismond"—they couldn't get my mom's name correctly—and I asked them, "Who are you?" They said they were detectives. I said "What is this in reference to?" and they said, "Ma'am, we need to speak to this person. Can you please open the door?" My heart just dropped. I opened the door and said, "What's going on?" and they said, "We need to speak to this person immediately." I woke my mother and my father. Then they said that there had been a shooting in Manhattan, an altercation between Patrick and *a man*—they never said it was an *officer*—and that they don't know what the fight was about and Patrick was shot. Then they said that Patrick was dead. At that point, my mother just dropped to the floor and my father was in shock. I was holding my daughter, who was nine months old. My knees buckled, but because I was holding her I didn't drop. But I yelled so loud that the next-door neighbor opened her door and her son, Steve, came running into our apartment. He was a good friend of Patrick's—we were all raised together—and he said, "What's going on?" When I told him, he started screaming, too.

I didn't know that Patrick was shot by an officer until the next day. A [*New York*] *Daily News* reporter called my cell phone and told me that Patrick was killed by a narcotics officer. I'm like, "What do you mean, a *narcotics officer*?" And he said, "Yes, Patrick was killed by a narcotics officer." I was in total shock. I said, "I didn't know that." He said, "You didn't *know*?" And that was the biggest blow to me, because these people made it look like it was just somebody in the street when it was one of *their* people. Most of the details were basically through television—New York 1, and all the other channels were giving it little piece by little piece. My father, my uncle, my cousin, and I went to Manhattan. I was working at St. Clare's Hospital with mentally disabled people at the time and I never knew that the building was connected to the morgue. I passed that entrance every day, not knowing that that was the morgue and not knowing my brother would be in there. We went in. I had to ID the body to make sure that it was him and it *was* him.

Then Kevin Kaiser came to see us and explained exactly what happened. They had put him in the opposite direction and put pressure on his body so he could hear what was going on but couldn't actually see what was happening. The way it was explained to us, these officers put handcuffs on my brother's body when he was already dead. This is crazy! What can he do when he's *dead*? Why go through all that? His cell phone was ringing and they were making jokes: Oh, a dead man's cell phone is ringing.

Derek Sells   They put him facedown in the street and cursed him. He was lying on the ground gasping for air, but help was not forthcoming from the Police Department. He had committed no crime, yet they treated him as if he were a farm animal. It was criminal! Then he was taken to a hospital and pronounced dead.

Enter Al Sharpton

The Reverend Al Sharpton   I was called by his sister, who told me about it, and I went out to the house right away because they called and asked me to help them tell the story of what had happened. When I got to the house, the family and I held a press conference and talked about what we would do.

Marie Dorismond   Sharpton embraced my family very well. He assured us that justice will prevail; he assured us that we were not alone and that he was going to be supporting us to the end. And he really was a very comforting person to be around. He brought us to his National Action Network, where we met his congregation, and we had a nice service over the phone with the Reverend Jesse Jackson; we met Mrs. [Coretta Scott] King [the widow of the Reverend Martin Luther King Jr.] and her son and they prayed with us. It was just very, very sweet of him to surround us with a lot of support. He fought with us, yelled for us. When we couldn't yell, he was yelling. He was the extra voice that we needed. And the apartment was flooded with people—people we didn't know came to give their support—and everybody was trying to find out what was going on. Kevin Kaiser's lawyer [Sanford Rubenstein] came to our house. And then somebody referred us to Johnnie Cochran.

Derek Sells   Having a public defender's background, I specialize in civil rights litigation and police brutality cases. Patrick's mother called our firm a day or two after her son was killed. She wanted Johnnie to work on her case. I then went to the Dorismond family's household in Brooklyn.

Marie Dorismond   Cochran came that same night—he flew in from California at eight o'clock in the evening—and said that he would represent us "because this doesn't look right; something doesn't look kosher." There was just so much, *so much*.

"He's No Choirboy": An Attempt
to Sully the Victim's Reputation

Mayor Giuliani had a major problem and he knew it. Patrick Dorismond's body was still warm when he began his misguided attempt at damage control. While urging the public not to "let their biases, their prejudices, their emotions, their stereotypes dictate the results," Giuliani was giving his own baggage full reign. First he sought to find some "dirt" on the shooting victim, and then when a juvenile record was discovered—at the age of thirteen, Patrick had been arrested on robbery and assault charges, which were dropped—he took the unheard-of step of unsealing the young security guard's juvenile record and ordering his police commissioner to make the details public. In his zeal, Giuliani uttered the three words that would inflame racial tensions in the city even further.

The Reverend Al Sharpton   When the next day Giuliani came out with "He's no choirboy," it was almost as if someone had driven a stake through the mother's heart. She was *already* heartbroken: it was like someone had resurrected Patrick and killed him again. I don't think people understand that a lot of the passion that I bring to fights is caused by being so close to the family. It touches you *personally*: I'm sitting there with the mother, who's sobbing and furious at what the mayor has done. What the mayor did in revealing the sealed documents and distorting them and trying to demonize this young man, even before they could bury him, really shook the Dorismond family.

Marie Dorismond   We have pictures of Patrick showing him wearing his altar boy suit. Patrick went to Immaculate Heart of Mary School, in Fort Hamilton, Brooklyn, New York—I was there as well—and on Sundays he was doing that and I was saying the Good News in church and I had my little part to say at the altar. And he went to Bishop Loughlin High School, but the tuition was high and my mother took him out and he went to public school.

Derek Sells   Anytime there was a police shooting there was a policy to demonize the victim—to put out as much dirt about the victim in the press as possible. That was done to reduce the public outcry that would go along with a police shooting. In this case, Giuliani saw that there was an arrest record and took off with it and basically lied. He said Patrick had been convicted of crimes when he had never been convicted of any crimes. The most Patrick was involved with was nuisance violations, which are not criminal offenses—things that don't rise to the level of criminal activity. When he was questioned on Fox News, Giuliani was asked point-blank: Were they arrests or were they convictions? And he said that they were convictions. That was *not true*; it was a *straight-out lie*. That was the way the Giuliani administration dealt with police shootings.

David Dinkins   [Of] the fact that his [Rudy's] father was supposed to have been a robber who stuck up a milkman and went to prison, Rudy said, "You shouldn't say that about him; he's dead." Well, this kid is just as dead. I'm fascinated by a thought process that suggests that one thing is okay and another is *not*.

Marie Dorismond   Patrick had solid, good steps all his life. He got into a little altercation when he was a little kid for a quarter and that was the case that was sealed and that Giuliani decided to *unseal*. He may have the power to unseal it to *view* it, but he can't expose it on the air and then add to it. Giuliani was just sticking his mouth in the wrong direction every time he talked about my brother. Maybe it's easy to pick on a young Haitian man. I guess that he wanted to just lay it on thick. And he laid it on the wrong thickness! My family is very classy; we're not thuggish.

Derek Sells   There is a sealing provision which the court puts in place in which records are not to be released to *anyone* in the public. The only way to get them released is to get the court to issue an unsealing order. Without that order it's a violation of law to release records and the information contained therein without court approval. That was the problem. Giuliani didn't unseal them, he just *released* them.

Mark Green   I sued him under a provision of the City Charter in order to prevent him from ever again unilaterally unsealing a juvenile record for whatever reason. I won the lawsuit. It was on appeal when term limits kicked in and we both left office. That was a very bad moment for him and the city.

Sanford Rubenstein   In using the bully pulpit of public office, get your facts straight *first*. And if you don't, you're going to pay the price. And in Dorismond, Giuliani paid the price. When it was eventually uncovered that he [Dorismond] really *was* a choirboy, it put his [Giuliani's] comment in perspective for what it was—another example of the policy of polarization coming out of City Hall. Damages were paid for that by the city.

Benjamin Brafman   It was a terrible public relations disaster to try and go into Dorismond's criminal record after he was shot because, at the end of the day, it wasn't relevant to whether or not it was a justified shooting at the time. You had a rabid press demanding answers and coming up with all sorts of their own theories, and the mayor is put in the position where he needs to respond almost instantaneously. And someone who's more seasoned, with more wisdom at that point in life, recognizes that whatever you say on the public record you're stuck with, so don't say *anything* until you sort it out.

Eric Adams   Giuliani learned something at the start of his administration: that reality is not what's real. If people, particularly in economically deprived areas, read it in the papers, it's real: they wouldn't have it in the papers if it wasn't real; if channel 7 said it happened, it *happened*. Giuliani controls the press. If he puts it out that Dorismond had a criminal record, it's here in the papers.

Derek Sells   Most administrations take a wait-and-see approach; they do some investigating before they jump to claim that it is the victim's fault. With this administration, it was: throw the dirt and let's see what shakes out and in the Dorismond case it backfired on them in a big way.

Marie Dorismond   I'll tell you, if Giuliani was in front of me, I'd rip him apart. It's disgusting to see somebody with so much education, like Giuliani, who used to be a prosecuting lawyer, to go such a negative route just to make his people look good. It really, really was disgusting. It was sad. I had to watch my mom, my father, every day, losing weight. I'm the only one there with my family, standing there, trying to shoulder all of this inside me with dignity and fight for my brother's rights. He wasn't even buried and he was being shot at in all kinds of directions, from Anthony Vasquez, who pulled the gun, to Giuliani demonizing him, making him look like a thug, a bum, who's got no family.

A Further Attempt to Sully Patrick
Dorismond's Reputation: A Damaging Leak

Derek Sells Shortly after we began our investigation, there was a leak about a toxicology report that said that Patrick had trace amounts of marijuana [in his blood]. We had been trying to get a copy of the autopsy report, but the Giuliani administration, intent on demonizing the victim, decided to leak the information to the public, although they told us they couldn't give it to us because of the criminal investigation. We then sued the City of New York and the medical examiner to obtain the leaked information.

Given the Mayor's Early Noble Sentiments about Removing Racial Tensions, How Did the Fiasco Following Patrick Dorismond's Shooting Come About?

Derek Sells You very rarely, if ever, hear of a situation where police shoot and kill unarmed white individuals in a city; it's black men who are being killed without having any type of weapon. The Louima, Diallo, and Dorismond cases came about because of the very aggressive and, I believe, illegal types of police procedures that were utilized under the Giuliani administration. The reduction of crime had such a high priority that they bent the rules. The attempt to get people off the street may have led to the "shoot first and ask questions later" type of approach that occurred in some of those situations.

Raoul Felder Rudy had taken a position: you're innocent until proven guilty. They were all dumping on the cops immediately and he took a position: you don't blame the cops until you know what happened, because nobody really knows what happens for some time. And he's a law and order guy. It's *that* simple.

Herman Badillo Those positions were unpopular in the black and Latino areas. I used to go to these town hall meetings. Giuliani and Bratton— especially Bratton—were very blunt about the need to take vigorous action, and that began to create tension between the black and Latino communities. And that's where it really began.

The Reverend Al Sharpton By the time of Dorismond, Giuliani had sensed he was losing his grip on a lot of things. He had declined a lot; even his cheering squad could find less and less to cheer about. And, rather than reevaluate and move differently, I think he acted like a stubborn child—he just overreacted—he just wanted to make Dorismond *bad* and I think that he reacted in a very immature and reckless and, probably, illegal manner.

Sanford Rubenstein   There's no question that there's a trial before the trial—a trial in the court of public opinion. It's an important trial: it may or may not get the potential jurors, but it certainly sets the tone for the case. And, also, in a civil case, when you have the court of public opinion deciding in your favor, you're going into negotiations to resolve the case amicably with a strong hand. But the prosecution doesn't usually do it: the federal prosecutors generally don't make statements at all, so the civil lawyers are the ones who end up sparring with the defense lawyers in this battle in the court of public opinion. In that trial, we sparred on a regular basis with defense counsel as advocates for our clients in the civil case. That's why it's so important for a client who ultimately wants to bring a civil case to have a lawyer early on to interface, not only with the prosecutors in bringing witnesses forward if they're unavailable, but also to be able to deal in the press with the intent to poison the jury pool against your client's point of view by defense counsel—and with *their* attempts to spin. You need someone spinning and advocating for the client early on.

Mark Green   When he's defensive and angry, he makes bad judgments. He is *technically* very smart—he has a very high IQ but a very, very low EQ [emotional quotient], and when the two collided on this issue of police misconduct, he made bad governmental decisions because he let his personal emotions and his political philosophy and his family story get in the way of good government. He rightfully would always tell how many people in his extended family were cops and firefighters and that is something to be properly proud of. But that doesn't mean that some cops didn't something terribly wrong—with Louima, Diallo, and Dorismond.

Benjamin Brafman   If it's a black-on-white issue, it's always much more of a story than if it's a white-on-white issue. If a white police officer shoots a white person ten times and it turns out that the white individual is not armed, it's not anywhere near the story as it is if a white police officer shoots a person of color. Rudy thought there was a double standard. He was an in-your-face kind of guy about this stuff and what he didn't get then— which he might get *now*—is that in the African American community, people are much more sensitive about these issues than the white community is. Hardworking parents in the African American community react differently when a black teenager is shot needlessly by a cop than do white people; white people don't worry about it, don't think it can happen to *their* kids. Black people immediately identify: this could have been *my* kid. And when you're the mayor of a city as diverse as this you need to be sensitive enough to keep your mouth shut until you sort things out.

Stephen C. Worth   Abner Louima and Amadou Diallo were unassailable victims, *pure* victims. And Mrs. Diallo was an extremely tragic figure and, to a lesser extent, his father—the ultimate grieving parents. Giuliani had lived through these two horrendous cases, which were public relations nightmares for him: what kind of city are you running here? And now Dorismond comes along and yet again all the same questions are being asked of him: what kind of Police Department are you running? He became aware that Dorismond had a bit of a past and it was simply too attractive for him to resist to get the pressure off him. These shootings were clearly public relations nightmares for the mayor—these are not calls you want to get in the middle of the night, so I think he was just so eager to differentiate Dorismond from the other two and when someone threw him a life preserver, he tried to grab it.

Was There a Bias in the NYPD against People of Color in the Giuliani Years?

Marie Dorismond   I believe so. I think he pressured them [the police], gave them some serious heat, that when they go out in the street it's: Shoot quick! Bring the bad guys down. Eliminate! Eliminate! Eliminate! It's like programming a bunch of robots. These guys are on the street and their first instinct is to shoot to kill, not shoot to *stop*. Look what happened with Kevin Kaiser: he was standing in front of the Wakamba nightclub with Patrick. They didn't really mess with Kevin. Kevin is Hispanic, but he looks white, and they went for my brother, who's a young, black male. Why did Patrick have to get shot? All because they asked him, "Do you know where I can get me some weed?" He said, "No." Why couldn't they leave him alone? Instead, for whatever reason, he [Moran] called for backup and the gun was not even in the officer's holster; it was in his hand, and he shot my brother in the aorta.

They could have shot my brother in the leg; they could have sprayed his face with pepper spray. They aimed and shot to *kill*, straight to the aorta, close range. A 9mm bullet, one shot, took my brother's life. And they tried to make it look like Patrick took the gun and shot himself. Patrick did not have any fingerprints on the trigger; there was no gun residue on his hands. That was clearly proved by the autopsy. The people who did the forensics showed me all of that. There was no proof of that. Basically through his [Giuliani's] time of administration, there was a lot of racism toward young black males. And the way he does it, the shooter doesn't seem to be a white cop; he seems to be a Hispanic cop.

Another Meeting with the Mayor That Never Was

Sanford Rubenstein   There was supposed to be a meeting with Mrs. Dorismond. She wanted Johnnie Cochran, who was her counsel, to be there and City Hall didn't want lawyers at the meeting. Whether it was an attempt to not meet with *Johnnie Cochran*, I don't know. The meeting was never held. And it was a time when there was a lot of fear in the minds of those who lived in communities of color that it could happen to *their* kids—a real fear that what had happened to Diallo, Louima, and Dorismond could happen to *their* sons and daughters.

Marie Dorismond   He tried to use a priest to intervene. He wanted to meet quietly, in the rectory of the church; he did not want to meet publicly with our lawyer and Mr. Sharpton present to say, "Sorry." And I refused to meet with him *privately*. We felt we weren't the only people he should apologize to, that he should apologize to everybody. But he didn't want to do it that way; he wanted to do it the coward's way. But we were not going to do that. I told the priest, "If Giuliani is really sincere, he would get on the air and apologize, not only to the family but to everybody else, in front of our lawyers." Patrick was not a piece of meat; Patrick was a human being and he deserved a better apology. But the mayor didn't even try to do that.

Derek Sells   Giuliani never reached out through his administration or through his corporation counsel to solve any issues with the family. They fought us at every turn: when we tried to obtain the autopsy report and when we tried to get some discovery. It was typical Giuliani style: fight, fight, fight. We had wanted him as our first deposition witness—many things could have been resolved if he had had to testify. But we were never able to get him on the stand, and by the time the criminal process took its course, he was out of office.

Patrick Dorismond's Funeral

On March 25, while Patrick Dorismond's funeral was under way at Brooklyn's Holy Cross Church, a melee erupted outside. As the crowd shouted "Giuliani must go!" rocks and bottles were thrown, police in riot gear fired tear gas, two police vehicles and a telephone booth were destroyed, and twenty-three members of the NYPD were injured.

Mark Green   It's good to be strong. It's good to be stubborn if you're right; but it's awful to be stubborn if you're *wrong*. Police misconduct was Giuliani's Iraq [a reference to President George W. Bush's decision to pursue military activity in that Middle Eastern nation]: he couldn't analyze his way to see that there was a problem that permitted a remedy. And by digging his heels in, he increased police–minority tensions in the city. And he ruined his reputation among communities of color. Giuliani is phenomenally popular in some communities, but he's phenomenally *unpopular* in communities of color. When I'm with black leaders or commentators in political circles or on radio or television, their venom against Giuliani is extraordinary and unhelpful; they just *hate* him. I can see African Americans not voting for George W. Bush—and they didn't—but there was not a level of personal hatred toward him in 2004 as there was, *and is*, in that community toward Giuliani now.

Marie Dorismond   Giuliani never sent flowers to the funeral, *nothing*. I heard rumors that he flew over Brooklyn the day of the funeral in a helicopter. Giuliani made a big mistake. People wanted to take the coffin and walk all the way from the funeral home to City Hall. But, of course, we could not let that happen because we had to bury him and we were very late and the cemetery was going to close. My main focus was to bury my brother the way he needed to be buried, correctly. And he went out like a real trouper.

———

There were calls for the mayor's impeachment and, according to a *New York Times* poll taken several weeks after the riot, his approval rating had fallen to a mere 32 percent. That was bad news, seeing that Rudy Giuliani had made known his ambition to run for the U.S. Senate.

Marie Dorismond   One of the reasons why he didn't do too well when he was running to become a senator was that the press was after him for the way he went about being so nasty to the family. Everybody wanted to know: Why are you being so insensitive? Why aren't you supporting the family? At least he could have said, "We're sorry for the family's loss." Instead, he just tried to make my brother look like a little guy. I don't know if he thought that Patrick didn't have a family—that he was just some little thug in the street. He picked the wrong person to do that to. You would think that the man would have had some kindness in his heart. He might have thought this could happen to his own son. Patrick was somebody's family member but he [Giuliani] didn't think about that. He destroyed my brother's name. That cop killed my brother and he [Giuliani] killed my brother *again*.

The Grand Jury Proceedings

The grand jury that examined the case did not indict Officer Vasquez. The officer's reinstatement in the Police Department—he was given desk duty for a time—infuriated the Dorismond family.

Derek Sells   There is a saying that you can indict a ham sandwich. My view is that [Manhattan District Attorney Robert] Morgenthau's office did not aggressively prosecute police officers. I have been able to look at some of the grand jury transcripts and from the little bit I have been able to glean from the questioning approach that Morgenthau's prosecutors took, it is clear that they were trying to protect the police officers and it's my opinion that the case was prosecuted in a way to justify *not* prosecuting the police officers. What is amazing to me is that Morgenthau put together a thirty-three-page report on the case. That was unheard of. It was almost as if they knew from the start that they didn't want this case to be indicted, that they wanted to quell any type of police outcry. At the *minimum*, Vasquez should have been charged with criminally negligent homicide. Even if you buy into it as an accidental shooting, the reason that there was a shooting at all is because he pulled the gun out and had it in close proximity to Patrick. Obviously, at a maximum you are dealing with murder two or a manslaughter count.

Sanford Rubenstein   The grand jury is a secret proceeding. I don't know *why* he wasn't indicted, but he *wasn't*. Morgenthau is an independent officer, who's acting totally independent of anyone else. The Manhattan District Attorney's Office did not see fit to indict him. We had met with the

D.A.—we had given full cooperation of my client in the companion case; he testified before the grand jury. In my view, Kaiser's account of what happened was credible and, ultimately, the city paid damages to him for his brutalization by police at the scene.

Eric Adams What happened to Dorismond should have played out in a courtroom to allow that that officer, under scrutiny, can tell his account of what took place that day. Dorismond was unarmed, he wasn't breaking any law, and he turned up dead, shot by a police officer. The mind-set is: you know what? There will be a civil suit and the family is going to get money and there's no reason to punish the cop—he was doing the best that he could; he was trying to make a judgment; he was trying to keep the city safe. So let's leave it like that.

The authors obtained a copy of a thirty-three-page report sent by Mr. Morgenthau on July 27, 2000, to Police Commissioner Safir. The authors were struck by its attempt to implicate Mr. Dorismond in his own shooting. On August 22, 2005, the authors placed a call to Barbara Thompson, director of Public Affairs in Mr. Morgenthau's office. At 5:50 P.M. that afternoon, she returned their call. When asked whether Nancy Ryan, head of the Criminal Division of the New York County District Attorney's Office at the time of the grand jury proceedings, would be available for an interview, Ms. Thompson replied that she would not. When asked whether anybody else in that office would comment on the report, she said no and, in an incredulous tone, asked why anyone would even *question* the contents of the report.

An Attempt by the Dorismond Family to Bring Federal Charges

Attorneys for the Dorismond family asked the Department of Justice to bring federal charges against Officer Vasquez. In response, James Comey, the U.S. attorney for the Southern District of New York—in an eerie reprise of the Justice Department's decision in the Diallo case—announced that federal charges would not be brought, characterizing that decision as having been "very, very difficult."

Derek Sells It's *nonsense* to say it was a "difficult decision" for the Justice Department not to charge Vasquez. The reason that Patrick was

approached was because he was black and he was standing next to someone who is Hispanic. That's the trigger for the civil rights violations. When
you ask the U.S. Attorney's Office to get involved, what they look at is what
civil rights are being violated. Here you basically have racial profiling. If
someone is not committing a crime, why are you approaching him? You
have violations of the Fourth Amendment. The law requires that there be
some nominal showing that a crime has been committed or that there is
some reasonable, articulable suspicion that a crime was afoot. In this
instance, the fact that a black man is standing next to a Hispanic man in
midtown Manhattan does not rise to the level of reasonable, articulable
suspicion. This was not a difficult decision for Comey at all. Based on
what I have seen, it should have been a very reasonable decision. I think
Comey was feeling the heat from Washington. If Comey believed it was a
difficult decision, that's why you have grand juries. As long as you have the
evidence, and you have a fair presentation, I'll put my faith in the grand
jury, whether or not criminal charges should be brought. Comey didn't
even give the grand jury a chance.

The Dorismonds would absolutely welcome the bringing of federal
charges. They feel that from a criminal justice standpoint they were not
given fairness. The failure of the state and the federal government to bring
charges has left a void for the family in their attempt to find closure. Until
a federal grand jury looks at this case they are going to continue to feel this
emptiness, knowing that these police officers are living their lives, enjoy-
ing their families without having to answer to the criminal justice system.

Marie Dorismond   I don't see why it was difficult. The man killed my
brother and he should have been convicted and sent to jail. We went to see
the attorney general. They invited *us*, as a matter of fact; they called us to
come to their office and we went with our lawyers. They told us how bad
and how heartsick they were about the situation, but they couldn't do
anything. We were like, There's no way this case can stay like that; it has
to go federal. But they weren't going to do anything further. This whole
administration—the Republican administration, the whole clan—was not
pushing to do anything further. That was *it*.

Are we still going to keep trying? Hell yes! As a matter of fact, we spoke
to Derek today [September 28, 2005]—he treats us more than just like
clients; he treats us like family—and whatever it takes, we're not going to
give up. There's no way we can rest completely every night, knowing that
this guy [Vasquez] is still running around and relaxing and eating and
drinking and happy and no problems in the world until he goes away. And

here we are, going to see Patrick's body in the cemetery in New York. I could grow old, with no teeth, and still press it. My brother was not just a piece of meat; he was a human being, an individual; he didn't ask to go out of life that way.

Have Things Changed for the African American Community?

The Reverend Al Sharpton There are still incidents, but the *tone* is different because whereas the police still have the support of City Hall, they know that if you go too far, this commissioner and this mayor are not going to go out there and support you. When [in 2003] the grandmother [Alberta Spruill, a fifty-seven-year-old woman with a heart condition, who died at Harlem Hospital one and a half hours after police mistakenly raided her West 143rd Street apartment] died in Harlem, Mayor Bloomberg came to the funeral and he said, "The buck stops here" [an echo of Harry S. Truman's view of presidential responsibility]—that if you engage in any kind of action, you'd better be right. Mayor Giuliani had a prosecutor's "us against them" mentality and he never came out of that—he probably still has it. That might be good for prosecutors, in terms of winning, but it's certainly no way to govern a city.

Sanford Rubenstein There's a different climate today—a different policy than existed during the Giuliani administration. There was skepticism during the Giuliani years and fear of the police. And there was a concern that the polarization was coming from City Hall. While we have our tragedies, there's a different mind-set today. Part of the reason that the [earlier] marches attracted so many people was that that was the only way they had of demonstrating how they felt about the manner in which people like Diallo and Dorismond were being killed by the police—the only method they had which they felt would make a difference.

The Dorismond Family Today

Marie Dorismond It's been very hard. When I was in New York, I didn't mourn my brother's death; I'm mourning his death in Florida. I quit my job because of the fact that my brother was in the morgue of a building that I had to walk past every day to go to work. I took two months off after the funeral. When I did decide to go back to work, I didn't know how hard it would be for me to look at every ambulance and wonder which one had had my brother's body in it. Many times, I attempted to ask the drivers, Which one of you carried my brother into the morgue? But I didn't do it. And then it just came to a point where I gave my letter of resignation and told them that I would be leaving in thirty days for Florida. And I left on October 1, 2000, my mother's birthday.

The family is still angry. To this day, I just can't believe my brother is gone; I still can't absorb it. We have Patrick's kids here every summer— that's our connection to Patrick. The children are doing very well. After Patrick passed away in March, the little one, Destiny, gave us a very big scare: she went into diabetic shock in May and her [blood] sugar went over a thousand and she went into the ICU. Now she's getting insulin twice a day. The girls are growing; they've gotten taller and they're speaking their minds. The older one, Infinity, said at one point that she would like to be a cop one day, just so she could go talk to the cop who killed her daddy. I told her, "By the time you get there, he'll be old and probably retired." She says, "I'll find him somewhere. I just want to ask him, 'How did it feel to shoot my daddy? Why did you do that?'"

PART VII

The Second Term: January 1, 1998– December 31, 2001

Chapter 15

ACT TWO, SCENE TWO: RUDY THE WINNER

*If you think that I've run out of enthusiasm for
the job because I'm a lame duck, watch out!*
—Rudy Giuliani, speaking during the 1997 campaign

The Campaign: Was Giuliani's Stated Campaign Intention of Bringing Racial Harmony Sincere?

The Reverend Al Sharpton   I don't believe he was sincere at all. I think that Giuliani really tried his best to race-bait his way in. He distorted Dinkins's role in Crown Heights: he appeared at any number of rallies there with Yankel Rosenbaum's brother, who clearly said that this was a pogrom, which meant it was a city- or state-sanctioned riot, which was absolutely absurd. There was no one that had a more unifying kind of spirit and track record and attitude than David Dinkins and he went out to Crown Heights, trying to stem the violence. And if they had asked, we'd have come out, along with the Cato family. And they knew that. And they knew that Dinkins did not hold the cops back. But Giuliani would appear at these rallies and never question those statements. And then, when the Crown Height Report came out, which hurt Dinkins, many of us felt that this was part of the policy between Mario Cuomo and Giuliani and their supporters and that it was that whole spirit of divisiveness that helped him to have that razor-thin victory in '93.

And he purposely sent signals that not only was he not going to deal with Dinkins, but not even with Carl McCall and Virginia Fields. How can one understand the poverty here when you're not talking to people elected to serve the City and the State? I think that it was part of his rhetoric to the more "respectable" crowd. But I also think he sent every signal to cool it to those that felt that this "us against them" mentality was appropriate, that he was definitely going to gear the city in that way. And he *did*.

Richard Thornburgh   I don't have any special insight into Rudy's problems with the African American community. But I find the notion of Al Sharpton being a burr under his saddle to be plausible; he'd be a burr under *most anybody's* saddle.

The Contenders

Mark Green   When I gave my swearing-in remarks as public advocate, I had absolutely no plans to run for mayor—I was just excited to hold high public office. I probably assumed I would stay eight years with term limits. In 1997, I *was* considering running for mayor and, of course, didn't because by then I could see how Giuliani was governing. When I said in April of '96 that I wouldn't run for mayor, he immediately called me in and we had a rollicking good meeting because I was then no political threat to him. He said, "Mark, how do you announce for one office—public advocate—and then imply, or say, that you're going to then run the next year for the U.S. Senate?" I said, "Well, I just *did*. I don't think the public likes evasive politicians, so I said, 'I'm running for reelection and don't be surprised if I run for the U.S. Senate because I could certainly do even better there.'" And he did an uncharacteristic thing: he told a newspaper that he was "relieved"—*his* word—that I had not run for mayor because I could have been competitive.

Ruth Messinger   I did not like Giuliani and I did not like the way he ran the city. Several substantive issues came out of the Borough President's Office. We said, for example, "Okay, we've done a comprehensive study of domestic violence, welfare to work, and we have a whole set of recommendations." And we would then reach out to the administration, saying, "We have a better plan." And there was no interest. They were hurting the schools, and, more important, they were hurting public higher education. Both the mayor and the governor were sort of siphoning money out, attacking the system, not seeing it as what it always has been: a route into the middle class. I felt there was something profoundly racist about it and I still do.

In the mid '90s I was showing my frustration. Racial divisions were mounting; income gaps were mounting. So, talking to advisers who were likely to be working with me, I got the notion that I would run for mayor. Now, I want to be absolutely clear: I was also motivated by the fact that '97 was the end of twenty years in city government and I had done about as many different things as you could do in the Borough President's Office. I had done some things that I really value and it was horrible to try to do those under *him*, even in the first two years, when I wasn't running. They were nonpartisan and there was no reason why they couldn't have been done.

I knew that if I ran for reelection as borough president that in 2001, with term limits, there'd be a huge field of people competing to be mayor. My personal guess was that the field would be big enough and young enough, not that I thought there was a sure chance of success in '97. I actually was probably a little optimistic, but I assumed, pretty comfortably in '96, that because of who would, or wouldn't, run that I could be the candidate in '97.

Mark Green   Incumbency has its values. Crime was down; he [Giuliani] was a very skilled arguer and candidate and, with the complicity of the media, they managed to marginalize Ruth in the media as some kind of freaky lefty. He out-raised her by a substantial amount in no small part because City Hall told donors—later denied till kingdom come: you contribute to Ruth Messinger and that's publicly reported, you're *dead*.

Ruth Messinger   I ran against him significantly on Louima. In fact, I was attacked by him and by others for how strongly I ran against him on Louima. And it turns out that at least a piece of what we did was wrong because it was reported that they [the police] said it was "Giuliani time" and I used that in a couple of speeches that I gave in the Haitian community. And then it appeared that it was not true—that someone made it up.

———————

On November 4, 1997, in the wake of the lowest voter turnout in decades, the incumbent mayor defeated Ruth Messinger by sixteen points. And although he barely carried the borough of Manhattan and lost the Bronx, he did garner 20 percent of the black vote, 43 percent of the Latino vote, and likely the same percentage of gay votes, rendering a stunning blow to the city's liberal constituency.

Ruth Messinger   I assumed—which is my worst assumption and probably the only thing I regret—that even though I might lose, given his popularity, we'd be able to have a serious campaign, since I'm a pretty serious, office-holding candidate, and that some of these issues would really be discussed and covered by the press. And the only thing in the whole time I spent in government, which I *love*, that I never got over, was the extent to which the press simply looked at the candidates, decided that he was going to win and, therefore, decided they didn't need to cover the candidates. And I was very, very frustrated.

Stanley Friedman   *Mickey Mouse* could have destroyed Messinger. She just never got off the ground. She didn't really have a core constituency other than the Upper West Side of Manhattan.

Frank Luntz   Crime was the obvious default response for why Rudy was a good mayor. But if you ask which was the greater accomplishment, getting all those people off the welfare rolls and back to work or reducing murders and other violent crimes, people actually said in my polling—it never gets reported—that welfare was more important. But what really matters is that Rudy wasn't necessarily a mayor about *issues*; he was actually a mayor about attributes and character traits. And the one attribute that no one in New York, not even Ed Koch, could equal Rudy in is the phrase "He says what he means and means what he says." I discovered in 1997 that that was the number one attribute that New Yorkers wanted in their mayor and it was the number one attribute that they used to describe him. That's one of the reasons why he won so overwhelmingly in that election. It wasn't about policy or issues. It was about *character*, about who he was as a person, and it's much more interesting. And it's much more *important*.

Election Eve

The November 3, 1997, edition of the *New York Times* carried a prediction by pollster Frank Luntz that the incumbent mayor "would get at least 60 percent of the vote" in the next day's election. Giuliani was concerned that potential pro-Giuliani voters, reading that figure, would stay away from their polling places. As Giuliani writes in his memoir, *Leadership*, "I called Frank in and told him, 'I don't understand why the hell you did that.' I told him not to repeat that ever again, and explained to him how damaging over promising could be."

Frank Luntz I don't know if there's any other candidate I would feel a greater personal human attachment to. There have been two times when he was *furious* with me—I had situations in '93 and in '97 where this happened—and, actually, both of them were legitimate. We got over both of them, thank God, because the first one was very early in the relationship. And only in a personal relationship would he know what to say to frighten me and make me feel awful.

Election Night

Ruth Messinger We followed the protocol, so we called to concede. I then did a concession speech, which was pretty dramatic and, perhaps, emotional. And then I remember being in a hotel with lots of disappointed people, watching him, and I was staggered by that speech: he certainly didn't say anything nice about me, or about the campaign, which is a common courtesy. He talked about how this is a new lease on life and a new opportunity and we're going to rid this city of the old. Give us a *break!*

I'm very happy now with my current job [with American Jewish World Service]. But after December 31, when I left the Borough President's Office, I was intent on finding a not-for-profit organization that I could direct, and I assumed—and many people assumed with me—that I would be able to run a not-for-profit that had to do with any one of twenty issues I had worked on in the city: homelessness, child care, foster care, or community development. I did some work as a private consultant and applied for a couple of jobs which were not-for-profits and twice I was headhunted in a search process. I had meetings with the boards of a couple of good organizations and then was the runner-up. And in one of these I was really surprised that they didn't choose me. I actually called a couple of people and said, "What's the matter?" And those people said to me, "You must be out of your mind; no one who runs a not-for-profit in the city is going to hire you, because they think the mayor will punish them!" The notion that people are worried about being punished by him just hadn't *occurred* to me until someone said it to me, because my premise was graciousness. My biggest joke [during the campaign] was "I got his kindergarten report card and it says, 'Does not know how to play well with others.'"

Some Major Second-Term Issues

Gene Russianoff   We had a giant dustup with the Giuliani administration in '98: [City Council Speaker] Peter Vallone, at the request of the government groups, changed the campaign finance law so that it would provide a match of four dollars to every one dollar of private funds—in my view one of the most progressive programs for campaign financing in the nation and an encouragement for candidates to seek out individuals and churches and people to match their money. The council passed it. Giuliani vetoed it—the mayor's argument was that it would cost a fortune. I can't even remember the number he used, but it was two or three times what it would end up costing. The council overrode his veto. In New York, when a bill is signed, there's something called a bill hearing—it's in the state law and it's just required—where it's either signed or vetoed, and the mayor has to sit and listen to New Yorkers high and low say whether they like it or they *don't* like it. Mayors tend to be testy and a little petulant during these bill hearings because why should they sit and listen to the public? When it came to this forum, they really organized. There were fifty to seventy-five people there, in the room that now the mayor works out of that used to be the Board of Estimate room. The Mayor was up on the podium and he was pretty dismissive. I was very angry at what he was doing. I really thought he was hurrying it along, not just that he was against the four-to-one match but, at the same time, he wanted to move the Campaign Finance Board quite away from the political process. So when I spoke, I said that the person who individually benefited the most from the law and had taken the most public funds in the history of the program was Rudolph Giuliani. And he *exploded*; I really sensed a feeling of tremendous anger from the stage. I looked at that in two ways: one, that he was, like all mayors, often scary and hard to challenge—even for someone like me, who was a regular advocate, it definitely was not the easiest thing—but also that he was *human*. Mayors live in insulated bubbles—all of them, not just Giuliani, and certainly Bloomberg—and they have their "yes" people around them and you don't get through to them. In Giuliani's case, they all told him that the program was very expensive and this was a terrible thing to do and I don't think he ever really got the other side of the argument. And I don't think he was the kind of politician who has people who give opposing sides of an issue and he then tries to sort them out in his own mind. I think that *he* sets the agenda and then gets "yessed."

"Sensation"

In 1999, Giuliani took on the Brooklyn Museum of Art, accusing it of distributing "sick stuff" by exhibiting paintings he perceived to be anti-Catholic in its "Sensation" exhibition. The mayor outraged the art world by threatening to cut off the city's subsidies to the venerable cultural institution.

Fred Siegel   That was a double con game: They had already tried this in Baltimore; Arnold Lehman [director of the Brooklyn Museum], the guy who brought the show, figured out in Baltimore that if you outraged Catholics, you would bring liberals to your side and make a reputation for yourself. He sees it in London and it's a sensation in the full sense. The full title is "The Sensation Show" and it's owned by [Charles] Saatchi. The irony here of course is that this is Margaret Thatcher's PR adviser. Saatchi has these commercial arrangements with auction houses, which are much less than ethical. He comes to New York with this show and he can't get support for it—everyone sees that this is an ethically compromised show, in a variety of ways, and he can't get any major sponsors. He goes to Trojan condoms; even *they* don't want to be part of it. So the idea is to hype the show, to get it sold, to help the Brooklyn Museum. Now some of the pieces of art that caused problems in England weren't even brought here—the handprints of a woman who had mutilated and murdered five children. It used to be that art created controversy; now controversy gives something the aura of art, whether it has any artistic value or not, so it was a double con. Giuliani's con was as follows: he didn't want to cave in to the Conservative Party on abortion, so he was looking for an issue. Now I can't prove this—I found no smoking gun, no memo—but I'm talking to people and watching it closely at the time. He was looking for a way to appeal to conservative Catholics without reversing his position and this was perfect. Lehman was a fraud; Lehman was corrupt; and he went after him.

Floyd Abrams   I've always thought that the position he took came from deep within him rather than simply being a political effort to gain Catholic or right-wing support. I always thought he meant basically what he said. He said he was angry and I believed him. That said, certainly among the political class there was a contrary view, reflected in newspaper articles, in which many people attributed to him an effort to defeat Hillary by attracting right-wing votes. Obviously, that could have been true. I've heard stories that after it was all over, he talked about both sides winning—we winning the legal battle and he winning on some sort of political level. But I've always thought that he was deeply offended by the Ofili painting as it had been described to him and he wasn't going to take it.

Steven Brill   I used to kid Floyd about when he was in litigation with Rudy, when Rudy was mayor, over the Brooklyn Museum, that those two were made for each other, because I don't think Rudy seriously thought that he was going to win those cases and Floyd seriously thought that *he* was going to win those cases—and he was obviously right, and obviously deserved to win those cases.

Floyd Abrams   I think he viewed himself as a tough guy—a guy who can't be pushed around, a guy who cannot accept other people's definitions of problems. Some of his success as mayor probably came because of that. With respect to the museum issue, he was angry and, as always, filled with a sort of self-assurance which led him to conclude that if he was angry enough he must be right and the law perhaps would even say he was right. I don't think he spends much time with self-doubt about whether positions he takes are correct. If the courts rule against him, as you see in this very case, the answer is: the court was out of touch, the court was left-wing liberal, the court was West Side Democratic. All those sorts of curse words he uttered when the case was over fairly reflected the way he thought of the court. I don't think he thought that he could be wrong, that, maybe, other values were more important than the values that he was trumpeting.

That was my first exposure to the Brooklyn Museum, my first meetings with the people there. They were stunned. I am an eyewitness to the leadership of the museum's having been stunned that Giuliani would go that far. I don't even think that they thought he would become involved. When do mayors become involved on matters like that? The museum had had an exhibition a few years previously which had dealt with censored works and it had never become a political issue. I think the museum officials were absolutely floored that the mayor would take this position. They also had what they understood to be—reasonably, in my view—a sign-off from the Giuliani administration. Now that was not from the mayor, but they did have it from the people in his administration who dealt with the arts.

Gene Russianoff   It was not our issue, but I followed it, like most New Yorkers did. I think it was political on the mayor's part: he decided that his constituency got very steamed up on these issues. And the Brooklyn Museum didn't have a lot of community support.

Floyd Abrams I always thought that we should win because, if nothing else, this was simply retribution visited upon the museum by a mayor who was angry at its art. There is much First Amendment law that says that political powers cannot limit First Amendment rights in an effort to punish people for doing something the leaders don't like. However, there were many hard issues in the case, for example, whether the Giuliani administration could prevail on the grounds that this was just a matter of funding art rather than banning speech flat out. The advantage that we had was the clarity of it all. Usually, people deny that they are trying to suppress speech. Giuliani, whether because of excessive self-confidence or because he thought that speaking out publicly was a good thing for him, made a record for us very rare in First Amendment case law. It is rarer that you have a situation in which that sort of personal venom is so transparent and undeniable and in which what is involved is so clearly a matter of punishing a cultural institution for pursuing its First Amendment rights.

With Rudy Giuliani as a client—someone who thought very well of his own legal abilities—it likely was not easy for a lawyer to give him advice that he did not want. I don't know what advice [New York City's Corporation Counsel] Mike [Michael] Hess gave him, but it is hard for me to believe that the advice was phrased so strongly as to lead the mayor to worry about what could happen in the case. I heard from more than one person that Giuliani said how unfair it was, how unjust, how little money he had. It seemed to me self-pity of a very unattractive sort. If you really want to play hardball the way *he* plays, you have to be prepared that people aren't just going to take it.

What brought the mayor to his knees was that his deposition was very likely to occur and that it likely would have been televised. I believe that at that point in a case that he was very likely to lose—we had already won in the court of appeals—some advisers must have sat with him and said, "What is the point of all of this?" He probably would have been an effective witness in his way, but he was well advised that a deposition would raise the newsworthiness of a case which was starting to fade—that the deposition would only harm him by unifying his opponents, leading to more criticism of him. To put the issue into more practical garb, even if he acted originally for purely political reasons, he had already served those reasons. If he had wanted to show what side he was on, to take a strong stand, he had already done that.

Fred Siegel   Every knee-jerk liberal in the city was talking about the second coming of Mussolini—which is the same thing that was said about La Guardia—and as soon as everyone got what they needed out of it, it was quietly settled. This is what the French would call *un grand guignol* [in reference to theater pieces featuring the gruesome and horrific that were performed at *Le Grand Guignol*, a small theater in the Montmartre district of Paris].

Was There a Threat to the Mayor's Second-Term Pledge to Unify the City?

Mayor Giuliani had begun his second term promising to bring unity to the city—a city already stressed by the arrest and torture of Abner Louima the previous summer. The downward cycle of police incidents involving innocent African American men, notably the gunning down of the unarmed Amadou Diallo and Patrick Dorismond, would intensify already severely strained race relations. In the wake of those killings, the question would be raised as to whether there was an antiblack bias in the NYPD.

Mark Green   Giuliani's skill is that he's a blunt instrument and his *liability* is that he's a blunt instrument. If you're a blunt instrument and the enemy is terrorists who have just killed nearly three thousand New Yorkers, he's a wonder to behold. But if you're a blunt instrument and your thesis is "Cops *good*; kids of color on the street probably *bad*," you have a problem in a diverse city.

Albert O'Leary   There's so much made of profiling, but the reality is that if a purple guy comes by and hits you with a stick every day, you're going to start being very wary of purple guys, right? Is it because the cops are racist? No, it's because the cops are used to dealing with black perpetrators or Hispanic perpetrators. It's just *conditioning*.

Sanford Rubenstein   There's a mentality that I just don't understand. They were coming out with the first verdict in the Louima trial and I was walking on Cadman Plaza [in Brooklyn, near Mr. Rubenstein's law offices]. As I got to the sidewalk, a police van sped by and there was a shout: "NYPD! NYPD!" It was almost like a football cheer and it was *police officers*! After a trial at which a police officer had admitted to this horrible act, to have a police officer, in front of the courthouse, stick his head out the car window and yell "NYPD!" was chilling, and it demonstrated a mentality that somehow has to be eliminated from those who serve as police officers in this city—in every city.

Gene Russianoff   There may be a lot of truth to those accusations about the police, but it comes out of a sense of grievance that we New Yorkers very often have. And, of course, if you're poor, or you're struggling, you have even more of a sense of grievance. From Rudy's point of view, it was more important politically to reduce crime than to get along with segments of the city in which you're going to lose some voters.

Benjamin Brafman   Rudy is, and always will be, very close to the police. He sees himself as their brother and their ally, someone who needs to stand by them. And he was an in-your-face type of mayor who wanted to be in charge right away; he was very eager to go public *before* he had all the facts because he thought the public expected it of him and, also, because he liked to be out front, being quoted in the newspapers and on TV. You're never going to have a white person look at these shootings [of Diallo and Dorismond] the same way as an African American person does. I don't think Rudy ever understood that and so he failed to recognize that simply saying you're sympathetic isn't the same as being a member of the African American community who believes it's open season where cops can shoot without responsibility.

Mark Green   I became worried, pre-Diallo, about a pattern of police harassment of innocent young black and Latino men and I asked for data from the [Police] Department about civilian complaints of police misconduct. I made the request under the City Charter provision, which entitles a public advocate to request such information. Giuliani said, Take a hike! So I hiked to the State Supreme Court, sued them, and won a unanimous decision and got the data. I then raised several hundred thousand dollars in philanthropic funds to hire people to analyze and categorize it. And we released a very sophisticated report showing how infrequently abusive cops were punished, which led to a rupture in cop-community relations and hurt race relations in the city as well. Giuliani was furious at my request, my lawsuit, my investigation, and my proposals, all of which got a lot of attention.

PART VIII

September 11

Chapter 16

HEROISM, GRIEF, AND DECISION

*My father used to say to me . . . whenever you get into
a crisis or an emergency and everybody around you is
getting very excited, you become the calmest person in
the room and you'll be able to figure your way out of it.*

—Rudolph Giuliani, recalling Harold Giuliani's words of wisdom

Had Rudy Giuliani not dropped out of the Senate race in 2000 and had he
won the election that November, he would have been in Washington on
the gloriously warm and sunny morning of Tuesday, September 11, 2001.

As fate would have it, Rudy Giuliani was still the mayor and he was in
New York on that morning. It was primary day, and as registered voters
were already arriving at polling places to choose their respective parties'
candidates to run in November to succeed him, the mayor was having
breakfast at the Peninsula, a hotel on 55th Street, just west of Fifth
Avenue, with his counsel, Denny Young, and his former assistant U.S.
Attorney, Bill Simon, to advise Simon on running in California's coming
gubernatorial primary.

Several minutes before nine o'clock, the three men were standing in
the hotel's entryway, saying good-bye, when the mayor was informed that
what was thought at the time to have been a two-engine aircraft had
crashed into one of the two towers of the World Trade Center.

As the mayor would recall in his testimony several years later, on May
19, 2004, before the 9/11 Commission, he went outside and, noticing that
the weather was fine, with excellent visibility, he concluded that the tower
had been deliberately attacked.

Lilliam Barrios-Paoli   It was eight-thirty. I had just voted and I was walking on Park Avenue toward the United Way [located at 2 Park Avenue, at 34th Street] on Park Avenue South where I was working at the time. I was on 33rd and Park when I saw a very low-flying plane going south. It was an American Airlines plane and it was flying very low and I remember saying to myself, What is that pilot *doing*? Then I looked south and I thought, He's going to crash and it's going to be a disaster in Manhattan! My God! If he crashes in Manhattan, it's going to change our lives because of the amount of people dead. I was never thinking, World Trade Center. I said to myself, Well, obviously, if he's in trouble, the pilot's going to go to the East River or the Hudson River. But looking at this plane, I'm thinking, LaGuardia's that way [to the east of Manhattan Island] and so is Kennedy; New York is the other way. Why is he *here*? By now there was a whole bunch of people looking up because you could hear the noise and the plane was very low and you could see it. I continued walking. I must have been on 31st or 30th because I was below the Empire State Building [which covers the entire west side of Fifth Avenue, from 33rd Street to 34th Street] and the plane was going straight down Park Avenue and I remember saying, "Oh, my God! This is so weird."

As the mayor was being driven in his sport utility vehicle, a black Chevrolet Suburban, toward the city's Emergency Command Center, located on the twenty-third floor of 7 World Trade Center, just north of the Twin Towers, he was informed—erroneously, as it would turn out—that twelve commercial jets were unaccounted for and that the Sears Tower in Chicago, then the world's tallest building, had been attacked.

The entourage sped south, cell phones ringing constantly, and when it reached downtown Manhattan the mayor could see that the North Tower of the World Trade Center was engulfed in flames. He and his aides then continued on, past St. Vincent's Hospital, where medical personnel were already marshaled, awaiting casualties. As the entourage reached Canal Street, the South Tower erupted in flames.

Glenn Corbett, professor of Fire Sciences, John Jay College of Criminal Justice   I was on my way to the college and had just driven past the Vince Lombardi rest stop on the New Jersey Turnpike. At that point there is a slight rise in the roadway and I could see the top half of the Twin Towers. I thought, Holy mackerel, it's an excessively large fire. I knew instantly that it was going to be a historic fire and that when I reached Manhattan

I would take my class down to the scene—that this was a once-in-a-lifetime situation for a fire sciences student. I never made it to the school. I got on a bus, but we were stopped about four hundred yards from the entrance to the Lincoln Tunnel. I had my scanner with me and heard live a good deal of the taped material that was eventually released [in 2005].

Now the Emergency Command Center was being evacuated and it was decided that the mayor should proceed to the area between the Merrill Lynch and American Express buildings on the western end of the Twin Towers site. It was then that the full horror of the attack and the desperation of its victims impacted on Rudy: looking upward toward the flames shooting from the high floors of one of the crippled towers, he observed first one person, then many others jumping from windows on what he estimated to be the 102nd floor.

Soon details of this deadly, unprecedented attack on U.S. soil began to emerge. At exactly 8:47 American Airlines flight 11, carrying eighty-one passengers and eleven crew members from Boston's Logan Airport to Los Angeles, had changed course and crashed into the North Tower of the World Trade Center, followed at 9:03 by United Airlines flight 175, which crashed into the South Tower, igniting a firestorm that would within a matter of hours cause the deaths of nearly three thousand innocent human beings from many walks of life and catapult the United States, and the world, into a new era of terror. That day's horrific events would be pressed indelibly into the memories of people throughout the States and abroad who saw those images on television or, more immediately, were at or near what would come to be known as ground zero as the Twin Towers were hit, burned, and imploded.

The Mayor Is Missing in Action

The mayor was driven to 75 Barclay Street, the site of the Police Department Command Center, where he set up an emergency post. Then there was an enormous thud. The South Tower of the World Trade Center had imploded and Rudy Giuliani was trapped in the now dust- and debris-filled building.

Rudy Washington   My driver says, "What do you want to do?" I say, "Well, Rudy's going to go over there" [to the World Trade Center]. I'm thinking, This is a little prop plane, a sightseeing plane, that somebody flew into the building and people probably got hurt and probably died; we'd better get down there. We start down the FDR [the highway named for President Franklin Delano Roosevelt that runs down the eastern side of Manhattan]. When you got to 34th Street, you'd see the World Trade Center pop up in the middle. I could see from the distance that there's this hole with black smoke billowing out of it. I told my driver, "This is serious. Get down there!" So we turn the lights and the siren on—I don't usually do that because it could cause an accident—and we shoot downtown. I've learned from experience that you never drive up to the scene because you won't get your car out—the fire trucks and stuff will block you in. So we park away from the building. I walk up to the gate and ask the cop, "Where's Rudy?" He says, "He walked down there already."

Herman Badillo   I was home [in the Bronx] and I was wondering where Rudy was. I told my wife, "I can't believe he wouldn't be out [on Primary Day], knowing him. He must be in trouble." And he *was* in trouble. I was worried that he had been killed because it took about an hour and a half before he surfaced.

Rudy Washington   I'm getting calls from the governor, something people don't know. "Where's Rudy?" I'm saying, "He went to the first building, Governor." He says, "Rudy, you're telling me he was *in it?*" "The last location I had on him was in the building." He says, "Rudy, are you trying to find him?" I say, "I've got cops on foot; I'm trying to. We lost our radios, we lost our cell phones, we lost everything." We had closed the schools and canceled the elections and I'm telling the governor that I'm doing all this and he's calling me every five minutes: "Rudy, did you find him? *Did you find him?*" I call the Pentagon and I tell the governor, "I've got fighter jets coming. As soon as I finish with this, I'm going to start a digging operation. I'm mobilizing." On my final call to the governor—like me, he assumes that Rudy is dead—he says "Rudy, I'm preparing to take over the city." "Fine, Governor, I'm here. I might relocate my command center. I've got to figure out where I'm going to go because I'm a sitting target till I know the air space is clear."

––––––––––

Also among the missing that morning were occupants of the Twin Towers, bystanders, emergency rescue workers, police, and several hundred of the firefighters from the city's five boroughs who had rushed into the burning buildings.

Edward Reuss   They had sealed all bridges because no one knew what was going on; there were no communications. You got all your news from home—this has since come out: you, as a TV viewer, knew more about what was happening than the 911 operators. The 911 operators didn't know and they were being inundated with calls from people in the buildings: Help! Help! Help! But *you're* watching the whole scenario: someone's calling up from the 110th floor and *you* know he's got a problem. And the poor firemen, with gear, trying to go up eighty stories with that on you! I'd drop dead of a heart attack, just walking up the stairs.

A Portrait of One Missing Firefighter

Sally Regenhard, mother of Christian Michael Otto Regenhard, a firefighter last seen alive in the lobby of the World Trade Center   It's impossible for me to start talking about Christian without crying and I hate to do that. You're talking aspirations and hopes. He was really like a young renaissance man respecting his background at the Bronx High School of Science, his IQ of 146, in a special talented and gifted program of the City of New York, when it was really going strong in the '80s, and then five years in the United States Marine Corps—I don't think many Bronx High School of Science graduates join the Marines. He just blossomed during that time; he mastered *so much*. He was a budding artist and a writer—it's been too painful for me to go through his notebooks and his journals from college. I just can't do it now, but I'm going to. He did everything, traveled everywhere. He loved life, loved people. He was writing a screenplay about children whose parents were killed by the Nazis. My son was a very strong supporter of the Holocaust [Museum and] Study Center at the Bronx High School of Science, so I'm sure that these things inspired him to be creative in the future.

For him to tell me about something he was doing meant it was extremely meaningful because there was so much of his life that we didn't know about because he traveled so much—he spent time at San Francisco State; he was in the military for five years; he lived in South America—he was bilingual in Spanish and English. He was hoping, I'm sure, to finish his screenplay, to continue his writing, develop his art. He had planned to apply to finish his studies here in New York—he was looking at Pratt [Institute] or Cooper Union and they would have grabbed him in a second. I'm sure he wanted to go back down to South America where he was a guide on a glacier in Patagonia. He loved Chile; he had a "promised one" there—kind of a pre-engagement. He loved being with the people. He wanted to remain down there as a rock climber and a mountain climber. I said to him, "Christian, you could fall off a mountain in the wilds of South America and no one could ever find you." It was a terrible, cruel irony that he was safer in the wilds of Patagonia than he was in his own city.

Dealing with the Situation on the Ground While the Mayor Is Still Trapped

Albert O'Leary   We knew nothing more about it until the second plane hit. Then there was an understanding: this is an attack. At that point, Larry Reuter, my boss, who was the president of New York City Transit [the Metropolitan Transit Authority]—he still is today—spoke to Joe Hoffman, the senior vice president for subways, and they made the decision, *instantaneously,* that they had to shut down the system. It was the first time in the history of the subway system they shut the whole system down. And they got everybody out—this was just a little after the peak of rush hour—and they got all the trains secure, there wasn't a *single person* injured in the subway, there wasn't a *single train* damaged by it. Of course, when the buildings collapsed, we lost the Cortlandt Street subway station on the 9 [New York City subway routes are numerically and alphabetically designated].

Rudy Washington   As I walked the site, I walked up on the nose gear; on it was a woman cut in half. I saw the wheel of the plane! It didn't register how big it was. Until six o'clock that night I operated on the notion that these were little planes out of Teterboro [an airport in neighboring New Jersey used by owners of small planes] with bombs on them. We're sitting in the command center at [One] Police Plaza and we've got News 1 on and they're talking about four hijacked airliners and I turn to the chief and say, "They hijacked *airliners* today, too?" He looks at me—he knows I'm not joking—and says, "Rudy, what do you think you've been *dealing with*?" Oh my God!

    Fuel had rained down on people and a lot of them were hurt. I could see them laid out there and ambulances were beginning to come up. I'm standing there with the first triage team. A woman is walking around fully masked—I don't know whether she's a doctor or a nurse—and she's got a garbage basket with a blanket over it. She uncovers it and puts something in; it's body parts. One of the cops says, "There are more planes out there!" And I'm thinking, Whew! Not only is this a terrorist attack, but it's going to be a *continuous* attack.

I'm looking for Rudy and I see Rosemary O'Keefe standing in the middle of all these injured people and she's got a helmet on. And I say, "Where's Rudy? Why are you standing there with a riot helmet on in the middle of the street?" She doesn't hear us and she says, "The *people*, the *people*! They're jumping out the windows. Don't go in; don't go in!" Debris and paper are raining down and she's saying, "Rudy's in there!" And now the cops are telling me, "More planes." I'm heading towards Rudy and I'm walking up on the [City Hall] plaza and I'm looking up. All the cops and all the firemen come running out. I don't know why they're running, but when you see *firemen and policemen* running, you know it's time to run. *I* turn around and start running. My driver is with me. We shoot past Rosemary, who's trying to run but can't. We can't leave her. We go back. My driver grabs one arm, I grab the other, and we're carrying her up the street. The cops are moving into a van and there's just room for her. We force her in, close the door and they take off. Now the building starts to fall.

The Mayor Is Found Alive and Takes Command

Rudy Washington The governor said, "Call me back if you hear anything on the mayor." I hang up. Ten or fifteen minutes later, a cop comes running in. He got close enough someplace where he got reception from their two-way radio and he could make out that the mayor was alive! I called the governor and I said, "I don't know where he's at; he's trapped in a building. They only said they have him in the basement of a building and he's alive." The governor gave a big sigh of relief. I said, "As soon as I get him, I'll put you in touch."

Rudy Giuliani's actions that morning at ground zero not only brought some measure of assurance to his grief-stricken, traumatized constituents in the immediate aftermath of that defining tragedy, but in demonstrating his great personal courage, dedication, and leadership, he succeeded in shedding both the baggage of his long career and more recent, negative image to emerge to most people as a superhero to his city, the nation, and the world.

Rudy Washington   He convened meetings every day, and not just of city agencies, but all the other agencies—federal, state, everybody; the governor went to these meetings. This was the first time people were getting a peek into Rudy's apparatus and how he functioned. This wasn't new to *me*; I had to report to Rudy every morning. They were scratching their heads: How do you guys live like this, under this kind of pressure? This was *Rudy Giuliani*. He puts his fingerprint on *every single thing*.

Henry Stern   People would report what they had done so that the mayor would know what to include in his press conferences. In these meetings I was able to observe his management style and how he coordinated things. He was terrific in a crisis. He asked sensible questions. He was in command.

Raoul Felder   They moved the whole city to a pier [Pier 94]. They put signs up: DEPARTMENT OF CORRECTIONS; SEWERS; DEPARTMENT OF SANITATION. Each department had a little desk and they would continue churning out these maps of the 9/11 area. They had another building, which was for survivors and their families. They had a place for kids, too, so that they were being taken care of. It was all a charade so that these people would think there was some hope.

David Dinkins   He rallied us. He called for former mayors; he called me and Koch. I remember at one meeting we went to in the first few days—it was a gathering of religious leaders that included us—we were all trying to help and I thought he behaved appropriately in that time and I was willing to do what I could to help.

Raoul Felder   One day, toward the end of the day, it was raining there [at the pier] and there was a line and Rudy says, "Why don't they have umbrellas?" And they say, "We don't have umbrellas." And he says, "Well, *get* them umbrellas." They said, "It's five hundred umbrellas." And he says, "What do I care? Get the *umbrellas*." And they got the umbrellas somehow. God knows where he got them; he got it together.

Herman Badillo   He reacted strongly to take direct and forceful action to reassure the people of the city and the country and to say that we were going to fight back against this type of thing and we should hold steady and meet the crisis. And it certainly helped: there were no riots; there was no looting. There were thousands of people in the street at that time and in other situations, like where there's been a blackout—I know because I've been in the middle of them—there has been looting, riots, and problems. And his forcefulness helped to make sure that people remained calm.

George Schneider   If I had to come up with one word for what we learned at Bishop Loughlin, it would be "integrity." You could see that he knew the right thing to do and he was going to make sure that he did it— that he was responsible for leading and he was going to make sure that everything was done to help New York recover and to help those who were directly affected recover as much as they could. It became clear to me that he was trying to deal with the whole thing in terms of people's safety, in terms of concern about those who had lost people, in terms of being determined—although he didn't have direct control over it—about justice for what had happened there. I just thought he was magnificent in the way he handled the whole situation.

Sanford Rubenstein   How do I react to him being known as "America's Mayor"? It's demonstrative to me how short a memory the public has with regard to things that may have been happening prior to 9/11when something as horrible as 9/11 occurs and one reacts in a way that is applauded by the public. It's demonstrative to me of what can happen in American politics. There's a saying: "It's a long time between now and November"— you never know what will happen in politics.

Mark Green   I can see some public officials overplaying the tough card, but I saw him close up during the weeks after 9/11 and he struck just the right note of toughness and compassion.

Steven R. Andrews   There were things Giuliani said on that day that can still make me cry. I remember him saying that the number of people killed was "more than we can bear." In my mind he achieved heroic status that day. But, of course, I'm not from New York. The wind changes and I get tears in my eyes.

Reconnecting with the Mayor

Rudy Washington   I heard where Rudy was: they had moved him to a firehouse. I called the governor and put the two of them together and I kept doing what I was doing. Now, at one o'clock in the afternoon, from

[One] Police Plaza, I get the admiral back and he says, "Rudy, I'm sending you a hospital ship; I've got the ship coming in to Morehead City [North Carolina] to pick up all the doctors and the nurses." "I'm not sure you should send these nurses and doctors. I just left the site and there are no injured people, just body parts." And he said, "Rudy, if anything comes up in that airspace that's not supposed to be there, we'll shoot it down. I've got half of it off the Chesapeake [River, off the coast of Maryland] and you've got the other half." Then I finally connected with the mayor. He got established at the police academy at about seven o'clock.

Mobilizing Resources, On-the-Spot Decisions, and Improvisation

Malcolm Hoenlein   We were in touch immediately with the administration and with the police and others and they were in touch with us. We had additional security right away. There was concern in terms of both individuals and institutions. We were concerned about a couple of things: one was physical security for the many Jews who were in there [World Trade Center]; and there was the second level of concern, which was the propaganda campaign saying the Jews knew in advance and they got out—the smoke hadn't even cleared and we were facing the PR battle against the imam from 96th Street and all the others. What Giuliani did with the Saudi prince [Al-Waleed bin Talal, who wrote a $10 million check for disaster relief to the city] was really quite remarkable. I'm not sure that others could have gotten away with it: people would have said you should take it. But Giuliani didn't. Again, I don't believe he did it to grandstand; to have gotten $10 million would have been good for him, too, but the fact is that he really does believe in those principles. That was an instinctive response on his part that that is not the right thing to do—that you don't take money from the guys who just blew up a building.

Rudy Washington   People are starting to call, offering their resources. Wilbur Chapman, who I later pushed for commissioner of DOT [New York City Department of Transportation], calls and catches me at [One] Police Plaza. I tell him, "I've just mobilized search and rescue; you're going to have to put people on." I'm working on all this and I've yet to talk to the mayor. I knew I was going to need a place for all the search and rescue teams. I had already reached out to the YMCA—I had already locked up their rooms, and we had the digging equipment coming in.

Lilliam Barrios-Paoli   That afternoon, the United Way and the New York Community Trust started a 9/11 fund, so my life was never the same for the next four months. I said to myself, My God! What's going to happen? This is going to change everything. And, of course, it *did*.

Rudy Washington   You've just got to keep going, you can't stop, and every second something else would come to my mind and I would do it. And when I got all the engineers together, I knew I was going to have a problem with the lights—something as simple as that. I had lights coming in from all over the city—from fire, police, the private sector, everybody—because we had lost power and I knew we were going to be out there in the dark. I took all the engineers down there and while I'm walking the site—we're bringing in all the heavy equipment, designating where the stuff is going to go—the city engineers are trying to determine if any of the [surrounding] buildings are going to collapse from damage.

In hindsight, people were going through emotional stress and not realizing they were going through it. I walked up on fights that were so mundane and trivial—people were caught in their own little world and couldn't let go. I walked up on a construction worker, a DOT worker, and a cop. The construction worker said, "I've got to put my piece of equipment here." The light pole is in the way and he wants to take it down. The DOT guy says, "You can't take down city poles; you've got to have permits." And the cop is like, "What are you, some kind of *idiot*?" I'm settling fights like this and I realize: people are in shock and they're just doing what they think they can do to make a difference.

A high-level city official at ground zero that day, who did not wish to be quoted for attribution lest he embarrass the NYPD, witnessed an exchange in which there was an individual standing on a mound, barking orders: "Get this water over here!" According to the authors' source, "He's about thirty-three years old and he's barking at sixty-year-old chiefs with white helmets and they're trying to reason with him. He says, 'We've got to get some water on this thing!' Who is he? He's a volunteer and people were *listening* to him!" His age was the giveaway for the witness to the episode, who reasoned that "if he were an older gentleman barking these orders, I might have said, 'He's a chief who's not in uniform.'" When the authors' source moved closer to the volunteer, he smelled alcohol on the young man's breath. "There were countless fights like that going on," the witness recalled.

Robert Volpe   I spent a couple of weeks down there working as a volunteer and only left when it became so organized that people were threatening to arrest us because we had a camera on us. But we weren't taking
pictures; it's history—you're living *history*. I lost a number of close friends
and so did Justin, people he went to school with, people he grew up with,
people who served with him who became firemen, and just friends in general. I sit with the families. My wife [an artist] has done, to date, about
thirty-three portraits of people we know personally because there were no
remains and she managed early on to do a number of them so they could
have something for the memorial services. And she's still getting requests
to do portraits. She was always a fantastic artist, and all of a sudden, I'm
watching this unbelievable portrait artist.

Edward Reuss   When you retire, you don't just leave the job. I knew the
borough commander [Assistant Chief Anthony] Tony Marra; he was our
chief of the Staten Island Command Center, the 122 Precinct. The retired
officers are all over the country, but a lot of them are still living in New
York City and we know who they are. So I go down to the 122 and I say,
"Tony, I'd like to bring all the retired guys." He was so busy, he says, "Yeah,
yeah, yeah"—he just dismissed me.
   I knew all the workings of Staten Island. We set up a mobilization point
and I called 1010 WINS [an all-news radio station in New York City] and
I called New York 1 on my cell phone and told them who I was. I said, "I'm
a retired police captain and I want all retired police officers to meet me."
I was in a big parking lot, where helicopters could come down, right on the
oceanfront, in an area called Ocean Breeze. I got over three hundred men
right away, within an hour. I knew a lot of them and some I didn't know.
What I did—I have no real authority—I kept records of who came and I'm
glad I did that. I knew who I had—their phone numbers and their ranks.
All different ranks came. A lot of the guys were saying: "I gotta get up
there." They didn't want to stay away. I knew that there were probably
thousands of people up there. They had nonprofessional people assisting.
It was just total chaos and the more people that flooded that area the more
they're going to be tripping all over each other. So I said, "No, let's get what
they *need* up there."
   The people in all the private industries were wonderful. Now, we're all
old-time cops so we did things in our day that they don't do now. I said to
the old-time cops, "Commandeer a couple of buses," meaning, "Seize the
bus!" They knew exactly what I was planning to do. So they commandeer
a bus and they're ordering all the people off the bus. The bus isn't going to

go anywhere because nothing was working. The ferries worked, but they wouldn't let people on. So they're ordering them and one of the drivers is saying, "What do you mean, you're taking the bus?" And the cop says, "We're taking the bus! You're commandeered; you're working for *us* now!" So they bring the bus over and he says, "Okay, now we've got to get supplies." We thought there were going to be mass casualties, bodies all over the place—this was an hour and a half after it happened—so all the hospitals were waiting: Where are all the bodies, where are all the casualties?

There was a medical wholesale house up the street, Ocean Breeze, right near the Staten Island Hospital, so we loaded the bus up with all kinds of equipment—what they really needed was the masks and gloves. I sent about five guys with the bus up to the grounds, which became known as the Pile or ground zero. And they got through. It was hard because they were very worried about more acts of terrorism. But they let them over because they had their [Police Department] shields. The best thing was, when they started saying what they needed—heavy gloves, boots, and masks, because they were going through this steel and metal and they were cutting their hands and their shoes were being ripped apart—we started getting that stuff.

But before they came to me, they went down to the ferry to try to get on. Imagine the cops, seeing a truck pulling these big bottles [of medical supplies], in the middle of 9/11: they'd worry about someone trying to blow up the ferry, right? And nobody knew who they were, so they had to come down to where we were. I knew who they were, so we gave them a police escort. I called the borough commander of Staten Island and they sent motorcycles because I knew all these guys and they knew me, so there was a level of trust there and we got them on the boat.

The Role of the Media

Edward Reuss   He [Mayor Giuliani] used the press to get the message out that the evacuation of the city was as orderly as could be expected: people were walking across the bridges. Why? That was the advice that they were getting. Use of the media was continuously critical. When Giuliani lost his headquarters and he had to actually flee from that area to save his *life*, the press was sticking those microphones in his face and he was on the air all the time, and the public knew that he was the leader. He was, in effect, leading the country at that time. That was his shining moment. He exhibited leadership in a crisis that's *unheard of*. There's no parallel to that; we've never been attacked like *that*. We had a total breakdown in order—there were no phones, no communications. The situation makes you a leader.

The Reverend Al Sharpton   Giuliani always romanced the media and they just blew him up. It was aided by the White House, fellow Republicans, Bush coming here, standing with him. So there was a lot of politics in it. I thought it was unbelievable how overnight they resurrected him. It was an unbelievable reinvention, unlike any I had ever seen.

David Dinkins   It was important that the people be encouraged and uplifted, so that part was good. I thought that that was fine.

Eric Adams   It was a minstrel show in my opinion. We as New Yorkers and Americans were never so vulnerable before, probably not since Pearl Harbor. We had never been attacked on our home soil and so it was difficult for us. I'm sure a psychiatrist would tell you that there's a need to feel that someone is going to be there for us. Rudy understood that and played on it: here I am at the lowest point in my polls; I'm just about on my way out; I'm just about ready to leave City Hall; I can never be president. He saw it as an opportunity for *Rudy*. And it turned out to be a great opportunity for Rudy. He was not "America's Mayor" until 9/11. People forgot and washed away all of his sins; it's as though he was baptized on September 11 and became this new person, Saint Rudy.

Glenn Corbett   How often did you see [Fire Commissioner] Von Essen or [Police Commissioner] Kerik speaking? Giuliani dominated the whole thing. The whole issue of disinformation in those first few weeks lies right at his feet. He should have had the fire and police commissioners going down the whole list of technical issues that were happening. *Giuliani* was the story. The whole nation saw only him over and over again and that is what led to this mythology about Rudy Giuliani.

Marie Dorismond   I said to myself: somebody must like him because they're giving him a last chance to look good. September 11 comes and he's being honored by the Queen. This is not *good*. This man does not deserve all this attention. And now I'm afraid that he may run for president one day and I don't think I want him to be anywhere near anything like that. It would be a big blow to my family *again* to be looking at his face all the time.

Sanford Rubenstein   The press clearly made Giuliani the hero of 9/11 in New York and that resonated throughout the country. And that's just the way it is.

Wouldn't Any Other Mayor Have Acted in the Same Way? Isn't That the Mayor's Job?

Carol Bellamy   Part of leadership is stepping up to the plate. I'm not a big fan of Giuliani's mayoral leadership, but it's awfully picky to pick at how he performed, not just that day but in that entire environment. He certainly performed superbly, but I don't think it would have been beyond the capacity of others to do that as well. The two that come to mind are Ed Koch and the present mayor. It would have been different, but both could have performed quite capably.

Jay Goldberg   Bloomberg would have done it; you would have done it; maybe I would have done it. I still can't figure out what *he* did. He didn't pull anybody from the rubble. But he got all that publicity and that propelled him back from a two out of ten to an eleven.

Lilliam Barrios-Paoli   Pataki didn't look that decisive; it was a great moment for *him* to shine and he didn't. Any of those people could have probably upstaged Rudy because he was a lame duck and nobody did. Nobody *could*. Rudy rose to the occasion and it was amazing to watch.

Raoul Felder   In a fight, you don't want anybody but Giuliani. If Dinkins could not handle a local disturbance in Brooklyn, Lord only knows what would have happened if somebody like him had been mayor at the time. Look even at Bloomberg. He takes these retreats and won't tell anybody where he's going. He says, "Don't worry, if anything happens, I can fly right back."

Fran Reiter   Where Rudy Giuliani surprised people is not the "take charge" part of it, but the emotional part of it and the way he very effectively brought hope to the people of the city and kept their spirits up. Anybody who has ever watched Rudy Giuliani at a cop's funeral knows that he is very emotionally invested in this part of the job—I always said it was "the priest" in him and there is an aspect of him that is very priestlike, in terms of comforting people who are in trouble. It's not the kind of thing you see on television as a rule; it's not the kind of thing you see when he goes to visit someone in the hospital; it's the thing you see when *you're* in trouble. That's the Rudy Giuliani that the world at large *doesn't* generally get to see. But it's there. And it's particularly there, I think, for strangers. I don't know that it's always there for those he's really close to. He's not made of ice; there are aspects to him that I love and there are aspects that I don't like and there are interpersonal ways that he has of relating that are fabulous and there are others that I think are *terrible*. He's a complex, complicated guy! But in *this* case he rose to the occasion, not only in terms of taking charge, but in terms of dealing with the families and with the group shock that the city was in.

John O'Leary, formerly Brother Aloysius Kevin   A cousin of mine lost her son-in-law and his brother—two young firemen—in the towers. Rudy came to the funeral of their son-in-law and it meant so much to her and to the whole family. At the time of that funeral and the comfort that Rudy offered, they didn't know that I had taught Rudy. It was subsequent to the funeral that I had an occasion to tell them. And they saw Rudy at another occasion and told him that they were related to me. They were very comforted and consoled and honored that Rudy would come to their son-in-law's funeral.

Glenn Corbett   The only time I ever met him was at a funeral for a firefighter who was one of my students. And it wasn't like he ran in with a hundred guys pushing people out of the way. It was really subtle; he came in with a couple of people and went right up to the family and said a few words to them. I appreciate that; it was a human thing to do.

Stephen C. Worth   I'd watch him during the services. He was remarkably humble in appearance and bearing; a remarkably modest speaker. There was nothing supercilious or arrogant about him. He was growing; he definitely seemed to find his humanity. He would hug the widows and he would look in the children's eyes and pat them on the head and talk to them and he would cry and it didn't seem artificial to me at all. He got in touch with himself. He wasn't the vicious, snide prosecutor that he was when he started.

Ed Koch   Mark Green said something which was absolutely stupid, that he could have done it better than Rudy, and people laughed at him, as they should have. Nobody could have done it better than Rudy. But I believe that many, if not most, mayors would have done it as well because that's your *job*. And that saved Rudy's reputation: he became Mayor for the World and you should not take any credit away from him. But to say that what he did was unique would be wrong. Others could have as well.

Mark Green   There are two views and I'm going to stay agnostic. One is that he did incredibly well by properly balancing toughness and compassion and rallying a city that had been dealt this blow. How did he do that? By putting the right words together with the right tone and by then taking concrete steps to organize the government to respond to this catastrophe. I saw him privately at this meeting; he's a guy with a lawyerlike ability to calmly elicit and pull together facts, arrive calmly at conclusions, and convey them to the public. He showed the skill of a lawyer giving a summation to a jury. Would someone else—Ruth Messinger or me or Dinkins—have done as well because the situation required that? I couldn't, and I wouldn't, say. You don't know until it happens.

Ruth Messinger   I was as caught up as everyone else, but it certainly did occur to me that that could have been *me*. I thought about what I would have done, but afterward, not on *that* day. I certainly did when I realized that on the one hand, the city wasn't going to be destroyed and on the other hand, that there was a gigantic change in people's sensibilities. This could have been *me*; would I have done it as well? And what other things might somebody be doing now, that they're *not* doing? I am with everybody in the city in thinking that he did it really well. He did it for the drama, he did it for the attention he *loves*, which is, of course, not *un*common in politicians, who love being in the center of the world. He and some other people handled themselves beautifully for that first minute. And he did it right and he got all the attention and recognition he needed for doing it right and he did it for six weeks.

Gene Russianoff   I know Ruth and she's a really good person and I would hope she'd do the same thing. Personally, I am skeptical about politicians. But in the wake of 9/11, because of my own personal experiences that day, I can't say I was worshipping a hero, but I did appreciate the mayor's leadership. Oddly enough, the mayor, whose politics are different than mine, was a stabilizing force. It still sticks out in my mind that someone asked the mayor about what the toll would be on the city and he said, "It will be more grief than we can bear." That really captured the spirit of it and every house in America was waving an American flag. I grew up in the era in which there were mixed messages. It seemed to me I was almost in a movie or an historic moment.

The Reverend Al Sharpton   I don't know any mayor that wouldn't have done the same thing. What was the mayor going to do, *run*? Look at Mayor Anthony Williams, in Washington, who suffered not only the plane crash, then not only the scare at the Pentagon, but the scare later over anthrax. *He* never ran; he didn't hide. He went through *two* crises and the national media didn't make a hero out of *him*; there was no *Time* magazine "Man of the Year" for *him*. And to lionize and make a hero out of Rudy Giuliani for doing his job! I think he should be given credit for doing his job; I don't criticize what he did, other than playing politics afterward, but I don't think that he did anything anyone else didn't do. I think the real hero was all the New Yorkers—ordinary people—that came together who did *not* have responsibilities of the mayor and did a tremendous job of trying to persevere.

Derek Sells   He presented an aura of strength and compassion. But in my view any mayor of New York would have done the same thing because when you are faced with that kind of tragedy, the hardest of hearts become compassionate. The true heroes were the citizens of New York City, the ones who even in the face of unquestioned fear of another terrorist attack went to work and kept the city going. Giuliani certainly reflected that spirit in the way he conducted himself.

Eric Adams   You have to understand this city to explain why I'm taking the position that it was a theatrical performance that made him this great hero. This city is a *great* city, with the history of a permanent government. No matter what happens to the person in City Hall, we have a built-in mechanism that the city operates with or without a leader. I know, without anyone telling me, that I have to go to the precinct and put on a uniform— captains know what they have to do in their geographical area; firemen know they have to put out fires. We don't need communications. This city has been doing its thing for so long and it will continue to do its thing. So Rudy didn't have to tell the truck driver, You've still got to drive the truck; he didn't have to tell the bus operator, If you can't get· down DeKalb Avenue [in Brooklyn], you've got to find an alternate route. The bus still has to move; the mailman still has to deliver the mail. Everyone knew their job; this is a city of professionals. And professionals don't sit home because a plane hit a building. They've been programmed to do what they have to do and they will get up and do it without any instructions.

Rudy gave the impression to America, to the globe, that the city stopped: I picked up the flag; they saw my leadership and everyone followed me down the Calvary Hill. Hell no! That did not happen. In fact, during that time, there was a state of total chaos until people regrouped and said, We've done this before. And there are unbelievable, heroic stories of new leaders, even while ground zero was taking place.

Benjamin Brafman Let's give Rudy credit: he knew that not just the people of the City of New York were going to watch his every move and listen to his every word, but that the *entire world* was going to be looking to him for guidance, for updates, for information, and Rudy rose to the occasion. Rudy is a seasoned politician with thirty years of law enforcement training to fall back on; he had all of his connections with the Justice Department, with the Police Department, with the law enforcement community, so he was a good mayor to have in place at the time. You were not dealing with just an act of trauma or a terrible act of natural devastation; this was an intentional act of criminal conduct, and he understood about preserving the crime scene but doing the rescue operation. He understood that more than other mayors would have, even if they were more popular. Rudy had command of that *naturally*, based on his experience, and that gave comfort to the world—that the person in charge of New York was someone who had brought the Mafia to its knees; who had taken on big business; who was not going to be intimidated. He rose to the occasion and a lot of people who *hated* him before 9/11 are among his biggest fans now. You know the old saying: a Liberal is someone who hasn't been mugged yet.

Fred Siegel In one sense they're right; in another sense, they're *not* right. It's precisely because a tight command structure was in place; it's precisely because they had been drilling and preparing; it's precisely because a team had been established that he could operate so effectively. A mayor rushes down there and heroically emerges to rally them and strikes exactly the right tone. Maybe *they* would have done that, too. But it wasn't just what he said; it's what he *did*; it's how quickly a new Emergency Command Center came up; it's how quickly services were put back into place. So could any one of them have done that? Absolutely *not*! Could they have done some of the theatrics? Probably.

Did the Mayor Experience an Epiphany That Day?

Herman Badillo   No, that was Rudy Giuliani as he was; he would take a very strong position and his position was that the city would be attacked and not knowing what else might be going on, his instinct immediately was to fight back and say, We've got to relax and let's take on this thing and let's get through this. And I remember, because I was invited to the meetings he had for days afterwards, he set up the command center on one of the piers and he got together with and had meetings every day after that with all of the commissioners, about what they were doing over by that pier, and kept people informed about what was going on. So he was very well organized and that was because he had always had meetings with the commissioners, so it wasn't a new thing that he pursued. But we were all worried about it because nobody knew whether there were going to be other attacks. But he made sure that the city was prepared.

Ed Koch   He did have an epiphany and I think he came close to death. There were people around him who were killed and I think that impacted on him and *still* impacts upon him. I say to people—I'm Jewish, I'm not Catholic; we don't have epiphanies, not on the road to Damascus, anyway—"It's my understanding that only saints have permanent changes as a result of an epiphany, so I expect him to revert to type." But he has not *yet*; there is still an effort on his part to be nice, and cordial, and collegial. But he wasn't *before*.

As the City and the Nation Grieve, There Is a Tremendous Outpouring of Emotion at Yankee Stadium

Rudy Washington   The mayor says, "We need to have some kind of get-together; we need to bring all the individuals together and we need to do it Sunday"—this is Tuesday. The mayor turns to me and says, "Rudy!" I'm going, Oh boy! He says, "Put this together!" I say, "Okay, boss. How much money do I have?" "You don't have any money." He wouldn't let me touch any of the money coming in for the families. The meeting is over. Rudy walks out and the secretary of state says, "Rudy, you're going to do this in *five days*?" I'm sitting there with a real sense of despair. I'm like, Oh my God! I haven't failed yet; I don't want to fail *now*. Now it's seven o'clock. It's a nice evening, so I say to my staff, "Let's sit in the little park and let's plan this thing." The wind changes and we get the stench [from ground zero], so we have to go inside. We have big fights about where to hold the get-together: there is a group that wants to put it on the lawn in Central Park. Everybody was really scared; we were waiting on that second attack. I figure: We can't protect Central Park. I convince the Police Department that it's a bad idea. But Henry's [Stern's] and my detractors had already run to the mayor: Central Park is the place to be. Fortunately, I had a former colleague, Randy Levine [who had become an executive with the New York Yankees], up at Yankee Stadium. I had to make certain commitments that I would not damage the lawn. The moment I started calling people to participate, I had all the mayors, all the senators, President Clinton. People's agents have got to get back to me. I don't have time, so I'm going to get two people for every slot, assuming I'm going to lose some. Now I'm working on *hours*. If I don't get Oprah [Winfrey] to be the emcee, I'm going to approach James Earl Jones. I approached about fifteen people. Lo and behold, every last one of them said yes! I went to the mayor and said, "Rudy, I have a problem. Not one person said no!" And he says, "Rudy, put *everybody* on!" I say, "You're talking about a five-hour program! By the way, I think I've got a network that's going to cover it." I had *five* networks and they covered it from beginning to end. Five days and no money!

Chapter 17

WEDNESDAY-MORNING
QUARTERBACKING

It's the same world as before, except now we understand it better . . . it's probably a safer world now.

—Rudy Giuliani, quoted in *Time* magazine, December 31, 2001

In the months following the worst terrorist attack ever to have occurred on U.S. soil, many questions were raised concerning whether the events of 9/11 could have been prevented; whether, in light of the previous attack on the World Trade Center, it had been a mistake to locate the city's Emergency Command Center in that complex; and why once the attack was under way the Police and Fire departments had failed to coordinate their efforts.

One of those who began to raise those questions was Sally Regenhard, who as her grief over the presumed death of her missing son gave way to outrage, began to realize that all was not as it had seemed in the immediate aftermath of September 11. She began to look back into the history of the construction of the World Trade Center three decades earlier and to question the actions of a long line of city officials, right up to Mayor Giuliani. Little more than a month after that terrible day in September, she announced the formation of the Skyscraper Safety Campaign.

Sally Regenhard   I had my first press conference at City Hall on December 12, 2001, and my first article in the [*New York*] *Daily News*. God bless the investigative reporter Joe Calderoni. There's a big picture of me and my son and it says, "Families Call for Further Investigation." That was the beginning of it and it was an uphill battle all the way and I'm still not at the top of the mountain. But you know what? My son climbed a mountain in Yosemite National Park and my inspiration is: if my son could climb *this* mountain—it's a three-thousand-foot sheer-faced mountain, and he climbed it the hard way—then I can continue to climb this mountain. And it's been a battle to expose the truth, expose the failure of our government, from New York City to Washington. All I want is *the truth*. And let the truth take care of Mr. Giuliani and his administration because the truth has its own life. The truth is that on 9/11 everything was not as it's portrayed to the public.

I'm looking at these buildings going down and, instinctively, I *know*: this is something that should not be happening. This is an outrage! They went down like a house of cards. And as the days went on and things evolved and I realized this massive loss of life and that my son was one of those people, I was outraged! But everybody was in such a state of shock that asking questions was not the common thing. And then I opened the [*New York*] *Daily News* one day in late October and there was an article, "Two Professors Call for Wider Investigation." They were from John Jay College. I called and got through to Professor Glenn Corbett, who to this day remains as chief technical adviser to the Skyscraper Safety Campaign, and his colleague, Professor Charles Jennings. They were open and kind and supportive and they shared their myriad concerns with me. Why isn't someone asking questions? I started a grassroots campaign and I started sending letters out to all the elected officials because Professor Corbett advised that we had to have an investigation, Congressional hearings. Now, the most horrifying part was that at this stage, and throughout the whole arduous journey, not one single elected official, including Mayor Giuliani and Governor Pataki, thought there should be an investigation. Isn't that horrifying?

The Troubling Chain of Command on 9/11: The NYPD vs. the FDNY

Edward Reuss When there's an attack in progress and you set up your temporary headquarters and you're coordinating all your troops, the FBI is the lead agency and they work with the Police Department because you have an ongoing crime in progress; you have terrorism going on. Now when 9/11 happens, after we have been warned we are continuously being attacked, FEMA's [the Federal Emergency Management Agency] in charge. FEMA set up their base in the Hilton Hotel; they set up their command post on Duane Street, in the firehouse. The Fire Department was the primary agency at that time; they controlled everything because there was damage and fire. Wait a minute, what about the ongoing terrorist incident? You can't have the Fire Department shoved in because there's a crime in progress that's going to require investigation and you need law enforcement in a position to determine how to handle it.

This is the bone of contention that came out of the current CIMS [Citywide Incident Management Systems] question. There was a hearing in the city council. I testified at the city council about a year ago [in the spring of 2004] about this very issue, when they came out with the McKinsey report [a McKinsey & Company report titled "Study of NYDP and FDNY Responses to World Trade Center Attack"]. I'm testifying—the fire commissioner was there—and at the end of the day, I mentioned how critical it was to have an incident command system for the police, not just the Fire Department, because you're working with the same language, the same methodology. And that's where we've arrived at: we have a system now in place. There was some resistance from the high-ranking members of the Fire Department. It's only natural; they feel it's their bailiwick. It's *not*. Terrorism is a whole new ball game—a massive crime that has to be dealt with, and the Police Department is more in a position to coordinate that than the Fire Department is.

They say that the police are doing the same work as the fire rescue companies, but they're not. And if you're trapped on the fifth floor and that bomb goes off and there's a fire, now what? You'd better get the firemen up there. Nobody's going to argue with the Fire Department once you've called them, right? But who's in charge? It's a crisis situation. That's the thin line that they're at. If you have a biological act of terrorism, do you think the wind is going to carry that to New Jersey or Connecticut? You have multiple jurisdictions—you can't be just the New York City Fire Department; you have the state police, you have the FBI, you've got federal agencies. That's why it's so obvious to me as a law enforcement officer, you have to go like that. We really haven't encountered this yet. We *will*—I don't see why we're *not* going to—unless we're born under the right star it's going to happen.

Henry Stern   These problems arise every day. While in general the departments do get along well, the police have long assumed that they are in charge of all emergencies and that the Fire Department puts out fires. But the Fire Department didn't have enough to do, so they became first responders. Firefighters can get to a scene more rapidly than the police because there are more firehouses than police stations. Fire trucks can move rapidly and are able to drive traffic out of the way.

Stanley Friedman   It's like the Yankees and the Mets, it's like the Brooklyn Dodgers and the New York Giants. It's the nature of the beast: you've got two very strong, very confident, very sophisticated agencies that will always be in competition—the finest, the bravest, the best—and they're never going to succumb to the other as being the superior force. Right now, they have as good a relationship as they're ever going to have; you're never going to have better. And if you do have better and one becomes subservient to the other, you may not have two effective departments, as you have now. They'll always have their differences. But when push comes to shove, bottom line, they'll work together to solve the problem. Maybe that's the bureaucrat in me speaking.

Could the Mayor Have Resolved These Rivalries Prior to 9/11?

Glenn Corbett   He did make it better by bringing in Jerry [Jerome] Hauer [director, New York City Office of Emergency Management], but it did not, by any stretch, fix the problem. The fundamental problem is the overlap. Giuliani didn't create the problem, but he didn't *fix* it. All of this stuff played out on 9/11 because you had that mentality. If you had had a truly integrated response where the police helicopters told the Fire Department what they were seeing overhead, things would have been different. But it is the mind-set of the Police Department that they cannot share: it's "our way or the highway."

Fred Siegel   There's an irony here. Part of the reason why the Police and Fire departments are so good is because they have battalion pride—the kind of esprit de corps you get in longstanding military units. That works against cooperation. On the other hand, the trouble with that argument is that Von Essen and Kerik were probably closer than any police and fire commissioner in recent history; there's less cooperation today.

Glenn Corbett   My biggest fault with Giuliani is that he was the sole person with the ability to change the dynamics of the relationships between those departments. He was the sole person who could sit down with their commissioners and say, Look, the days of duplication and rivalry are to end *now*.

Was It a Mistake to Have Located the City's Command Center at 7 World Trade Center?

In the wake of 9/11, questions began to surface concerning the wisdom of Mayor Giuliani's insistence in 1993, following the first Trade Center bombing, of locating the city's emergency reaction center right there, where there could—and would—be another, truly devastating, attack. It was later revealed that the fuel tanks required to service that command center were in large part responsible for the destruction of the 7 World Trade Center building, which had not taken a direct hit by hijacked aircraft.

Glenn Corbett   It was a stupid place to put it. One reason that had been suggested for doing so was that 7 World Trade Center was close to City Hall, but I don't buy into that. It assumes that the mayor is the only person who should be there. Many other officials should be in the emergency operations center, and it should be located in a safe, secure place that cannot be compromised by a natural disaster or terrorist attack.

Fred Siegel   When Giuliani builds the Emergency Command Center, he puts it in the wrong place—although not unreasonably so, since FEMA and the FBI are there—but he gets tremendous flack: he's paranoid; he's inventing problems that don't exist. And he was taken as an egomaniac for doing this. But the preparation paid off; hiring Jerry Hauer paid off. What was expected was a chemical and biological attack. There's an all-day brainstorming session about what's going to happen and no one anticipates *this* scenario. Some people, [NYPD Chief of Department] Lou Anemone and others in the Police Department said, "This is really a bad idea. They hit this target once and they're going to come back; we should put it in Brooklyn." And Anemone was right. That floor [in 7 World Trade Center] was the nerve center; all these other agencies were there and so there was a certain seeming synergy to have it there. It seemed to make sense. No one expected this kind of attack and so the drills that were going on around the World Trade Center—because people knew that the buildings were targets—were at the base of the building.

A source, who would not speak for attribution, stated:

> It had nothing to do with the 1993 attack. This was supposed to be a bunker. A bunker, like, for example, Hitler's bunker, is

normally underground. It is a place where you dig in. In your command center you should be safe from enemy attack, so you don't put a bunker on the twenty-third floor of an office building. But Giuliani got into a situation where he met opposition, where his enemies were claiming that the command center was a waste of money. It wasn't a waste of money. On the contrary, it was enormously sensible to have an emergency management headquarters. This one was beautifully done, with maps and charts on the wall, but it was just located at absolutely the wrong altitude. You couldn't say this because then you sided with the enemies who were trying to discredit him by attacking the whole idea.

It was a good idea, but it was in the wrong place. The debate was not over where to put the center but rather over the need for such an expensive headquarters. It was the Democrats griping. After the fact, Giuliani was criticized for being complacent. But if you weren't complacent, how could you live? Could you live in fear every day since 1993 that the enemy was coming to get us? It is human nature that we have a certain complacency.

Ruth Messinger   Everything about the bunker was ridiculous. We were opponents of the bunker because of the cost: it seemed to me we were probably going to protect ourselves by spending a huge amount of money in a not very practical place. It was not in the center of the city and it was up several floors—if you think about anything, you think in terms of a large, first-floor place. Certainly the location seemed to be tempting fate, which turned out to be temptable.

Edward Reuss   When the first bombing happened [at 12:17 P.M. on February 26, 1993, a rented Ryder truck, a Ford Econoline, carrying a 1,500-pound bomb exploded in a garage on the B-2 level of the World Trade Center, killing six people], where they tried to topple the buildings, they didn't lose masses of people and the buildings didn't go down, thank God! If I have any critique of that at all, from the city, it was that I don't think they reacted enough; it didn't wake us up. I don't know why. We weren't like, Gee, look what they tried to do! I don't think anyone thought that it [the bombed building] could have toppled. Imagine if it had toppled, with all those people in it. It would have hit the other one and they both would have gone over. Now, Giuliani puts his command center in 7 World Trade Center. I had a problem with him putting it on the twenty-third floor because when there's a fire, you can't use elevators. I don't know why that was done. It might have been a fiscal decision. It turned out to be a fortune because that building collapsed too.

Mark Green   In retrospect, it was as stupid as could be to put the bunker in the sky, given that there had been this attack on the World Trade Center before—and given all kinds of intelligence reports that planes could be used as weapons. But Jerry Hauer recommended it and he's as smart on municipal preparedness as they come. I assume Giuliani regrets it.

Eric Adams   This mayor is not afforded the luxury of pointing to someone else and citing poor judgment on their part because he had his finger in *everything*, on every aspect of running this city. In spite of people saying it was a bad decision, a waste of money, he articulated his belief that that was where he was going to put the center anyway.

Glenn Corbett   If the emergency operations center had been in operation, you would definitely have had Fire Department personnel present. They would have been able to see what was going on by watching television and would have been able to communicate with the people on the ground. They would have been able to say, Look, there is a really big, big fire up there; we have to rethink this whole operation of sending guys up there with hose packs. Unfortunately, all the senior commanders were at ground zero; there wasn't anybody very senior at headquarters or at Manhattan dispatch watching what was going on at a distance. The really large issues of command and control were taking place in the lobby and then out onto West Street. That's where the rubber met the road as far as command and control issues go.

Albert O'Leary   Hindsight is twenty-twenty. The command center was a remarkable place. I've been there. It was state-of-the-art. Hey, I don't remember any stories when they announced it saying: Gee, that's a bad place to put that. Nobody said: Why'd you put it *here*? But we all learned a lot from September 11.

Glenn Corbett   That's where Kerik and Von Essen needed to be, along with the mayor. The problem was resource allocation and you really need a place where you can make that happen, where you have telephones, televisions, radio communications, and you can call in additional resources rather than trying to accomplish this from a corner out on the street. If the command center had been operative, it would have played a role. But it is hard to say whether it would have changed the outcome. You have to remember that the whole event was a hundred and two minutes from beginning to end, so there was not a lot of time.

Albert O'Leary   OEM [the Office of Emergency Management] under Rudy Giuliani was a powerful agency because they carried their boss's shield at that point—the commissioner of OEM was the mayor's emissary—and whenever there was a problem among city agencies, whether it was police or fire or sanitation or EMS [Emergency Medical Services], whatever OEM said, went, under Jerry Hauer. If Jerry said, This is what the mayor wants, this is what you *did*. And that was fine. But they were a fully independent agency and why they decided to put it *there*—or if they even considered the fact that the Trade Center was an obvious target—I don't know.

David Dinkins   When I was in office, I was condemned by some for being in Japan when they bombed the World Trade Center in 1993: How *dare* you be away when they're bombing the World Trade Center? Like I knew it was coming. But it was suggested at around that time that we ought to take a hard look at these structures and how they were built. And we didn't. I'm not saying that it's Rudy's fault, by any means, but he was the guy who was the mayor and I don't know how much looking at such things anybody did. There's a conspiracy theory now that there were explosives in that building—that it would not have come down as quickly. I have not the remotest idea whether that's true or not. What do *I* know?

Albert O'Leary   I thought the [Atlantic and Pacific] oceans protected us. I think most Americans thought the oceans protected us. I don't think anybody perceived it as this really major threat to the United States that there were these religious zealots over there who *hated* America.

Fred Siegel   Giuliani got involved in the terror issue in '85 when he got involved with the Klinghoffer business and he was really ahead of the curve, all the way. And he understood how dysfunctional the FBI was; he understood that the NYPD was much better than the FBI. In the late '90s, I gave talks here at Cooper Union on terrorism. You couldn't get people interested; they would not take it seriously. So I sympathize with [former

White House counterterrorism adviser] Richard Clarke—he's turned into a horse's ass—I really admired him in those days because he was signaling the clarion call.

Criticism of the Giuliani Administration
re the Malfunctioning Radios

Glenn Corbett Isn't Giuliani the mayor who presided over the whole radio debacle in the Fire Department? The reason why these guys didn't get the message to evacuate was because they couldn't hear it, and there is a direct relationship as to why there were so fewer police officers who were killed; it's because they had a much better radio system.

Eric Adams You can't take the credit and not take the criticism. If you're going to take the credit for the decrease in crime and the success of the Police Department, you've got to take the criticism for not dealing with some historic conflicts between the police and the firefighters. There's been a long tradition, but it needed leadership to quell the conflict. There was a failure to do so and to come up with a very clear set of guidelines of: this is how it's going to be done. So he has to take blame for the lack of communication between the two.

Lilliam Barrios-Paoli A lot of people don't know, or want to know, that between what the mayor wants to happen and what *really* happens is the Office of Management and Budget [OMB]; they make cuts and decisions that I don't know if the mayor is always a hundred percent aware of. The bottom line is the mayor's, but the budget is negotiated between OMB, and not necessarily the head of OMB, but the head of a task force and a commissioner, and sometimes not the commissioner, but the first deputy. And horse-trading happens: they [the radios] probably went to the lowest bidder; they probably thought the radio was fine, but the radio *wasn't* fine. But in the scheme of things, it wasn't the end of the world because how often do they really use the radio? I mean, nobody could have foreseen the World Trade Center. Who would have thought a plane was going to become a kamikaze bomb? For crying out loud! Up to that moment, it wasn't something that normal human beings would have factored in. So the decision was fine, and probably would have been fine for another thousand years if that hadn't happened. The mayor is ultimately responsible. But I'm sure the mayor didn't know that the radios were there; I don't think

that he gave an order and they bought faulty radios. Can you imagine anyone doing that?

Eric Adams   There was total chaos with the firefighters' radios; no one
was able to hear each other communicate. While he was busy holding
press conferences to show him as the great leader, he was sneaking up to
Albany to change legislation so he could become mayor for life! You have
to understand this man: he used the people when they were hurting the
most. He is the great manipulator.

Chapter 18

THE AFTERMATH

*A big part of leadership is consistency—letting those
who work for you and others you lead know that you'll
be there for them through good times and bad.*

—Rudy Giuliani, *Leadership*

The Yom Kippur Eve Surprise

While still deservedly basking in the admiration and appreciation of the city, the nation, and the world, Rudy yet again revealed his *other* side: on the eve of Yom Kippur, the holiest day of the year for people of the Jewish faith—a day of fasting, prayer, introspection, and atonement—he floated a trial balloon in a clumsy attempt to override the city's term limits legislation and extend his final term in office for at least three months.

Mark Green   When he met with me at five o'clock that afternoon in his office—there were just the two of us in the room—I had no idea what he was going to say. I went down there with two aides and we waited in a room for him and then someone said, "The mayor will see you now" so I went in alone. There was no chemistry there. He's an outgoing mayor after America's greatest tragedy and the person not running against him but because of term limits is seeking to succeed him. He was matter-of-fact. He said, "Look, the city has had this catastrophe and this is an unusual circumstance, and I have this team together and I think I need three more months after the normal term has ended to complete what we know we can do." And I said, "Wait a second. We had a normal election in 1864 [in

285

the midst of the Civil War] and the Civil War was worse than this. I presume regularity in law and so I have a hard time supporting this." So my first reaction was "no," with the Lincoln analogy and my second was "no." Then, after consulting with just family and a few friends—I couldn't speak to other people because it was Yom Kippur—my third reaction was "yes" when I thought of the enormity of the problem and his argument for it. I decided that the circumstances were unique and unprecedented enough that I would agree in this situation. So at about eight thirty I called him and told him that I *would*.

Lilliam Barrios-Paoli   I think everybody was terrified and nobody knew what was going to happen. And the thought of changing mayors at that time made a lot of people very, very, very scared. When he came up with that idea, Mark wanted to do what was right for the city. Interestingly, Bloomberg didn't think so. The only thing I can think of is that Bloomberg was being very closely advised by Koch, who probably understood the dynamics of politics better than anyone, and might have said to him, It's a mistake; you can't change constitutional terms.

Derek Sells   If you really want to do what is best for the people, you follow the law. Your term is up; why would you want to extend it? But he wanted to use it to benefit himself. That's typical Giuliani, that's why he is so divisive. If his views conflict with the law, he'd rather use his views as if they *were* the law.

Ruth Messinger   He announced he should be mayor for life! That was such a *shock*. It reminded me and, I think, probably, other people, that this man is not in touch with the real world in some fundamental way because he's done this great job—and, by the way, that great job still is catapulting him into all kinds of other options—but the notion that: Hey, I'm doing this for us all, so we should suspend all the rules, is really bizarre. It was a little bit like Alexander Haig [in 1981, immediately following the attempt on President Ronald Reagan's life]: I'm in charge.

Floyd Abrams   September 11 was such a world-changing event and the mayor behaved so well in connection with it that that will be New Yorkers' first, second, and third memories of him. I wasn't surprised that Mayor Giuliani could be persuaded that his services were needed longer. And from his side, it should be said that many people were saying this. I was more taken with the public than angry with the mayor. He wasn't behaving in a revolutionary way—he wasn't breaking the law; he was going to *change* the law. But for the city, notwithstanding the valor with which he behaved, to say in effect, "These are the rules, even for *you*," was pretty remarkable.

Gene Russianoff   I was horrified by the notion, and it didn't have that much to do with *Giuliani*—it obviously *did*—but the notion that you would rip up the city's Constitution and the rules of the game to me is, as an amateur historian, like going back to the Civil War and habeas corpus gets suspended. We put in a lot of effort—we held a news conference, we wrote letters, we talked to the [*New York*] *Times*. The leadership of the city's big business community were willing to give them some more months. And, to my horror—but to my eventual feeling good about it—he called in Freddie Ferrer and [Mark] Green, and Green agreed to it and Freddie said, "No, no way I'm going to do it." And you think Mark is the liberal politician. I always use the Y in Prospect Park [in Brooklyn] as my test run, and all of these Prospect Park liberals are going, "What's the deal with Mark Green? How can he possibly . . . ?"

Mark Green   I'd appreciate it if some day you gave him truth serum and asked him if he did it on the eve of Yom Kippur knowing that I really couldn't confer with anybody and had to make an instantaneous decision.

Ed Koch   That was the craziest thing! That was one reason that I supported Freddie Ferrer. I hadn't decided what I was going to do in the Democratic primary with Mark Green, but when Mark Green folded and said to Rudy, "They'll give you three months"—it's *illegal*! It can't be done! But the demand! It's *insane*! And then Mark Green said "yes"; at that time, he didn't want any problem. Although I don't believe I would have supported Mark Green under any circumstances, it was one reason I gave at the time because neither one of them was, in my judgment, terrific. But that was the worst thing that Mark Green did. He came up here—I asked them both to come up here—and he wasn't happy about it, to my recollection, but he thought it was okay. And Freddie said, "No," and I said, "You're absolutely right, Freddie."

Fred Siegel   When Giuliani asked for ninety days after 9/11, he was pummeled, but he was absolutely right. As we're sitting here [on July 7, 2005] more time has passed since 9/11 than it took to defeat the Germans and the Japanese in World War II, and other than repairing the subway and the

PATH line [a major underground rail system connecting Manhattan with New Jersey], nothing has happened. Giuliani was right: for ninety days, he would have had the full attention of the Congress. As the months went on, we were on to the next political cycle: we were on to the 2002 elections; other issues came up. What did Giuliani want in that ninety days? One of the things he wanted was not an aid package; he wanted to change the federal funding formulas that constantly undermine us—for every dollar we send to Washington we get back about eighty cents. That would have helped us in the long run; it would have paid enduring benefits.

Mark Green   I got a lot of abuse for that from my opponent in the runoff, Freddie Ferrer, and from some media analysts. Of course it never happened because, basically, [State Assembly] Speaker Sheldon Silver had to pass on it and wouldn't allow it. Then it just died.

At the time of the mayoral runoff election, Giuliani did make one last attempt to extend his mayoralty by attempting to undo term limits.

Mark Green   He was seriously talking about trying to overturn term limits so he could run again. I was disappointed when I saw him try to use the attack [on the World Trade Center] to start to argue to undo term limits. It would be hard to imagine it happening and it *didn't* happen. It would have had to have been state law superseding city law, but it's one thing and extraordinary, I thought, to seek a onetime extension right after an attack—whether that was right or wrong I'll leave to others—but it's quite another to use the attack to change the law permanently, which I thought was exploitative and improper. And just as he was starting to try to do that so he could run himself for a third term, he was persuaded to drop the idea.

Then, despite the city's straitened financial situation in the wake of September 11, there were negotiations for the construction of new stadiums for both the Mets and the Yankees. And there was a deal giving the father of his consumer affairs commissioner a $40 million subsidy for the construction of film studios on the site of the old Brooklyn Navy Yard. By engaging in these last-ditch, lame-duck acts, was Rudy extending favors in anticipation of calling in some big political chits up the road?

There was *more*.

The Issue of Control of the Mayoral Archives

Stanley Friedman   Why did he put his archives in his briefcase and take them home? You don't have to be a genius to figure that out.

Gene Russianoff   It's another issue which we were very involved in. Wayne Barrett did the piece ["Rudy Heists City Archives to Shape His Own Legend"] in the [*Village*] *Voice* [published in the January 23–29, 2002, issue of the weekly newspaper] saying the mayor had stolen history and so we lobbied very hard for the bill in the City Council to seize control of the documents. I considered them to be tainted: if the chain of record is broken and you don't really know for sure that they have been manufactured or disappeared, that casts a cloud on the records. And it's very wrong that he didn't consider the Municipal Archives worthy of his records. We held news conferences with archivists; we testified; we had strategy sessions. They eventually passed a bill that no future mayor can do this.

By the time the council—it's not always the strictest of bodies—got around to passing the legislation, the mayor really had control of the documents. If I have to peg a motivation to that, I just thought that he wanted them out and about and available as soon as possible and that the Municipal Archives, the Department of Records and Information Services, would be assigned to him. And I know that others, like Mike Wallace and CUNY [the City University of New York], really feel they're tampering with the documents. And those are [Wayne] Barrett's feelings too: look at Barrett's book [*Rudy!*]. How could Giuliani have been elected without people knowing that his father [Harold Giuliani] had been convicted of a federal crime? But he was. They [the facts] are out there and you need a lot of work to dig them up.

Fred Siegel   I worked in the archives. When I stopped working there, the material was still coming in. My sense of the administration is that while there is some interesting material in the archives, so much of what happened that was important actually took place in the eight o'clock meeting—that's where the decisions were made; the decisions were not made in typical interoffice fashion, thirty memos going back and forth. There's no record of that, or if there is, I don't know of it.

———————

While Rudy Giuliani remains a heroic figure, after September 11 he was heavily criticized—his knighthood by Britain's Queen Elizabeth on

February 13, 2002, notwithstanding—by families of some of the 430 rescue workers who died on that terrible day for the way in which he sought
to control and expend the proceeds of the city's Twin Towers Fund, which,
he calculated, would take several years' time to distribute. Only after the
threat of a lawsuit did Rudy change his tune and agree that the funds
would be distributed within sixty days. But the damage had been done.

Eric Adams   He turned 9/11 into his own private cash cow. He raised
this enormous sum of money, $120 million, and then when he left office,
he darn sure tried to take the money with him. What the heck happened
to our surplus? We went into his last administration with an enormous surplus. It was as though he felt Mark Green was going to beat Bloomberg
and the coffers were, all of a sudden, empty. The level of unethical behavior was unbelievable, from Harding, the Liberal Party chairman's son, not
being qualified to hold a position and just robbing the city of money. There
was a level of unethical behavior and he has to take blame for some of that
behavior. Now a lot of people forgot about that behavior because he was
cleansed in the waters of 9/11. So now we have a "new" Giuliani in the
eyes of many.

The 9/11 Commission Hearings

Following a vigorous campaign in which victims' families and their advocates picketed in front of the White House and attended Joint Intelligence
Committee hearings, the 9/11 Commission was convened in May 2004 at
the New School for Social Research, in New York City.

   Mayor Giuliani appeared before the commission on May 19. Asked a
series of what his critics characterize as "softball" questions, he appeared
to be passing with flying colors; that is, until a firestorm of protest was
ignited by victims' families and their advocates who believed that he and
his administration had been grossly negligent before and on September 11,
2001.

   As the mayor suggested that the firefighters had heard orders to evacuate the doomed towers yet had decided to stay and die, several observers
began to shout.

Sally Regenhard   What a lie and an outrage! Do you know that the age
of the average person who got killed on 9/11 was thirty? What young firefighter, or any person, would make a conscious decision to stay and die if

they knew that that building was going to collapse? The worst thing was the sullying of the reputation of my son and the other firefighters by saying that they made a conscious decision to die. That is a filthy lie and that is why I started screaming. Maybe there was a very small number of firefighters that heard the order to evacuate and either didn't understand the urgency or wanted to finish saving a person. I give them all the credit. God bless them. They were heroes. However, the vast majority of people did not hear orders to evacuate. The 9/11 Commission basically backed up an aura and a myth of the Giuliani administration; they did very little to expose the truth.

Glenn Corbett   You could cut the tension in the room with a knife. I was also feeling the tension because I had given technical questions to the commission to be asked of the former Giuliani commissioners [Bernard Kerik, Thomas Von Essen, and Richard Sheirer] who accompanied him to the hearing. Only one of my questions was asked. So I was frustrated. I was thinking, Ask the *real* questions. All the family members present were also thinking what I was thinking. I had provided the commission legitimate questions that Giuliani and his people should have been able to answer. But the members of the 9/11 Commission didn't ask them. There was this pool of hot gasoline in the room, ready to ignite, and a man in the back of the room was the match. He stood up and basically said, "Stop kissing ass; ask about the radios." The insult of course was that Giuliani and his commissioners were not asked the hard questions. It was only their successors who were.

The mayor appeared momentarily to have been stunned by the outburst but recovered and went on to complete his testimony.

Glenn Corbett   Giuliani basically said, "These guys [the firefighters who died on 9/11] were heroes; they chose to stay behind." Bloomberg said the same thing in a letter he sent to the 9/11 Commission, and that is what the commissioners put in their report because after going to great pains to describe—in chapter 9—the communications problems, the commissioners concluded in a footnote that all on-duty members of fifteen to twenty fire companies knew there was an order to evacuate, but, for whatever reason, didn't get out. What Giuliani, Bloomberg, and the 9/11 commissioners are basically saying is that these firefighters chose to die in the building. That drives the families nuts. When I received the transcripts that have thus far been made available, I found evidence to the contrary. If you read the transcripts you cannot come to the conclusion that all of the firefighters knew to get out. Some of them *did* know, but I believe that the majority did not know to get out.

The Release of the 9/11 Tapes

Eric Adams   You have to hand it to Norman Siegel for forcing them to release those 9/11 tapes because Giuliani controlled the press so well that they created a story that didn't actually happen. They created a hero of this person that helped us rise up out of their fears and he led the city. Nobody was willing to say the emperor had no clothes on because if you said it you were anti-American. Even when he went to the hearings, he lashed out at the panel: Stop this foolishness! He made you feel as though if you questioned anything, you were un-American: How *dare* you question this sacred time of 9/11?

Sally Regenhard   What the Giuliani administration did was to have it become part of myth. And when he and his administration were questioned about what had happened to this city, what he did at the 9/11 Commission in New York was to flip it around and make it that people were questioning the heroics of the emergency workers. He has a blurred vision between him and his administration and the emergency workers, so that when some of the commissioners, like John Lehman, started criticizing the communications, when he said the communications system wasn't worthy of the Boy Scouts, the Giuliani press machine flipped it around and made it seem that Lehman was questioning the performance of the emergency workers. This man is brilliant in PR and he was able to do it and pull the wool over everybody's eyes—that *he's* the big hero. The emergency workers were lambs going to the slaughterhouse; they were sent into a hopeless situation, with no plan.

A Question of Legacy: Will the Mayor's Real Accomplishments Be Eclipsed by the Events of 9/11?

Raoul Felder   I've been in different places abroad and he's a major figure abroad. It's amazing. If you say, "Name me five Americans," they'll come up with him. I suppose that's what he's going to be remembered for most of all.

Sally Regenhard   September 11 should have destroyed this man's reputation. He was at the nadir of his life; people hated this guy! They hated the way he treated his former wife. He used to be portrayed in drawings in the papers as a Hitler-like character. September 11 is the best thing that ever happened to this man. I just want the truth to come out—is that there was a denigration of the truth, a contamination of truth about that day.

Ed Koch   It's not terrible. I mean, he deserves the reputation he established. But the people who are aware of that, who didn't live in the city, are unaware of how much animosity existed. And, also, [there's] a lot of affection for him; I mean he does have in New York City people who *love* him. I like Bloomberg. What I have said about him [is that] his weakest trait and his strongest trait are the same: it's his personality; he doesn't *have* one! When they talk about mayors and personalities, they generally talk about Giuliani and *me* and La Guardia; among the modern ones, they talk about Koch and Giuliani. And we do have personalities. And my strength is that people know that if they ask me a question, I'm going to tell them what I think, whether they like it *or not*. I don't mean to insult anybody— I'm not going to say it in a way that's insulting—but I'm going to tell them what I think. And that's my strength; it always had been.

Gene Russianoff   It's as if his eight years as mayor didn't happen—that this one event defines him, and defines all the thinking about him. There are a lot of people in New York who have reasons to be unhappy with what the mayor did. I think if you were in Omaha or Denver, you'd think that everybody in New York just thought the world of Giuliani and you're surprised to hear that they don't like him.

Ruth Messinger   If it hadn't been for September 11, it's staggering to think about how we would actually evaluate him as a mayor, given those first two great years and the six years in which *nothing happened*. After September 11 it was clear that the way in which he performed for those six weeks was going to translate into money on the lecture circuit forever, and a new wife.

Edward Reuss   He turned the city around. People say there was a renaissance. There *was*. In my own personal experience, when my son was sworn in as a police officer in January 1985, in Madison Square Garden, we came from Staten Island. We took the ferry and I remember getting on the train at South Ferry. You couldn't see anything in there. It was a disgrace: human defecation. My daughter was shocked—she grew up in Staten Island and she was kind of sheltered—she said, "Dad!" I said, "Yeah, this is New York City." That's how bad it was. And that was the beginning of the crack epidemic, too; it was raging. That was 1985; he wasn't the mayor yet. We didn't come out of that until the '90s. He actually took this city—and people thought it was ungovernable—and made a point about the so-called homeless people. Remember Tompkins Square, the homeless shelters? They had a Hooverville up there. Giuliani would go after the problem right away; he didn't let it fester.

Just to show you what it was like being a police officer: you'd question someone in the ferry terminal who's homeless and you had a feeling about this guy—he may have been wanted—and you couldn't do any checking; the courts wouldn't let us do a check. And there was a law for loitering; we would lock people up for that. They just threw out the law; they didn't just throw out the case—the judges ruled this was unconstitutional—and we were very discouraged because every time we had a loiterer, they threw it out.

PART IX

Life after City Hall

Chapter 19

GIULIANI PARTNERS, OR RUDY THE
VERY, VERY, VERY RICH MAN

*His unique success at transforming New York and
his strength in dealing with the September 11
terror attacks has given him a legacy of
honor and respect the world over.*

—from a Giuliani Partners press release

At midnight on December 31, 2001, Rudy ceased being mayor of the city
he had loved, promoted, and protected so heroically on September 11. His
achievements would quickly be recognized by *Time* magazine, which
named him 2001's "Person of the Year." Other accolades would follow,
including his knighting by Queen Elizabeth at Buckingham Palace in February 2002, his receipt of the Ronald Reagan Presidential Freedom Award
on March 8, and his characterization by the president of France, Jacques
Chirac, as "Rudy the Rock."

As the mayor sought in vain in the immediate aftermath of 9/11 to
extend his term by three months, he was very likely already setting in
motion his new career: within a matter of months, he had founded Giuliani
Partners, a security consulting firm. Very shortly thereafter, in the spring of
2002, he was named "Consultant of the Year" by *Consulting* magazine.

Giuliani Partners would within three years mushroom to include an
association in May 2002 with Nextel, to "improve public safety communications," according to a Giuliani Partners press release; Giuliani's chair-
manship of the board of advisers of Leeds Weld Equity Partners, described
as "the largest private equity fund in the United States in the education,
information and training industry"; a "strategic alliance" in March 2003
with CB Richard Ellis, the largest commercial real estate services company in the world; and the founding, in December 2004, of Giuliani

Capital Advisers, LLC, which offers "independent advice to leaders deal-ing with complex business challenges, strategic transaction or financial distress," with offices in Atlanta, Chicago, Los Angeles, New York, San Francisco, and Troy, Michigan. Most recently, in 2005, Giuliani became a partner in the four-hundred-member Texas-based law firm Bracewell & Patterson, now known simply as Bracewell Giuliani. Its clients include—or have included—Enron, Chevron Texaco, and Pacific Gas & Electric.

Is Rudy Taking On Too Much with His Many Acquisitions?

Herman Badillo   He's out there: he does a lot of campaigning for candidates—he raises money for a lot of people. And the business runs pretty much by itself; it's not being a lawyer, where you have to be in court every day—it's more of giving advice orientation—so it doesn't take away from it; it enables him to have money to make contributions to people who are running for the Senate or the Congress, and then make friends within the Republican Party, which is good. But I don't see how he makes friends with the Christian right wing of the Republican Party.

Fred Siegel   There's a synergy here. He *is* making a lot of money and he's also making the contacts he needs to run for national office, and his Texas law partners will come in very handy in a national campaign. There's a kind of implicit agreement—or, maybe, it's explicit—between Giuliani and Bloomberg: if Bloomberg doesn't screw up welfare and crime reform (and he's free to screw up anything else he wants), in return, Bloomberg gets to write Rudy an enormous check when Giuliani runs for president.

Floyd Abrams   While I don't have any reason to doubt his expertise, I don't think there's any doubt that he is trading on, and profiting off of, his 9/11 activities. It's a bit off-putting because of the nature of the event. I'm just not sure whether to criticize him.

Carol Bellamy   People's careers are based on what they've done. Perfor-mance is what the world is about—or ought to be about—and he per-formed well, and if that has helped him in his life subsequent to being the mayor of the City of New York, so be it. I don't subscribe to those kinds of complaints. That's sour grapes.

Steven R. Andrews   I don't have a problem with what he has done and I don't think most Americans have a problem. It's unfair to say he has traded off 9/11. I am a lawyer who practices in a state capital where everybody trades off contacts in state government. I'm no Giuliani apologist or supporter. All I'm saying is that if you choose a life of public service and in doing your job you become famous, or if you are called to service at a time of national stress and you achieve notoriety, not because of who you *are* but because of the perception of *what you accomplished*, then it is certainly appropriate to use what you learned when you were in public life to help you privately. What would you have the guy do? He wasn't going to apply for the Second Circuit Court of Appeals. He wasn't that sort of intellectual type person.

Steven Brill   Trading on 9/11? I'm not sure I know what that means. Everybody who goes out of the government trades on what they did in government. It allows the private sector to take advantage of all the wonderful experience he had in government. It depends on what he does, what he's getting paid for, and what he's doing. So what?

David Dinkins   Putting whether he's trading on it or not aside, he's a very fortunate fellow in many ways. I'm not one who thinks that one's private life should play a role in these kinds of discussions, but if others had behaved remotely as he has in the past it meant the end of their careers—but not *Rudy*.

Stanley Friedman   It's sort of funny what life produces. Some people are in the right place at the right time and he should count his blessings because he was in the right place at the right time and took good advantage of it. And I say, "Good for him!"

Helping Out a Loyal Friend

In 2004, with the announcement by Tom Ridge, President George W. Bush's head of Homeland Security, that he was retiring, Rudy Giuliani recommended to the president that he appoint Bernard Kerik, who had risen from a hardscrabble childhood as the son of a prostitute to become the police commissioner of New York City.

The president had already announced Kerik's appointment when, in an embarrassing series of disclosures, it was revealed by Kerik that he had a "nanny" problem [he had failed to pay Social Security tax for his children's nanny] and had carried on simultaneous affairs with the publisher of his memoir and a high-ranking officer in the Bureau of Corrections. Kerik then said he would not seek that position and shortly thereafter resigned his position with Giuliani Partners.

Edward Reuss   I felt terrible when Bernie Kerik fell from grace and I think it hurt Giuliani, too. I mentioned in an article I wrote about it. [Niccolò] Machiavelli's [1469–1527, the Italian philosopher and political figure known for intrigues] advice to the prince: it's very important who your lieutenants are; they can be smarter than you; they can be more talented than you; but they've got to be *loyal* to you. A lot of people who are great leaders will sort of shy away from people who are, maybe, smarter than they are. It's a mistake. You're looking for loyalty. You've got to get their loyalty; they can be smarter than you, but they've got to be loyal. I don't want to talk the guy down, but Kerik had flaws, obviously, and Giuliani didn't see them. Everyone is entitled to make mistakes. But when I look over his whole career, how many mistakes can he make like that?

Ed Koch   I thought it was terrible what he [Kerik] did. And I don't think we've heard the end of that. I have no personal knowledge about Kerik. In fact, Kerik has been very nice in his comments about me. On the occasion when he was sworn in, he invited me—I didn't know why and he made it very clear why: he said he had applied to the Police Department. He was in Saudi Arabia at the time and the Police Department had rejected his application, saying that they couldn't take one from out of the country, or from Saudi Arabia—I don't remember which—and he wrote to me and I, in turn, brought it to the attention of [Police Commissioner] Ben Ward and Ben Ward sent him an application and that's how he became a member of the Police Department, so he ascribed his ultimately being in the situation where he became the commissioner as a result of my efforts and he invited me to the swearing-in.

I think what he did was a disgrace in not telling the president, not alerting him to all the things—and I don't even know what *all* means here—but it's a lot. You can go back and look at all the papers around his association with different people—I don't want to get into it because I don't know what the facts are—but disreputable connections. And it's hard for me to accept the statement which at least most people think Rudy has made, or conveyed, that he didn't know anything about it. It's hard for me to accept it. Now, maybe he didn't. Because I don't think it's simply that he didn't pay the Social Security tax for his [children's] nanny. And why *didn't* he? But I don't think that's the only reason. But how could Rudy appoint him police commissioner and not be briefed by DOI [Department of the Interior] and rely on whatever he had filed as corrections commissioner two years before? It doesn't make any sense to me; it's not what *I* would have done.

Fred Siegel   Bush was charmed by Kerik—I get this from talking to people in Republican circles—and Kerik is enormously charming. He was completely outside of Bush's orbit. Kerik sold himself; the Giuliani connection didn't *hurt*, but I don't think he pushed him on Bush. The tragedy of Kerik is that he actually did a very good job; his first six months as police commissioner are magnificent. And the other thing the Bush people liked—it's an incredible story: the streetwalker who was found murdered—Kerik is a truly self-made man. Part of the reason Kerik was so good is that he came out of the demimonde and he understood it. Part of the reason Kerik got into trouble was that he never completely left the demimonde. The moment you know that something has gone wrong, that he's so taken with himself, is when he begins to send busts of himself out to all the precincts; you know that he's taken with his own accomplishments.

Gerald Lefcourt   If I had made the kinds of arguments to Rudy when he was U.S. attorney that he made publicly on behalf of Kerik, he would have laughed. The absurdity of this guy, Kerik! I had thought that Rudy was much savvier. He defended Kerik not knowing the facts. Imagine him wanting Kerik to be in that position [Secretary of Homeland Security] to begin with. He was *his driver*!

Raoul Felder   Bush went out of his way right afterwards—he had him [Giuliani] ride in the car with him and right after that, and then invited him for dinner at the White House and it seemed to me that was to deliver a very clear message: that he didn't hold that against Rudy personally.

Joining Forces with Ed Koch in Support of George W. Bush in 2004

Ed Koch   I announced, independent of the Republicans, whom I had had no discussions with, that I was voting for George Bush and I didn't agree with him on a *single* domestic issue—that's in all my statements; if you want them, we can give them to you—but I believed that his position on fighting international terrorism was more important than *any other issue* and that the Democratic Party and its candidate, John Kerry, didn't have the stomach to stand up to international terrorism. That's what I said. So then I got calls from two people: one, Bush's former press secretary, Ari Fleischer. He came here with the head of the Republican Jewish Committee and they said to me, "We would like you to go campaigning in Philadelphia and Florida." Ultimately, I went to Pennsylvania, Florida, Michigan, Iowa—I don't know why they sent me to Iowa; I think there are two Jews in Iowa and I met both of them, but they wanted me to go campaign in Jewish areas, primarily Ohio and Florida—and I went. And they say I had an impact.

Then they asked me, "Would you do a commercial with Rudy?" and I said, "Sure." It wasn't done together. I would have done it together—I did it with Cuomo; Rudy and I did a commercial together—but it was done separately, taped, but not because of any negative feeling on *my* part. And I have never had a problem with meeting Rudy in a social circumstance—shaking his hand, chitchat of the day. There's never been any tension, even though I make my comments about Rudy. He never did bring up the Barricade Books [*Nasty Man*]. And I'm proud of that book because the title was *mine*; I insisted on that title. I don't run into him. But were I to, there'd be no tension.

Time Out for Personal Matters

As he sought to advance his professional—and by extension, political—agenda, Rudy took time out to marry Judith Nathan, his companion of three years. The ceremony, which took place on May 24, 2003, at St. Monica's Church, on Manhattan's Upper East Side, was the finale in a series of misadventures, including his rumored liaison with the unpopular Cristyne Lategano and his messy divorce from the well-liked Donna Hanover.

The Failure of a Sixteen-Year Marriage

Lilliam Barrios-Paoli City Hall is very intense; it's a bunker mentality and you bond deeply and everybody else becomes an outsider. Donna was out there, looking in, but she wasn't *part* of it. And he had an incredible capacity for work and wasn't home a lot for the conversations about whether or not Andrew did his homework. I think he tried the first year, but the intensity of what was happening in government overtook the whole thing and so there was a separation. It's very difficult when somebody you love is totally, intensely involved in something and *you're* not and your work is not that intense, no matter how good or fabulous or important it is. They both tried for a period of time. They had dinners at Gracie Mansion, with music, and they would dance. I think they *loved* each other. I'm sure that when he was in love, it was very intense as well, but his intensity went all to work. They just grew apart and there were other people that took his time and his interest. He, like many, many men, didn't know how to blend the private with the work, and the private suffered. And she woke up one morning and realized that he didn't feel that way anymore. The sad part of it was that there wasn't a dialogue going on, or it couldn't end more amicably, especially for the kids.

Although very much married to Donna Hanover and the father of their two young children, Rudy had clearly been *smitten* with Cristyne Lategano and angered almost everybody in his administration by keeping them out of the loop while sharing confidences—and likely other intimacies—with the adoring protégée who was young enough to be his daughter. One evening during Rudy's second term, the day of the annual Greek Independence Day Parade, the authors were having dinner with several of their children in a favorite Upper East Side Greek restaurant when in walked Rudy and Cristyne, with another man and Rudy's security detail in tow. As the authors observed the Giuliani party, it became clear to them that the extra man was, in fact, Rudy and Cristyne's "beard." Lest one assume that the situation was lost on the younger Strobers—not to mention other diners—they began to poke one another, one of them exclaiming, "Look at the lovebirds!"

Much gossip about the lovebirds ensued. The August 4, 1997, issue of *Vanity Fair* carried a story in which it was alleged that an affair was in progress—an allegation hotly denied by the two. On June 24, 1999, however, Cristyne went on extended leave from her official duties. A little more than two months later, she announced that she would become the head of the city's Convention and Visitors Bureau. And on February 6, 2000— almost six months to the day following that announcement—she married Nicholas Stratis Nicholas. Had Cristyne found a better job and then true love with Nicholas? Or had Rudy the Pragmatic, prohibited by legislation from seeking a third term as mayor, had her thrown out of both City Hall and Gracie Mansion so he could clear the air for his next political move, his candidacy for the U.S. Senate?

Rudy Airs His Marital Linen

On May 3, 2000, one week before he announced that he and Donna Hanover were separating, Rudy and Judith Nathan—"Rudy and Judi," as they were dubbed by the media—were photographed by the *New York Post* looking very lovey-dovey with each other. While Rudy coyly described the attractive Judi as being merely "a very good friend," he wasn't fooling anybody, except maybe Donna, who tried to hold on to what was left of their marriage. Did his illness have something to do with his decision to leave Donna? After all, Judi, a former nurse and pharmaceutical company executive, could offer him special guidance and encouragement, which she did, helping Rudy to choose his course of treatment.

Despite Judi's obvious presence, Donna weighed in as First Wife on May 6, declaring that she would "be supportive of Rudy in his fight against his illness, as this marriage and this man have been very precious to me." But Rudy wasn't buying. He decided to ratchet up his and Donna's private war, announcing their separation on May 10, but without informing Donna beforehand. Thus continued the protracted marital strife that would lead, eventually, to their divorce and to his marriage to Judi. But not before Donna got in a few licks. In a statement to the press, ignoring Judi's presence in Rudy's life and referring specifically to the long-departed Cristyne, she confided that "it was difficult to participate in Rudy's public life because of his relationship with one staff member."

Lilliam Barrios-Paoli   When people ask me, "Do you think that Donna didn't know?" I say, "I'm very sure that she *didn't*." In Rudy's mind, it evolved from "I love you" to "I don't love you anymore." And when he gets to "I don't love you anymore," he assumes that everybody understands that. The fact that there has never been a conversation doesn't get factored in so, in *his* mind, she should have been aware of it.

Was Donna's Divorce Settlement a "Spectacular Victory," as Her Lawyer Claimed?

Raoul Felder   The fullness of time will show whether it was a spectacular victory or a miscalculation. I saw the ultimate settlement. Why was that a good settlement if she claimed he was worth millions?" I said, "I can't discuss it." And I never did. I knew there was no question there would be a settlement. We were prepared to try the case and I had cartons of records when I showed up in court. They [Ms. Hanover's counsel, Helene Brezinsky, and other members of the law firm Kasowitz, Benson, Torres & Friedman] showed up in court with a *briefcase*. Somebody should have told them in law school that if you tell somebody you're going to try a case, you bring more than a *briefcase*. I took a look at them—a couple of kids there with their briefcase—as soon as I walked in; I knew they had no intention of trying the case.

His personal life now less frenetic, Rudy Giuliani is showing every intention of going on to the next chapter in his ever challenging and rewarding life—a return to the political arena.

Chapter 20

GAZING INTO THE CRYSTAL BALL:
THE PRESIDENCY IN RUDY'S FUTURE

I think I'll return to politics.

—Rudy Giuliani on October 5, 2005, during a question-and-
answer session following an address to a gathering
of business leaders in Washington, D.C.

A few days earlier, the globe-trotting former mayor–turned very, very rich
Giuliani Partner had told an audience in Denmark that he would consider
tossing his hat into the 2008 presidential race "next year." Was Rudy being
ambivalent or indecisive as he had been in 2000? Or was he very astutely
hedging his bets, surveying the list of potential rivals for his party's nomination as well as sizing up potential opponents?

As he looks toward 2008—and possibly beyond—Rudy is not only
richer but, apparently, happily married. By day, both he and Judi are
engaged in good works. And by night, they are often seen on the black-tie
charity circuit, she beautifully dressed and coiffed and he likewise, his
ghastly comb-over a style of the past. Happily, too, there has been no
recurrence of Rudy's prostate cancer.

As of the fall of 2005, it appeared that Rudy would likely make the race
in 2008, thus fulfilling the burning ambition he has harbored since his
high school years of becoming the first Italian American president. Would
he be doing so in the hope of completing some unfinished political business, the defeat of Senator Hillary Rodham Clinton?

Richard Thornburgh   It was fortuitous that he didn't run, as it turned
out. When you're in public life, you have these decisions to make and you
have to take your best shot at it. There was some degree of misgiving

among his friends and supporters about his Senate race, but it didn't last long enough to really give vent to it.

Herman Badillo   I think if he had been smart that's what he would have done because, having served in Congress and knowing the people in Washington, I know he's not popular with the Republican Party. They don't like anybody from New York; as far as they're concerned, they could all float out to sea—they don't like Jews, Italians, Irish, blacks, or Latinos. And he's pro-choice, he's pro-gay, he's pro–gun control; he's against all the things that the average Republican in the heartland is for. If he had beat Hillary in 2006, then the party would owe him *big*; then he would have an excellent chance of getting the presidential nomination.

Richard Thornburgh   Rudy's an ambitious guy. I wouldn't want to venture a guess on what he's going to do. If he does run for president, he has a lot of hurdles to overcome, but he's faced *that* before. The last time I saw him, at a memorial service for Judge Waldman, in Philadelphia, we had a brief conversation and he clearly indicated that he hadn't ruled it out.

Fred Siegel   He's *running*. And he's running in an interesting way, a bit like Wendell [Lewis] Willkie [1892–1944, a Republican and President Franklin D. Roosevelt's opponent in the 1944 presidential race]. In other words he's done some of the rubber chicken circuit stuff, but he's involved in business deals all across the country, sometimes with friends of W's [President George W. Bush's]. He's had a chance to meet with business-people in all these major cities, so he's taking a somewhat unconventional route to building a national network.

Sanford Rubenstein   Two thousand eight is a long time away. A lot can happen in three years, and I wouldn't speculate. I think it's a long road that he has to walk to be able to present himself to those communities which felt that there was a policy of polarization when he was mayor, to demonstrate that he would be different in any other office he would seek to hold. I just hope that the work that we did in representing these victims ultimately ends with what Louima had said early on in his case—that he doesn't want it to happen to *his* son or *anybody else's son*. If we, by raising these issues, by shining the spotlight on these glaring examples of police misconduct, can prevent acts such as these from happening in the future—whether it's Louima or Diallo—then we've accomplished something. That's how I see the issue, not so much whether someone who has been in political office gets an opportunity to run for another political office, or is elected or not.

Benjamin Brafman   If Rudy runs, he will market his strengths—his training as a prosecutor, his leadership abilities that came out in 9/11. But the Rudy of today is a much different person than the Rudy of twenty-five years ago: 9/11 has brought out a softer side of many people, who will *never* be the same. There was a time in Rudy's life when he wanted, necessarily, to be known as the toughest guy in the neighborhood—and *was*—and he made it a point to bring it up whenever he thought it would be helpful to advance his agenda. I'm not sure he has that agenda anymore.

Marie Dorismond   September 11 saved his butt. He has to be remembered by the things that he did that were negative, not only by the good things of 9/11 because it seems that 9/11 has wiped out the bad things. He's looking bigger, better, meaner, and richer post-9/11. But he's not a hero; he's a killer.

The Reverend Al Sharpton   Rudy Giuliani is a power-hungry person. But I also think he knows that the honeymoon he's had with the media since 9/11 would be over if he ran and had to defend things that they don't now bring up. I think he's going to *flirt* with it; I think he's going to constantly keep himself in the papers because of his ego. But I don't think he'll ever pull the trigger because he knows that he will have to go back and explain everything—from Dorismond to Diallo to how his family separated—a lot of things he doesn't want to explain. It's better to live the reinvention than to have somebody move the veil and see that the wizard really isn't the wizard. So right now, he can lead all the media and the national pundits on the Yellow Brick Road. He'd better *never* let us get near that veil. I know what's back there; I've pierced it before.

If Giuliani Is Doing So Well Financially, Why Would He Even Want to Run?

Raoul Felder   I really don't think money is where it's at with Rudy. The man could literally walk around with no money in his pocket or $10,000; it doesn't mean a thing to him. There is one great photograph of him: he's at some town meeting and his cuff is held with a *paper clip*. That's Rudy. I got a call from a tailor on 57th Street. He says, "Let me make him a suit

as a present." I said, "First of all, you don't know who you're talking about;
he doesn't take presents. Second of all, a suit is the last thing on his
mind."

Ed Koch   I don't believe he's going to *be* the presidential candidate of the
Republicans because the good things about Rudy are why the Republicans
won't take him—his substantive positions. He supports the right of abortion; he supports gay rights; he supports gun control; those are the three
matters of passion for Republicans, and the news that I read was that he
was told by Trent Lott, the senator from Mississippi, who I know—I
served with Trent Lott in the House of Representatives—that he couldn't
possibly get the nomination because of his substantive positions. And I
believe Trent Lott is right. So I don't expect him to be the presidential candidate, as much as he thinks he *will* be.

What Kind of President Would Rudy Be?

Saikou Diallo   He's a good leader, a *very* good leader, and very intelligent.
If he changes his character, he may be a good president. But he has to
change.

Derek Sells   When I see Giuliani, I see someone who really isn't compassionate. His policies are very divisive. If he is elected again as a public
official you may see the same divisiveness. When you are a representative
of the people you have to understand where the other side is coming from.
You can't just look at the world with blinders. And I'm afraid that's Giuliani.
The country is so divided, as the last election demonstrated. To put Giuliani in office at this point in time is just going to further the divide and
make matters worse. We need someone who will build bridges.

Jay Goldberg   I think he might have a little bit of a problem because
when he was mayor, *he* called the shots and a president has to be able to
interact, with his staff and with Congress, and be more collegial. Giuliani,
if he lacks anything, it's collegiality. And he may not be as attractive once
he's in office because he has a tendency to not be warm. You see, people
go for Bush because they tend to think he's a nice guy, but Giuliani is a
harsher person and he takes a stricter approach to things, so I don't know
that he'd be able to build a consensus.

Gerald Lefcourt   There is a lot of controversy about what he did in the U.S. Attorney's Office for himself. That was pure ambition. And I thought it was very, very dangerous for a city like New York to have a mayor like that and that he would be a similarly dangerous president. He shot from the hip like crazy in all these police cases and with the power at a president's disposal, I would rather have a more reflective person.

Floyd Abrams   I would be disturbed by his ascension to the presidency. His behavior as mayor gives reason for great concern about how he would perform in unpredictable and difficult circumstances. I say that believing that he behaved not only with valor but with enormous skill on 9/11. He may have been better mentally prepared for a major act of terrorism than any other American political leader. But that skill takes you just so far. The next major threat doesn't have to be terrorism, it could be a Katrina. Then the question is, How would he interact with a Democratic mayor and governor? Would he send troops in too quickly? We needed troops in New Orleans but would he send in troops in a storm that was only half as bad as Katrina? You'd have to ask how he would react with the mind-set that led him to his superior achievements at the time of 9/11 and yet to repeated acts of what were at best insensitivity for the principles of civil liberties, constitutional law, and living in a society where people disagree with those in power. I'm not comfortable that he would react well. I'm not comfortable that he understands that if he were president good, decent, serious people would disagree with everything he did.

Fred Siegel   The pre-9/11 accomplishments haven't gotten nearly enough attention because if you're going to look at how he'd govern as president, you have to look at how he governed as mayor. And so it's important to see how he operates—the kind of tight staff style he has, where he brings things together; he breaks down barriers. Giuliani is a student of government and I suspect that right now he's studying the federal government. Our vulnerabilities are considerable. If, as we're approaching the presidential campaign, you get something like today's [July 7, 2005] London bombing, that will give his campaign an enormous boost.

Richard Thornburgh   He would be Reaganesque in the sense of providing—or at least seeking to provide—inspiration; I think he'd be very good at that. But Rudy is more a hands-on guy than President Reagan was. I served in the Reagan administration for a spell myself as attorney general and he didn't leave many fingerprints. He was a marvelous president in providing credible leadership, but he was not a nuts-and-bolts guy. I think Rudy's track record is keeping an eye on things, finding good people, delegating the primary responsibility to them, but being darn sure of what's going on. If Rudy were to be president, it would be a *Giuliani* presidency.

Stephen C. Worth   He's natively intelligent and he's smart enough to know what he *doesn't* know. One of his biggest faults is his need to fight his vendettas and to abuse his enemies in a personal way. He's got the ability to inspire and to lead and there's no doubt that he's got *charisma*. Rightly or wrongly, he cloaked himself in the mantle of 9/11 and he is the modern-day Winston Churchill. Would I be frightened to have him as president? No. We've had far dumber men doing the job, and he inspires and can lead.

David Dinkins   Rudy as president is kind of frightening. My question would be, Will I move to Bermuda? Where will I go?

Eric Adams   It's inevitable that he's going to be elected because people think he's "America's Mayor." Americans search for heroes and Giuliani represents Red White and Blue right now and Middle America, for whom Red White and Blue means everything, is going to make sure that Giuliani becomes president. Giuliani is a master manipulator. He now represents the symbol of antiterrorism. Here on the East Coast and on the West Coast our thought processes are different. In Middle America, that Christian right is so fanatic that they believe that they are right, that there's no room for discussion. In their minds, this is not "God's country," it's "God's globe." There's an arrogance in Middle America that on the sixth day God made America, not man, and that's all that matters to them. Giuliani understands that. His mind-set is, the heck with the rest of the globe; the only man that is important is an American, and he plays on that. I am so afraid of this man taking office in one of the most powerful positions on the globe. He will bring the same arrogance that he brought to City Hall to the halls of the White House. Instead of shutting down vendors and turning away blacks in Bedford-Stuyvesant, he's going to turn away blacks in Africa and the entire globe, with the AIDS crisis choking the life out of some of those people. And instead of saying, "So what?" to Puerto Ricans in the Bronx and Spanish Harlem, he's going to say, "So what?" to the Hispanics down in Central America. The same level of locking up every person that didn't agree with him—if an artist drew a picture of him and he didn't like it, he'd raid their house—he's going to do to people who disagree with him outside this country. And he's going to think he can make us into isolationists when, in fact, we can no longer live that way. That is probably going to be one of the most dangerous periods in American history. I hate to sound like I'm saying, "Run for the hills!" But even if he doesn't beat Hillary Clinton *this* time—as he didn't beat Dinkins the first time—he will be consistent and *per*sistent until he occupies the White House. And he will no longer be in control of the largest police force; he will be in control of the largest military might on the globe. That is so frightening.

INDEX